CASSELL

英語寫作技巧

THE CASSELL

GUIDE to
WRITTEN ENGLISH

James Aitchison 著

趙福利 譯・姚乃強 審校

中文大學出版社

《CASSELL英語寫作技巧》
James Aitchison 著
趙福利 譯、姚乃強 審校

本書為英國Cassell出版之*The Cassell Guide to Written English*
一書之中文版

中文版 © 香港中文大學 2003

本書版權為香港中文大學所有。除獲香港
中文大學書面允許外，不得在任何地區，
以任何方式，任何文字翻印、仿製或轉載
本書文字或圖表。

國際統一書號(ISBN)：962–996–106–7

英文原著 © James Aitchison 1994

2003年第一版
2006年第二次印刷

出版：中文大學出版社
　　　香港 新界 沙田 • 香港中文大學
　　　圖文傳真：+852 2603 6692
　　　　　　　　+852 2603 7355
　　　電子郵遞：cup@cuhk.edu.hk
　　　網　　址：www.chineseupress.com

The Cassell Guide to Written English (Chinese Edition)
  By James Aitchison
  Translated by Zhao Fuli
  Examined and approved by Yao Naiqiang

Chinese edition © The Chinese University of Hong Kong 2003

All rights reserved. No part of this publication may
be reproduced or transmitted in any form or by any
means, electronic or mechanical, including photocopying,
recording, or any information storage and retrieval
system, without permission in writing from
The Chinese University of Hong Kong.

ISBN: 962–996–106–7

Original English Edition © James Aitchison 1994

Cassell
5 Upper St. Martin's Lane
London WC2 9EA

First edition 2003
Second printing 2006

Published by The Chinese University Press,
　　　　　　The Chinese University of Hong Kong,
　　　　　　Sha Tin, N.T., Hong Kong.
　　　　　　Fax: +852 2603 6692
　　　　　　　　　+852 2603 7355
　　　　　　E-mail: cup@cuhk.edu.hk
　　　　　　Web-site: www.chineseupress.com

Printed in Hong Kong

目　錄

第二部分　應用篇

前 言

　　「懂得使用標準書面英語真的很重要嗎？」這是學生們時常會問起的一個問題。可以這樣說，對於日常生活中不需要用書面英語的人來說，這並不很重要，就像航海技術對於從不出海的人無關緊要是一樣的道理。但對於需要用書面英語的人來說，規範的英語就變得至關重要了。

　　標準書面英語作為英語公認的國際準則，在所有說英語的國家中使用，這樣，能夠讀懂倫敦《泰晤士報》(*The Times*) 的讀者，同樣也能看懂《愛爾蘭時報》(*Irish Times*)、《紐約時報》(*New York Times*) 或者《印度時報》(*Times of India*)；為一家報紙撰文的記者，也同樣可以為其他報紙撰稿，只要其寫作風格稍作改變即可。書面英語的標準是由印刷商和出版商逐漸規定出來的，目的在於規範作者所使用的英語，有一個統一的規則，只有遵從這樣的規則所寫出來的英語才能得到認可，否則就不能讓讀者很好地理解。

　　不管是學生還是其他作者，如果沒有很好地掌握書面英語，就不能清晰地表達其思想，遑論表達其思想的精妙和複雜之處。即使他有足夠的能力構築並分析深邃複雜的思想，但如果其書面表達不能恰如其分地展示其思想，也會讓人覺得他並非才思敏捷或者思想不夠成熟。

　　不管是寫短文、寫報告，還是寫學術論文，也無論是為報

刊雜誌撰文還是著書立說，作者都有責任將其思想表達清楚。如果把一篇寫得很糟糕的東西呈現給讀者，讓他們去費心推測其中的意思，作者就會失去讀者的信任。試想，如果讀者對作者所使用的語言產生了懷疑，他們又怎能相信作者所表達的思想呢？

　　文章寫得流暢準確，不僅能贏得讀者的信任，而且較高的語言質量本身也能增加文章的權威性。要使所寫的文章流暢、準確，只能通過不斷的寫作實踐以及對書面英語規範和技巧的深入理解才能達到；也只有這樣，才能寫出好文章，才能瞭解其他作者是怎樣寫出好文章的。即使作為一個普通讀者，如果不懂得作者為了達到其寫作目的所採用的手法，就會很容易人云亦云地受到政客、廣告創作人或者記者們思想的蠱惑，而失去辨別是非的能力。

　　英語書面語和英語口語的差別很大，它們是英語的兩種不同形式。我們先學會說，然後才會寫，這是因為人們幼年時在家庭環境中先學會說話是自然而然的。在這樣的環境下習得的語言也因此缺乏規範性。

　　然而，書面語的習得並不是一個自然過程。字母和書寫體系完全是人創造出來的，需要一代人又一代人的繼承。寫作是一種需要事先經過縝密思考規劃的個人行為，而口語則是一種社會性或集體性的行為，往往是事先沒有經過規劃，具有自發性、即時性的特徵。

　　與口語不同，書面語不受時空限制，可以在廣大的地域範圍內久遠地流傳。這一特性使得書面語比口語更具權威性。當書面語被用來記錄諸如戰爭、宗教、法律、生死、婚姻等人類活動時，它的這種權威性就進一步加強了。

　　書面文字的權威性有時與作者的權威性是不可分的。例如，過去為教堂抄寫經文或教義的神職人員曾經控制著宗教，原因就在於只有他們才知道教義原稿上所寫的內容。即使到了今天，仍然是歷史學家們掌握著歷史，新聞編輯們控制著新聞。如果發生的事情沒有在歷史書籍或新聞媒體中得到記載，那麼這些事情就不會為多數人所知。

　　書面英語的規範化進程早在盎格魯—撒克遜 (Anglo-Saxon) 時代人們抄寫文稿的時候就開始了。這一過程由早期的印刷商和出版商又重新繼續，直至使英語的多數規則都得以規範化。在這期間，西敏寺 (Westminster) 的出版商威廉・卡克斯頓 (William Caxton) 出版的第一本書於1477年問世。到1755年塞繆爾・約翰遜 (Samuel Johnson) 出版的《英語詞典》(*Dictionary of the English Language*)，在單詞的拼寫、意義和語法，句子及段落結構，以及標點等方面都有了公認的規範標準。

　　這些公認的規範標準是有一定靈活性的，本書後面的各章節將向大家表明英語是處於怎樣一種不斷發展的狀態。社會文明在不斷發展變化，這就需要在語言中添加新詞或給業已存在的詞賦予新的意義，以反映這種發展變化。例如，有些詞的拼寫發生了改變，有時把兩個已經存在的詞用連字號 (hyphen) 連接就構成了一個複合的新詞，當這個複合詞逐漸被接受而變成標準的英文單詞時，連字號就慢慢被省略掉，使得原來的兩個詞變成了一個詞；語法和句法也在發生改變，但變化的速度比詞彙要緩慢。現在英語的語法比五十年前要顯得簡單並且不那麼嚴格；句法規定出句子和段落的結構及長短，是構成寫作風格的根本所在，不同的作者之間均有不同，但目前總的趨勢是傾向於使用更加簡潔明快的句法結構。儘管有上面所提到的這

些靈活性,標準書面英語還是保持相對穩定的狀態,在單詞的拼寫、意義以及詞法句法方面都不容過多的靈活性。

在現今的英語中,口語也在採用一些以前為書面語所獨有的特徵,這是因為電話、電腦和通訊衛星等這些電子技術革命的產物,已經使得口語也能超越時空的局限。伴隨著電子技術革命的進一步發展,一些狂熱的改革者曾預言,用手書寫的時代將告結束,報紙、雜誌、書籍將逐漸消亡,無紙化辦公的時代即將到來,一句話,就是書面語的使用即將成為歷史。但這一預言已經被證明是一個錯誤,標準書面英語仍然是最有效的交流載體,也是英語國家中受過教育的人之間進行溝通的最重要的媒介。

第一部分

基础篇

第一章 | 詞類和語法

　　英語較其他語言有著更多的詞彙，但其超過五十萬的標準詞彙及成百萬的科技詞彙可歸為有限的十類。其中四個主要詞類為名詞、動詞、形容詞和副詞，另外六個小的詞類為代詞、介詞、連詞、限定詞*、數詞和感歎詞。

　　把詞彙適當分類，可以使我們更清楚地瞭解具體詞彙的形式與功能，以及詞彙之間怎樣相互結合並相互作用，以產生特定的意義。這些特定的意義是受語言的標準或規則所規範；如果沒有規範，語言將是一團亂麻。因此我們需要用規則來賦予語言以意義，這與多數團體或社會活動需要用規則來賦予其意義是同樣的道理，比如遊戲或體育、駕駛車輛、安排假期活動、租屋或買房等，這些都需要有定規。本章將介紹英語詞彙的分類以及各類詞彙的主要特點及使用規則，但我們首先要對詞彙的某些概念和特點有一個初步的認識。

曲折變化

什麼是曲折變化？　　**曲折變化** (Inflections) 是指由於單詞形式的改變引起其語法功能的改變，從而使其意義也產生細微的變

---

* 編者註：語法學家對於限定詞作為一個詞類，還沒有取得一致的意見。有關限定詞的解釋，可參看本書第32頁。

化。曲折變化通常是由在單詞尾部加上一個尾碼來完成的，而尾碼一般是由幾個字母構成的一個簡短詞素。

名詞的曲折變化　最簡單的曲折變化是加在名詞尾部使之由單數形式變為複數形式的 s，如 computer（單數）/computers（複數）。代詞也有單複數形式的變化，如，I, you, he/she/it 是單數，we, you, they 則是相應的複數形式。

　　與曲折變化 s 相類似，'s 和 s' 這兩種曲折變化可以加在名詞尾部來表示該名詞的所有格形式。單詞的格是有關名詞和代詞的一個語法範疇，用來表示名詞或代詞在句子中的功能。幾百年來，英語中的格已經大大簡化，名詞只有兩種格，即原形和所有格。

代詞的曲折變化　代詞則有三種格，即主格、賓格和所有格。代詞還有另外一個語法屬性 —— 人稱。代詞有三種人稱，第一人稱、第二人稱和第三人稱，分別指不同的敘事角度或書面語言中所採用的不同視角。I 和 we 是第一人稱，是說話者或評述者，you 是第二人稱，指說話時的直接受話對象，he/she, they 是第三人稱，是說話者所談論的對象。

　　現代英語中第二人稱的單複數形式一般都用 you，但也有一些例外。在蘇格蘭和北愛爾蘭的口語語法中，第二人稱的複數形式為 youse；美國南部有些州的口語中則用 you-all 來作第二人稱複數。

動詞的曲折變化　由名詞或代詞所表達的數的概念在動詞的使用上也有體現，在這方面英語語法在發展過程中也經歷了一個簡

化的過程。現代英語中，動詞用一種形式來表達單數概念，如，he/she/it walks，而用另一種形式同時表達單數和複數概念，如 I (單數) walk, they (複數) walk。此外，動詞還可以通過詞形的變換來表達語態、情態和時態等語法特徵 (詳見第54–74頁)。

形容詞和副詞的曲折變化 形容詞和副詞通過曲折變化形式來表明規模或程度的大小，它們的標準形式 (未經曲折變化的形式) 稱為原級，另外還有兩種形式則稱為比較級和最高級，如 tall (原級)，taller (比較級)，tallest (最高級)。

實義詞和功能詞

實義詞 (Content Words) 和**功能詞** (Function Words) 是英語語法中另一種對詞彙的區分方法。一篇文章的絕大部分內容或意義是由實義詞來表達的。前文所述的詞類中的幾個主要類別，即名詞、動詞、形容詞和副詞都屬實義詞。

功能詞的語法作用與其自身所具有的詞義同樣重要。有時功能詞對句子的意思影響不大，但在表明句子中詞與詞之間的關係上卻起著舉足輕重的作用。連詞和介詞就屬於功能詞。動詞則有些特殊，原因在於所有的主要動詞都同時既是實義詞又是功能詞，也就是說他們對句子意思表達及所起的語法作用都非常重要。

可見，不能把實義詞和功能詞兩個概念絕對化。實際上，句子中的每一個單詞都或多或少既對句子的意思有所影響，同時又具有一定的語法功能。

瞭解了上述這些概念，下面我們就開始對各詞類分別進行介紹。

名 詞

　　名詞 (Nouns) 是實義詞中的一個大類，表明人或事物的名稱，如人名、地名、動植物名、自然現象 (如天氣)、商品名、人類的價值觀念和情感等。名詞不僅是我們理解語言的基礎，也是我們認識事物的根本，因為我們是通過名詞來認識世界和適應環境的。

　　按照類型和功能，可以把這一大類詞分為若干小的類別。

◆ 專有名詞和普通名詞

● 專有名詞

　　專有名詞 (Proper Nouns) 是某個 (些) 特定的人、地方、機構或事物的專有名稱。為了表明其獨有性，專有名詞的第一個字母通常要大寫，例如：

> Anna Desai, Miriam Levy, Matthew Ray; India, Taj Mahal, River Ganges; United Nations Organization, International Monetary Fund, European Court of Justice; Boeing 757, Spitfire Mark IV, Jaguar XJ40.

有些專有名詞還要加上引號或用斜體字來表示，例如詩和小說的標題、電影片名、樂曲標題、報刊雜誌的名稱以及書名等 (詳見第127–29頁)。

● 普通名詞

　　普通名詞 (Common Nouns) 是具有相同特徵的一類人或事物的名稱，例如：

> dentist, guitar, poem, student, tree, whale.

當然普通名詞也可以是日用商品、現象或物理特性的名稱，
如：

aluminium, money, fire, snow, heat, noise, speed.

◆ 具體名詞和抽象名詞

● 具體名詞

顧名思義，**具體名詞**(Concrete Nouns) 一般是指看得見、
摸得著、及實在的物質。一個名詞可以同時既是具體名詞又是
普通名詞。看下面的例子：

axe, computer, guitar, paper, student, tree, telescope

也可以既是具體名詞又是專有名詞。例如：

Mount Everest, Lake Tanganyika, River Nile, the House
of Commons, the Kremlin.

● 抽象名詞

抽象名詞(Abstract Nouns) 是指那些沒有物質存在的事物，
一般包括人類的價值觀念 (values) 和情感 (emotions) 等。例如：

anger, courage, fear, greed, hatred, humour, love, zeal

還可以是概念 (concepts)、思想 (philosophies) 和理論 (theories)
等。例如：

capitalism, justice, liberty, relativity, tyranny.

另外，上面所用到的那些概括性的詞本身，如values, emotions,
concepts, philosophies, theories 也是抽象名詞。

◆ 名詞的來源及構成

現代英語中的許多名詞都是由古英語發展而來，並且可以

通過英語所特有的一些尾碼來辨別，如 **-dom, -er, -hood, -ness** 等。

- ● 後綴 -dom

dom 這個詞在古英語中的意思是審判或司法，但在現代英語中變形為 doom。dom 作為後綴表示狀態、職位、性質等。例如：

> boredom, chiefdom, Christendom, freedom, kingdom, martyrdom, officialdom, serfdom, wisdom.

- ● 後綴 -er

後綴 -er 保留了它原有的意義，一般用來表示職業，如：

> archer, baker, barber, brewer, butler, carter, cutler

或者表示某種活動的參與者，如

> lounger, scrounger, dancer, romancer, loner, moaner.

以上兩種表示職業或活動參與者名稱的名詞在語法上稱為施事者名詞 (參見頁 13)，因為這樣的名詞所代表的人是動作的實施者。由於從事某種工作的人常常與其職業緊密聯繫在一起，其所從事的職業就漸漸成為用來指稱其家庭的別稱，例如：

> Cooper, Hooper, Fletcher, Porter, Salter, Thatcher, Turner.

- ● 後綴 -ier

從中古英語和法語而來的後綴 -ier 也可構成施事者名詞，例如：

> cashier, collier, courier, farrier, furrier, glazier

-ier還可用來構成與軍事相關的職業，例如：

> bombardier, brigadier, cavalier, chevalier, fusilier, grenadier, soldier.

• 後綴 -hood

由古英語中的had一詞轉化而來的後綴-hood，起初用來表達級別或次序之意，現在則表示生命的階段和狀態。例如：

> childhood, boyhood, girlhood, brotherhood, sisterhood, fatherhood, motherhood, manhood, womanhood, parenthood.

• 後綴 -ness

除-dom和-hood之外，後綴-ness也可用來表示生命的狀態或者某種物質的質量或特性等。在現代英語中，用這一後綴幫助構成的名詞很多，例如：

> madness, sadness, goodness, rudeness, quickness, home-sickness, spotlessness, thoughtlessness.

• 後綴 -er, -ier, -ery

後綴-er和-ier表明工作的人（或實施動作的人），而源自中古英語和法語的-ery則用來表示行業或工作的地方。如：

> bakery, bindery, chancellery, colliery, creamery, drudgery, ironmongery, midwifery, piggery, scullery, surgery.

◆ 動詞和形容詞用作名詞

英語語法具有很強的靈活性，表現之一就是動詞和形容詞可以用作名詞。

• 過去分詞用作名詞

有些動詞的**過去分詞**形式 (Past Participle，跟在 has/had 或 have been/had been 之後的動詞形式) 可以用作指代某一類人或事物的名詞。例如 forbidden 這個詞用作名詞時表示被禁止的事物。還有很多類似的例子：

the beaten, the bereaved, the dispossessed, the educated, the fallen, the lost, the repatriated, the wounded.

• 現在分詞用作名詞

動詞的**現在分詞**形式 (Present Participle，即在動詞尾加上 -ing 的動詞形式) 也可用作名詞。顯然，這類名詞多表示某種動作或活動。看下面一段話：

Fat Sam tried various forms of exercise: *swimming*, *cycling* and *running*. He even tried *dieting* for two days, but Sam finally gave up all hope of *slimming* because he could not put his favourite pastimes — *eating* and *drinking*, and *dreaming* and *thinking* about *eating* and *drinking* — out of his mind.

上面這段話中所有以 -ing 結尾的動詞形式都用作名詞，其中 swimming, cycling 和 running 表示 Sam 所作的各種運動；dieting 和 slimming 兩個名詞與其動詞本身的意思相同；eating, drinking, dreaming 和 thinking 則是說明 Sam 日常習慣行為的名詞。

用作名詞的 -ing 形式的動詞有時也叫作**動名詞** (gerund)。至於語法概念上所說的 a gerund-grinder，是指那些吹毛求疵的學究式的語法學家，因為不管有無必要，他們非要把動詞的現在分詞與動名詞形式區分得清清楚楚。這一名稱也提醒我們，本

書的目的在於告訴讀者應該怎樣在寫作中恰當有效地使用語法，而不是僅對語法生搬硬套。

• 形容詞用作名詞

形容詞也可用作名詞。這類名詞最常見的用法是用來指代那些具有該形容詞所表明的特性的人，如 the good 與 the bad, the weak 與 the strong, the rich 與 the poor。還有更多的例子：

> the beautiful, the dutiful, the meek, the sick, the blameless, the homeless, the grotesque, the picturesque, the lecherous, the treacherous, the uneatable, the unspeakable, an academic, a schizophrenic, a mystic, a romantic.

◆ 單數名詞、複數名詞和集合名詞

• 名詞的數

名詞可以是**單數** (Singular) 也可以是**複數** (Plural)，單數是指數量上只有一個，複數是指數量上有兩個或以上。名詞所具有的這種單數和複數的特性叫作名詞的**數** (Number)。

• 名詞複數變化規則

絕大多數英語名詞的複數形式是在單數形式後加上字母 **s** 構成的。例如：

> car/cars, house/houses, submarine/submarines.

有些名詞，尤其當該名詞是以 **ch**, **sh** 或 **s** 結尾時，變成複數形式時要在其單數形式之後加上 **es**。例如：

> arches, churches, thrushes, wishes, gases, kisses.

當一個單數名詞是以輔音字母加 y 結尾時，其複數形式就要把單詞末尾的 y 變成 ies。例如：

> armies, delicacies, remedies, tragedies.

有些以 f 結尾的名詞變成複數時，其尾部要變成 ves。例如：

> calves, halves, hooves, knives, lives, selves, wolves.

這一規則也有許多例外，如：

> roof/roofs, chief/chiefs, belief/beliefs, proof/proofs.

還有一些名詞複數的不規則變化形式是通過改變該名詞單數形式中的母音來實現的。例如：

> man/men, foot/feet, mouse/mice, woman/women

也有一些名詞的單數與複數形式相同。例如：

> aircraft, arms [weapons], cattle, deer, measles, milk, salmon, sheep, trout, trousers, wheat.

英語從其他語言中吸收或借用的名詞，其複數形式往往更加複雜多變，對此我們將在第四章中討論。

• 集合名詞

集合名詞 (Collective Nouns) 用來表示若干人或事物集合的名稱。例如：

> a board of directors, a cast of actors, a platoon of infantrymen, an armada/flotilla of ships, a squadron of aircraft, a school of porpoises.

雖然集合名詞是指兩個以上的人或事物，但它在語法上卻是屬於單數名詞，如：

an archipelago（單數）of islands（複數）

a constellation（單數）of stars（複數）

a miscellany（單數）of essays（複數）

◆ 可數名詞和不可數名詞

● 可數名詞

可數名詞（Countable Nouns）與**不可數名詞**（Non-countable Nouns）是英語中對名詞的又一種區分方法。可數名詞所代表的事物可以用數目來計算，如：

lorries, computers, shoppers, shoplifters

● 不可數名詞

不可數名詞則無法用數目來計算，或者說不可數名詞所代表的事物的量或許可以度量，但該事物卻無法就其個體進行計數，看下面的例子：

freight, information, business, crime.

從下面的句子中可以更明顯地看出可數名詞與不可數名詞的區別：

Fewer lorries were needed because *less freight* arrived at the depot.

A few computers can process *much information*.

Many shoppers create *much business*, with *fewer shoplifters* there is *less crime*.

標準英語是不容許以下這些表達方式的：

less lorries, fewer freight, less computers, many

information, much shoppers, many business, less shoplifters, fewer crime.

可數名詞與不可數名詞的區分決定了用來表明事物的量的集合名詞的用法，也就是說，用來描述可數名詞集合的集合名詞必須具有可以單獨計數的特性，而用來描述不可數名詞集合的集合名詞則必須具有數量不可單獨計數的特徵。比較下面兩組例子：

可數	不可數
the number of vehicles	the volume of traffic
a series of accidents	a great deal of distress
a number of ten-pound notes	a sum of money
a succession of visitors	the amount of interest

以people這個詞為例，該詞為可數名詞，在標準英語中就不容許有諸如the amount of people這樣的表達方式，因為amount這個集合名詞通常是與不可數名詞搭配使用的。

以上所作的這些區分非常重要，可以使我們更精確地描述現實的真實情況，並且可以通過加入一些相關的語法上的細節和限定來對事物加以界定。如果沒有語法上的這些區分，我們寫出來的東西就會顯得粗劣含混，缺乏說服力。

◆ 名詞的性

● 陰性和陽性

在現代英語中，名詞的性 (Gender) 是與生物學上的性相一致的，分為陽性、陰性和中性。這與古英語或現代德語、法語是不同的。這些語言中名詞的性既有生物學上的區分，也有語

法上的區分。例如，在古英語中，ham (home) 這個詞是陽性，而stow (place) 這個詞卻是陰性；在法語中，arbre (tree) 是陽性，而fleur (flower) 卻又成了陰性。英語當中有不同的陽性和陰性名詞形式來表示各種動物的雄性和雌性，例如：

> bitch/dog, cow/bull, dam/sire, doe/buck, duck/drake, ewe/ram, colt/filly, mare/stallion, goose/gander, hen/cock, pen/cob, sow/boar (前者雌性，後者雄性)

- 陰性後綴 -ess

當沒有專門的詞來表示雌性動物時，後綴 **-ess** 可以起到這樣的作用，如lion/lioness 和tiger/tigress，這些詞將長時間存在於英語中。另外一些表示貴族成員的詞也是如此，例如：

> duchess/duke, countess/earl, marchioness/marquis.

人們對於性別的看法在改變，連帶對於語言中的性這一概念的態度也在改變。除去表示動物和貴族成員的詞之外，有些名詞的陰性形式已經被陽性形式所取代，或者有些曾經是陽性形式的名詞現在變成了陰陽兩性通用的詞。語言上的變化反映了社會的變化，隨著法律的進步以及人們對於兩性態度的變化，現在已經沒有什麼職業是被男性所壟斷的了。因此像authoress, instructress, manageress, poetess 等這樣的詞已近銷聲匿跡了；那些表明動作發出者、職業從事者或具有某行為特徵的人的施事者名詞，過去有的以尾碼-trix來表示陰性及-tor來表示陽性，如下面這些例子：

> administratrix, curatrix, directrix, executrix, inheritrix, mediatrix, proprietrix, prosecutrix.

用現在的眼光來看，這些詞都已顯得不合時宜了。

然而，英語中陰陽兩性通用的過程並未完結，也沒有一致的規則。陰性名詞仍在使用，但有些詞已經非常孤立，有些詞只能專門用於女性，有些則是出於女性的自我意識的需要而仍然保留著。例如：

> barmaid, heroine, housewife, lady, midwife, mistress, suffragette, usherette, waitress.

在很多施事者名詞中，可以用後綴-woman來代替-man，例如：

> countrywoman, forewoman, horsewoman, policewoman, saleswoman, spokeswoman, sportswoman, townswoman.

像to man the exhibition這個短語中的動詞to man可以換成to staff，即to staff the exhibition。但是，盡量多的使用陽性名詞這一傾向是英語這種語言所固有的，例如下面這些詞就很難找到兩性通用的形式：

> craftsmanship, human, husbandry, man-eating tiger, man-hole, man in the moon, manslaughter, masterpiece, mastery.

◆ 名詞的格

● 古英語名詞的格

在古英語中，名詞和代詞按照它們在句子中的位置及功能會有不同的格 (Case) 及曲折變化形式，例如，古英語中的scip (與ship義同) 一詞，單數有三種形式：scip, scipes和scipe；複數也有三種形式：scipu, scipa和scipum。也就是説一個名詞有六種變化形式。

• 名詞的所有格

現代英語語法已經有了很大的簡化，名詞只有兩種格，一種是單詞的原形，一種是**所有格** (Possesive Case) 形式。所有格一般通過在單詞末尾加's或s'來表達 (詳見第132–41頁)。現代英語的發展變化有時並不遵循一定之規則，或甚至讓人覺得不合邏輯，比如名詞在發展過程中失去了表示格的屬性的詞尾，而代詞卻仍然保留著這些詞尾 (參見第19頁)。

代 詞

代詞 (Pronouns) 起替代作用，是替代名詞的詞。它雖是一個比較小的詞類，但仍可分為幾種，並且其中大多數在標準書面英語中使用頻繁。

◆ 人稱代詞

人稱代詞 (Personal Pronouns) 是代詞中最主要的一類，有數、性、人稱、格四種語法特徵，因此它是除動詞之外，語法變化形式最多的一個詞類。

• 人稱代詞的數

像名詞一樣，人稱代詞有單數和複數之分，如：

單數	複數
I	we
you	you
he/she/it	they

- 人稱代詞的性

　　人稱代詞的性也像名詞一樣，主要從生物學角度來區分，如：

陽性	陰性	中性
he/him/his	she/her/hers	it/its

I, you（單複數同形），以及we, they這幾個人稱代詞既表示陰性，也表示陽性，they還可以表示中性。嚴格來說，中性代詞並不能稱之為人稱代詞，因為它不是用來指代人的。

- 人稱代詞的人稱

　　人稱代詞除了指代人之外，還可表明語法意義上的第一、第二和第三人稱：

	單數	複數
第一人稱	I	we
第二人稱	you	you
第三人稱	he, she, it	they

第一人稱代詞I和we用來指代說話者，表明的是說話者的敘述角度；第二人稱代詞you指聽話者或說話者的直接授話對象；第三人稱代詞he, she, it和they用來指代被說話者所提及的人或物，即說話者和受話者之外的人或物。

　　代詞用作主語時，其數和人稱就決定了句子中動詞的語法形式。在現代英語語法中，動詞只有兩種表達數的形式，一種是動詞的原形，另一種是原形尾部加-s，如：

代詞	動詞
he, she, it	walks
I, you, we, they	walk

代詞與動詞之間的這種呼應關係在語法上稱為人稱與數的一致。

• 人稱代詞的格

　　人稱代詞的格有不同的形式。所謂格，這裏是指代詞的語法範疇及形式，依該代詞在句子中的功能而定。人稱代詞的三種格分別是主格、賓格和所有格。

　　人稱代詞的主格形式有：

　　I, you, he, she, it, we, they

顧名思義，作為主格的這些人稱代詞形式主要是用來作與之相關的動詞的主語，如：

主語	動詞
he, she, it	walks
I, you, we, they	walk

在語法術語中，**主格** (Subjective Case) 有時也稱為Nominative Case，而前者的用法更普遍，因為它能更清楚地表明主格代詞作主語的特性 (因為英語中「主語」一詞為subject，而subjective是subject的形容詞形式)。

　　作賓格的人稱代詞有：

　　me, you, him, her, it, us, them.

毫無疑問，賓格人稱代詞是用來作動詞的賓語，如：

主語	動詞	賓語
The reporter	interviewed	me, you, him, her, us, them

當人稱代詞出現在介詞之後時，也要用賓格形式，如：

主語	動詞	介詞	代詞
The reporter	wrote	about	me, you, him, her, it, us, them

因此，我們應該說 between you and me，或者 from him and me，而不是 between you and I，或者 from him and I。賓格有時稱為 Accusative Case，但在英語中，同樣由於 Objective Case 這一說法能更明確地表明賓格代詞作動詞或介詞賓語的特徵，所以人們也就習慣使用 Objective Case 這一術語。

　　以上關於人稱代詞的規則有兩種例外情況，一是當代詞作系動詞 be 的賓語時，該代詞要使用其主格形式，因此在較規範的標準英語中，我們會看到這樣的句子：

　　They are the winners; it is *we* who are the losers.

　　The best candidate was *she* who spoke first.

代詞在這兩個例句中的用法時常被認為有些陳腐，卻不能改成下面的形式：

　　They are the winners; it is *us* who are the losers.

　　The best candidate was *her* who spoke first.

因為這是不符合語法要求的。為了既避免使用這種陳腐、呆板的主格形式，又避免使用賓格而造成語法錯誤，目前人們傾向於用下面的句式來表達：

　　They are the winners and we are the losers.

The best candidate was the woman who spoke first.

另一個例外情況是當代詞跟在某些表示比較的表達方式之後時，該代詞要用主格形式。這些表示比較的表達方式有more than, more fearful than, less than, less able than, worse than, better than, no better than, as good as等等。例如：

You need this even more than *I*.

I am probably more timid than *she*.

We are just as important as *they*.

為了便於記住這條規則，可以假設句子中前面出現的動詞要在代詞後重複出現，即：

You need this even more than I need this. 或者：

You need this even more than I do.

I am probably more timid than she is.

We are just as important as they are.

人稱代詞的所有格形式(所有格代詞)有：

mine, yours, his, hers, its, ours, theirs.

所有格形式的人稱代詞和名詞表示擁有或所有權。人稱代詞的其他所有格形式還有：

my, your, her, our, their

而這些形式的所有格被稱為所有格形容詞，或所有格限定詞。所有格代詞與所有格限定詞(形容詞)的區別在於，所有格代詞用來做句子的主語和賓語，或者作介詞的賓語，而所有格限定詞出現在它所修飾的名詞或名詞短語之前。下面列舉的幾對句子中，每對的第一句中使用的是所有格代詞，第二句中使用的是所有格限定詞：

Mine is the smallest car in the car park. 或者：
The smallest car in the car park is *mine*.
My car is the smallest in the car park.

Even so, I would not exchange this car for *yours*.
Even so, I would not exchange this car for *your* car.

I cannot remember which suitcase is *hers*.
I cannot remember which is *her* suitcase.

Theirs is an early morning flight; *ours* is at noon.
Their flight is early in the morning; *our* flight is at noon.

所有格 (Possessive Case) 在英語中有時也稱為生成格 (Genitive Case)，但人們更習慣於使用前者，因為它能明確地表示所有的意思。

上面所講到的人稱代詞的各種屬性，即數 (單複數)、性 (陽性、陰性和中性)、人稱 (第一、二、三人稱) 和格 (主格、賓格、所有格) 可以用下表作一小結：

人稱	單數			複數		
	主語	賓語	所有格	主語	賓語	所有格
第一	I	me	mine	we	us	ours
第二	you	you	yours	you	you	yours
第三	he/she/it	him/her/it	his/hers/its	they	them	theirs

• 人稱代詞的拼寫

英語中少數幾條絕對規則之一，就是人稱代詞的所有格形式後永遠不加撇號 (')，如：

yours, his, hers, its, ours, theirs.

同樣，關係代詞**who**的所有格**whose**的後面也從來不跟撇號。

至於 its 和 it's，以及 whose 和 who's 這兩對詞則很容易使人產生誤解，但它們也不是很難區分。It's 是 it is 的縮略形式，意思也顯而易見，如下面的句子中方括號所示：

> When it's [it is] winter in Sweden it's [it is] summer in Australia.

把這句話與下面沒有撇號的所有格代詞 its 的正確用法比較一下就更清楚了：

> Three features of the city of Edinburgh are its historic Castle, its varied architecture and its annual Festival of the arts.

在 its historic Castle, its varied architecture 和 its annual Festival of the arts 這三個短語中，its 的意思是「……的」或「屬於……的」，這裏的意思當然是「Edinburgh 的」或「屬於 Edinburgh 的」。

而 who's 是 who is 的縮略形式，意思即「誰是……」，如：

> Everyone who's [who is] elected to Parliament has an entry in *Who's Who* [Who is Who].

下面是所有格代詞 whose 的正確用法的一個例子：

> Mark Mason, whose favourite putter was stolen the night before the tournament, took six strokes at the fourteenth hole.

句中的短語 whose favourite putter 意思是「屬於他的 (Mark Mason 的) 高爾夫球輕擊棒」。

要想正確使用 its, it's 和 who's, whose 這兩對詞，重要的是看你在使用它們時是想表達 it is 還是 belonging to it 的意思，或者

是想說who is還是belonging to whom的意思。為了避免在使用
這兩對詞時造成拼寫錯誤，可以採用這樣的簡單方法：當要表
達it is的意思時，就寫成it is而不用it's；當要表達who is的意
思時，就寫成who is而不用who's。It's和who's這兩個縮略形式
的完全形式it is和who is也正符合標準英語的要求。關於撇號
的其他用法，詳見第129–40頁。

◆ 反身代詞

反身代詞 (Reflexive Pronouns) 是代詞中的一個小類，包括：

myself, yourself, himself, herself, ourselves, yourselves,
themselves.

它們被稱為反身代詞，是因為這些代詞用來指代同一個句子中
出現的人稱代詞或名詞，如：

They cooled *themselves* with chilled drinks.

The *bowler* was disgusted with *himself* when he was
hit for six.

在以上兩個例子中，反身代詞themselves用來指代人稱代詞
they，是動詞cooled的賓語；反身代詞himself指代的是名詞
bowler，是介詞with的賓語。

◆ 強調代詞

強調代詞 (Emphatic Pronouns) 與反身代詞在形式上完全相
同，但它們在句子中的位置一般是緊跟在它們所指代的人稱代
詞或名詞之後，這樣就起到對該人稱代詞或名詞的強調作用：

He himself admitted he bowled badly.

The *pitch itself* was not to blame.

◆ 疑問代詞

疑問代詞 (Interrogative Pronouns) 也是代詞中的一個小類，用來提出問題，包括：

who, whom, whose, what, which.

疑問代詞常出現在句子開頭的位置：

Who chose the team?

Whom did you consult in the selection?

Whose idea was it to include that bowler?

Which batsman will open the innings, and *what* is his average this season?

至於why和where等其他wh-詞，一般被劃分為副詞或副詞性介詞 (詳見第85–86頁)。

◆ 關係代詞

有些**關係代詞** (Relative Pronouns) 與疑問代詞形式相同：

who, whom, whose, which, that, what.

這兩者的語法區別在於，關係代詞通常與其前面出現的從句中的名詞或代詞相關，並且位於從句的首位。有關關係代詞的詳細說明，請見第259–72頁。

◆ 指示代詞

指示代詞 (Demonstrative Pronouns) 包括this, that, these和those，其功能是指明該代詞所代替的名詞。如：

This is the *handbook* for the IBM computer.

在這句話中，指示代詞this用來指代名詞handbook。同樣，在下面的句子中：

Whose compact *disc* is *that*?

指示代詞that指代名詞disc。再如：

I tried other *print ribbons* but I prefer *these*.

這裏的指示代詞these指代的是名詞print ribbons。

如果一個指示詞後緊跟一個名詞，則這個指示詞可稱為指示形容詞或指示限定詞，或簡單稱為限定詞。

◆ 不定代詞

不定代詞 (Indefinite Pronouns) 用於指代不確定的人或物。用來指人的不定代詞有：

one, anyone, someone, anybody, somebody, everyone, everybody, no one, nobody.

Everyone assumed that *someone* would order new ribbons. *Anyone* could have done it but *no one* did.

其他不定代詞可以用來既指人又指物，如：

all, few, enough, several, many, more, most, others.

如果不定代詞後緊隨的是一個名詞、其他代詞或形容詞，那麼這個不定代詞的詞類就變成不定指限定詞，也稱為不定指形容詞。在下面的兩對句子中，第一句中用的是不定代詞，第二句用的是不定指限定詞：

Most had entered the industry straight from university.

All the best software designers were promoted.

Some joined the research department and *others* joined the marketing department.

Several designers were transferred to the training unit so that *enough* new designers would be available.

對代詞this和it的濫用或含混的使用是常見的錯誤,尤其在用這兩個詞作句首時更要小心。只有在明確指代前一句話中的名詞或名詞短語時,才能用這兩個代詞。

形容詞

形容詞(Adjectives)是詞類中的一個大類,並且變化多樣,往往緊接在名詞之前,其功能是通過加入細節或定義來對名詞進行修飾和描述。細節可以是外表的、具體的,如:

loud music, black coffee, new shoes, toxic waste.

這幾個例子中,loud是形容詞,用來修飾名詞music;形容詞black用來描述名詞coffee;形容詞new修飾的是名詞shoes;形容詞toxic用來描述的是名詞waste。

另外,形容詞所描述的細節也可以是抽象的,如:

an insoluble problem, a fair decision, a melancholy mood, a controversial topic.

這幾個例子中,insoluble, fair, melancholy和controversial是形容詞,problem, decision, mood和topic則是形容詞所修飾的名詞。

形容詞還可表達比喻的意義,以加強名詞的語氣或給名詞增添一些比喻色彩,如:

a bright future, a soft option, galloping ambition, a flimsy idea.

bright, soft, galloping 和 flimsy 這四個形容詞是用來修飾 future, option, ambition 和 idea 四個名詞，這裏的每個形容詞如果單獨來看，表示的都是某種物理特性，但由於它們所修飾的名詞都是抽象名詞，這樣就產生了一種比喻的修辭效果。一般來説，形容詞放在名詞之前，但也有一些例外，例如，英語的習慣用法中不容許如下的表達方法：

> an afraid child, an aware student, a glad mother.

正確的説法應該是：

> the child was afraid, the student was aware, the mother was glad.

習語 (Idiom)，或者習慣表達法是經過長期使用而約定俗成的，是一種為人們所廣泛接受的單詞組合形式。正如社會其他現象一樣，約定俗成的東西對於語言也具有很強的約束作用。

下面幾個習慣表達法中，形容詞就被放到了名詞之後：

> the body politic, chairman designate, crown imperial, heir apparent, inspector general, letters patent, malice aforethought, president elect, princess royal.

在法語中，形容詞通常被置於名詞之後，而上面這些短語也如下面這幾個從法語中借用的專業性短語一樣：

> court martial, band sinister, lion rampant.

形容詞及其所修飾的名詞或代詞有時會被動詞或副詞隔開，例如：

> Miriam Levy was confident in rehearsal but she felt extremely nervous in performance. Her friend, Anna Desai, always seemed calm in front of an audience.

這句話中，形容詞confident修飾的是專有名詞Miriam Levy，卻被動詞was隔開；形容詞nervous修飾的是代詞she，但這二者之間卻插入了動詞felt和副詞extremely；形容詞calm描述的是另一個專有名詞Anna Desai，之間也是插入了副詞always和動詞seemed。

◆ 形容詞的來源及構成

現代英語中的很多形容詞都來自古英語和中古英語，如：

alive, dead, good, bad, weak, strong, ghastly, wonderful, heavenly, hellish, hard, soft

還有表示顏色的形容詞：

black, blue, brown, green, grey, red, white, yellow.

像古英語一樣，從日爾曼語發展變化而來的古挪威語也是英語形容詞的來源之一，如：

flat, gusty, odd, ugly, ragged, rugged.

● 添加後綴構成的形容詞

有時本來是**詞根詞** (root word) 的形容詞，如good, bad, low, flat等，卻被毫無理由地看作是**詞幹** (stem)；還有很多其他形容詞可以由在詞根詞上加尾碼來構成，例如，把尾碼**-ful**加到名詞pain後面，這個詞就由名詞變成了形容詞painful。**-less**這個尾碼與-ful的意思差不多相反，這兩個尾碼都是由古英語而來，如：

skilful, wilful, blameless, shameless.

形容詞full中有兩個字母l，而形容詞尾碼-ful中只有一個字母l；名詞skill和will中有兩個l，而變成形容詞時就省去了一個l，拼寫成skilful和wilful。

　　還有大量其他形容詞由古英語中的尾碼-ish，-ly，-y和-some構成：

> devilish, outlandish, English, Scottish; beastly, ghastly, godly, manly; filthy, healthy, stealthy, wealthy; handsome, wholesome, loathsome, lonesome.

由古英語的尾碼-ward或-wards構成的形容詞一般表示方向：

> backward/backwards, forward/forwards, eastward, westward.

還有少量形容詞由尾碼-en和-like構成：

> wooden, woolen, ladylike, lifelike.

來自法語的尾碼-esque和-ique的拼寫和發音在一定程度上保留了法語的特徵，如：

> grotesque, picturesque, antique, unique.

拉丁語尾碼-osus和-utus到英語中變成了-ous和-ute：

> hilarious, precarious, absolute, resolute,

來自希臘語的尾碼-oid和-oidal構成了很多科學和醫學中的詞彙：

> cuboid, rheumatoid, gyroidal, typhoidal.

有一些形容詞後綴滲入英語的途徑還不十分清楚，有的是從拉丁語或希臘語借入法語，然後再從法語借入到英語中；有的是

仿造法語、拉丁語和希臘語尾碼的形式。這種多重轉借造成英
語中很多對形式上幾乎完全相同的後綴，如：

-ant 和 **-ent**：
arrogant, elegant, affluent, effluent

-able 和 **-ible**：
deplorable, ignorable, audible, legible

-ary 和 **-ory**：
necessary, voluntary, accusatory, introductory

-atic 和 **-ic**：
aristocratic, ecstatic, classic, heroic

-al 和 **-ial**：
clerical, spherical, cordial, primordial

-an 和 **-ian**：
Anglican, Lutheran, Churchillian, Gilbertian

-ane 和 **-ine**：
humane, mundane, equine, feminine

-ate 和 **-ete**：
considerate, desolate, effete, obsolete

-ac 和 **-ic**：
ammoniac, cardiac, drastic, ehthusiastic.

• 添加字首構成的形容詞

通過添加字首，即把詞素加到詞根詞前面，也可構成形容
詞。「字首」(prefix) 這個詞本身的「pre-」部分就是一個字首。字
首與尾碼都能改變詞義，所不同的是，形容詞字首往往是添加
到形容詞之前，這樣雖然改變了詞義，但並不改變原詞的詞
性。很多形容詞字首可以把原來的形容詞變成其反義詞，即添
加字首後的形容詞與原詞的意義相反或是對原詞義的否定：

abnormal, amoral, anticlockwise, counteractive, contradictory, disgraceful, distasteful, illiterate, illegitimate, immortal, immoral, indefensible, indispensable, irrelevant, irreverent, undrinkable, unthinkable.

• 由動詞和名詞轉化而來的形容詞

動詞的過去分詞，即跟在助動詞has或had之後的動詞形式，常用作形容詞：

the beaten team, a dispossessed tenant, a lost child.

至今，很多這樣的形容詞仍在不斷生成，例如：

computerized production line, pressurized water reactor, recycled paper, televised debate.

以 -ing 結尾的動詞，即現在分詞，也可用作形容詞，如：

humming bird, stinging nettles, washing machine

下面是一些較新的例子：

alternating current, central processing unit, cooling cycle, expanding universe, leading/trailing edge, oscillating forms of energy, scanning electron microscope, sweetening/emulsifying agents.

形容詞還可以由名詞構成，只要把一個名詞放到另一個名詞之前即可：

brain waves, wave power, power boat, boat people
communications satellite, satellite transmission
cell culture, culture shock, shock wave, wave motion.

◆ 形容詞的比較級

在 extremely nervous 這個短語中，副詞 extremely 用來表示 nervous 這個形容詞的程度。下面是一些類似的例子：

acutely anxious, desperately sad, naturally fat, peculiarly pink, very small, wholly innocent.

不同的程度可以單獨用形容詞的不同形式來表達，這些形式在語法上稱為原級、比較級和最高級，多數形容詞的變化形式是這樣的：

原級	比較級	最高級
sad	sadder	saddest
fat	fatter	fattest
pink	pinker	pinkest

上面這些形容詞，其語法變化形式是規則的，下面則是一些語法變化形式不規則的形容詞：

原級	比較級	最高級
bad	worse	worst
good	better	best
little	less/lesser	least
many/much	more	most

有些形容詞要在前面加上形容詞 more 或 most 來表示比較或加強語氣，如：

原級	比較級	最高級
anxious	more anxious	most anxious
careful	more careful	most careful
helpless	more helpless	most helpless

有些形容詞帶有絕對意義，因此是不可比較的，也就是說，它們沒有程度上的高低、大小、強弱、優劣之分，使用的時候只有一種形式：

> complete, dead, eternal, faultless, final, finished, incomparable, infinite, perfect, ultimate, unique.

與此類似，表示次序的序數詞也不能進行比較：

> first, second, third

然而，the very first這樣的表達方式卻是人們所認可的。數量詞可以看作是形容詞，但把它們歸為數量詞更加簡單明瞭（關於數量詞另見第36–38頁）。

限定詞

　　限定詞 (Determiners) 的語法作用是對名詞或名詞短語的範圍加以限制或界定。正由於限定詞的這種功能，使它具有形容詞的作用。限定詞包括了少量的不同種類的功能詞，這也體現了英語語法的簡化趨勢。限定詞這個詞在意義上含混不清，是因為它包含了曾經屬於甚至目前仍屬於其他一些詞類的詞。正是這個原因 —— 即把幾個詞類壓縮為一個詞類，我們可以說限定詞標誌著語法的簡化。

　　像形容詞一樣，限定詞一般放在它所修飾限定的名詞或名

詞短語之前。最常用的限定詞有 **a/an** 和 **the**，它們也分別被稱為**不定冠詞** (Indefinite Article) 和**定冠詞** (Definite Article)，如：

a party, an opposition party, the political party.

常用的限定詞還有下面幾個：

this, that, these, those

這些詞有時也稱為指示詞，因為它們用來指出或者表明所涉及到的名詞或名詞短語，例如：

this cinema, that supermarket, these new town-centre offices, those building society branches.

與上述幾個限定詞相似的還有：

which, whichever, what, whatever, whose

這些詞可以用在一般陳述之中，如：

Jack can afford to buy *whichever* computer he chooses.

He knew *what* discount the dealer gave to students.

這幾個詞還可以用於疑問句，用來提問，如：

Which computer did you finally choose, Jack?

Whatever reason led you to buy a Millennium X12?

Whose recommendation was that?

表示所有的限定詞，即：

my, your, his, her, its, our, their

可以明確表明擁有、所有，或歸屬，如：

my computer, your pocket calculator, her expensive video recorder, their antique gramophone.

當這些表示所有的限定詞以下面的形式出現時：

　　　　　mine, yours, hers, ours, theirs

就被用來代替名詞而不是修飾名詞，因此應屬於代詞（見第21–
22頁）。限定詞與代詞不同，它們不能單獨出現，一般後面要緊
跟一個名詞或名詞短語，有些限定詞可以表示名詞或名詞短語
的範圍或數量，如：

> most vehicles, some family cars, all motor cycles, many
> furniture vans, every horse-box, much traffic congestion,
> each motorway filling-station, enough petrol, no car
> parks, less bad temper, few accidents, several slow-
> moving farm tractors, whole families.

名詞和名詞短語前還可以有兩個或更多個限定詞，如：

> a few vintage cars, this whole stretch of motorway,
> each and every driver, all the many miles.

　　上面出現了諸多語法術語，如定冠詞、不定冠詞、指示詞
和表示所有的詞等，甚至限定詞本身也是一個術語。這些術語
只對語法學家來説有意義，大多數作者只要能明白限定詞不過
是提供一些使他們的寫作表達得更清楚和更精確的方式就可以
了。

數量詞

　　數量詞（Numerals）是用來表示數目的一類詞。在語法中，
之所以用numeral這個單詞來表述數量詞，而不用number，是
因為number這個詞常用來指「數」這個語法概念，即單數、複數
而不是指數學意義上的數位記號。

　　把數量詞歸為一種詞類，使英語語法得到了簡化。像限定

詞一樣，數量詞曾被劃分到不同的詞類中，但現代語法認為，從零到無窮大的數量詞共有的數學特性比它們多種多樣的語法特性更為重要。過去的語法中對數量詞的分類在本節的最後有所論及。在現代語法中，我們只須考察一下數量詞的兩個小類，即基數詞和序數詞。

◆ 基數詞

基數 (Cardinal) 這個詞來自拉丁語，意為「絞鏈、關鍵」，後來它的意義逐漸引申為「基本的、主要的或首要的」，因為次要的事物總是跟著首要事物轉動。

那麼基數詞就是那些基本形式的數量詞，如：

> one, two, three, four, five ... ninety-seven, ninety-eight, ninety-nine, 100.

在標準英語寫作中書寫數位時，人們普遍認可的寫法是從一到九十九的數位用英文拼寫，從一百到一百以上的數位則直接用阿拉伯數字。而在英國的報刊雜誌上和許多書籍中，是把從一到九的數位用英文拼寫，十和十以上的數位則用阿拉伯數字。這種做法在書寫成千上萬的大數位時就顯示出了優勢，例如 17,475,739 這個數位這樣寫，即使對於不太識數的人，也是既易寫又易讀，比寫成下面的形式要簡便容易得多：seventeen million, four hundred and seventy five thousand, seven hundred and thirty-nine。

◆ 序數詞

序數 (Ordinal) 這個詞源自拉丁語的 *ordinalis*，意指順序或位元次。下面是序數詞的例子：

— 37 —

first, second, third, fourth, fifth

100th, 101st, 102nd, 103rd, 104th, 105th

此外，數量詞還有一個小類，其中包括once, twice和thrice三個副詞。

　　過去的語法曾把數量詞劃分為三個詞類：形容詞、副詞和代詞。下面是三個數量詞作形容詞的例子：

> Mark Mason, the *second* golfer to tee-off, took *six* strokes at the *fourteenth* hole.

這句話中序數詞second作形容詞修飾名詞golfer，基數詞six修飾名詞strokes，序數詞fourteenth修飾名詞hole。下面的例子中，數量詞用作了副詞：

> Geoff Gratton, who had won *twice* before on the Blue Pines course, was lying *first* at the end of his round but finished *third* in the tournament.

這裏，數量詞twice, first和third作副詞，分別修飾動詞won, was lying和finished。

　　下面是數量詞作代詞的例子：

> *Forty-two* played in the tournament. *Two* equalled the club record of *seventy-three* and a *third* scored *seventy-four*, but the winner was Sean Kelly with a round of *sixty-eight*.

這句話中，有的數量詞代表golfer, competitor或player等名詞，有的作動詞的主語或賓語，有的作介詞的賓語。Forty-two是動詞played的主語，two是動詞equalled的主語，seventy-three是介詞of的賓語，third是動詞scored的主語，seventy-four是scored的賓語，sixty-eight是介詞of的賓語。

動 詞

　　動詞 (Verbs) 是詞類中的一個大類，是用來表明動作、變化及存在狀態的詞。動詞既是實義詞又是功能詞，在句子中既有表義功能，又有比其他詞類更多的語法功能。

　　語法上，一個標準英語句子，至少要有一個**限定動詞** (Finite Verb，即帶主語的動詞)，這是最低要求。限定動詞的主語也就是包含該動詞的從句或句子的主語，是該動詞所表明動作的施事者或動作發出者。

　　主語可以是名詞：

　　　　Authors (名詞) write (限定動詞)

也可以是名詞短語 (由一個名詞做中心詞或主導詞的一組詞)：

　　　　Some modern authors (名詞短語) write (限定動詞)

還可以是代詞：

　　　　They (代詞) write.

當動詞用來表達命令的語氣時，主語可能是暗指但並不在句子中出現的 you：

　　　　Write!

動詞的類型和形式決定了該詞所要表明的動作、變化或存在狀態的性質及範圍。

　　動詞的作用範圍受到下列因素的影響：是規則動詞還是不規則動詞；是主要動詞還是助動詞；是及物動詞還是不及物動詞；是限定動詞還是非限定動詞；是主動語態還是被動語態；是單數還是複數；是陳述語氣、祈使語氣還是虛擬語氣。此外，動詞的形式還表明了時態，用來表達不同的時間概念。

◆ 規則動詞

　　規則動詞(Regular Verbs)是指可以在詞尾加上屈折變化-ed 來構成其過去式(見第61–65頁)的動詞。以規則動詞walk的過去式為例:

　　　I walked　　I have walked　　I had walked.

就其所有的時態和功能來說,walk這個詞有四種不同的變化形式:

　　　walk　　walks　　walking　　walked.

同樣,所有其他規則動詞都有四種形式,如:

add	adds	adding	added
love	loves	loving	loved
zip	zips	zipping	zipped

大多數借入英語或創造出的新動詞都看作是規則動詞:

　　　anodize, breathalyse, bulldoze, clone, degauss, demote, interface, metricate, overkill, streamline, telephone, televise, transduce, zap, zip.

◆ 不規則動詞

　　不規則動詞(Irregular Verbs)打破了前面提到的規則動詞變化的常規,其過去時態採用不同的形式,例如不規則動詞think的過去式為thought,並且其三種過去時態的形式都是thought:

　　　I thought　　I have thought　　I had thought.

動詞think的所有時態和功能共有四種形式：

think   thinks   thinking   thought.

有些不規則動詞的過去時態有兩種形式：

I drank	I have drunk	I had drunk
I drove	I have driven	I had driven
I swam	I have swum	I had swum

這種過去時態有兩種形式的不規則動詞，其所有時態和功能有五種形式：

drink	drinks	drinking	drank	drunk
drive	drives	driving	drove	driven
swim	swims	swimming	swam	swum

最為常用的不規則動詞be有如下變化形式：

be   am   are   is   being   was   were   been.

不規則動詞的過去時在非標準語法中，或稱通俗語法中得到了簡化，這在英國非常普遍。例如在通俗語法中，採用I have drank和she had drove這樣的表達形式，而不用標準英語中的I have drunk和she had driven。通俗語法還創造了標準語法中不存在的動詞過去時形式。例如在標準英語中burst和hurt這兩個詞的過去時和現在時同形，而通俗語法中卻容許bursted和hurted這樣的非標準形式出現。

下面列出了不規則動詞的標準語法形式，其中除了pay這個動詞是來自古法語之外，其他所有列出的不規則動詞均來自古英語或中古英語。用星號（*）標出的動詞在列表之後有更詳細的講解：

不規則動詞

arise arose arisen	fly flew flown
beat beat beaten	forbid forbade forbidden
become became become	forgo forwent forgone
begin began begun	foresee foresaw foreseen
bid bid bid*	forget forgot forgotten
break broke broken	freeze froze frozen
build built built	give gave given
burn burnt/burned burnt/burned	go went gone
	grow grew grown
burst burst burst	hang hung/hanged hung/hanged*
cast cast cast	
catch caught caught	heave heaved heaved*
choose chose chosen	hide hid hidden
cling clung clung	hold held held
cost cost cost*	hurt hurt hurt
cut cut cut	kneel knelt knelt
deal dealt dealt	know knew known
dig dug dug	lay laid laid*
do did done	lean leant/leaned leant/leaned
draw drew drawn	learn learnt/learned learnt/learned
dream dreamt/dreamed dreamt/dreamed	
	let let let
eat ate eaten	lie lay lain*
fall fell fallen	light lit lit
find found found	lose lost lost
fling flung flung	mean meant meant

mistake mistook mistaken	spend spent spent
outdo outdid outdone	spill spilt/spilled spilt/spilled
overcome overcame overcome	spit spat spat*
pay paid paid	spit spitted spitted*
put put put	spread spread spread
putt putted putted*	spring sprang sprung
ride rode ridden	steal stole stolen
ring rang rung	sting stung stung
saw sawed sawn	stink stank stunk
see saw seen	strike struck struck*
seek sought sought	string strung strung
sew sewed sewn*	swear swore sworn
shake shook shaken	swell swelled swollen
show showed shown	swim swam swum
shrink shrank shrunk	swing swung swung
sing sang sung	take took taken
sink sank sunk	teach taught taught
slay slew slain*	tear tore torn
sleep slept slept	throw threw thrown
sling slung slung	wear wore worn
slink slunk slunk	weave wove woven
sow sowed sowed/sown*	weep wept wept
speak spoke spoken	wring wrung wrung
speed sped sped	write wrote written
spell spelt/spelled spelt/spelled	

Bid	過去式bade和過去分詞bidden現在是屬於較陳腐的用法。
Cost	Costed的形式只在表示估算生產成本的意義時使用。
Hang/ hung	在標準英語中，hung用來指無生命的東西，如Portraits have been hung in the gallery. 而hanged是指用絞刑把人處死，如The prisoner was hanged at dawn.
Heave	其過去式hove現在只用在較古舊的有關航海業的術語中，如hove to.
Lay	這個動詞的原形和現在時形式是lay，意思是放置在地上或放到平面上，例如，Hens lay eggs. 其過去時形式為laid。這個詞的引申義可以表示放置，如He laid a bet或She is laying paving stones.
Lie	其原形和現在時形式為lie，意思是處於躺臥的狀態，如to lie in bed；這個動詞的過去式為lay，如He lay in bed until noon；其過去分詞為lain，如Litter has lain in the street all week.
Lie	意思是「說謊」時為規則動詞，其過去式和過去分詞形式相同，都是lied.
Put	這個動詞中有一個t，其過去式和過去分詞都是put，當變成現在分詞時，要雙寫t，即putting.
Putt	這個動詞中有兩個t，其過去時形式為putted，它只是用於高爾夫球和鉛球兩項運動中。
Sew	中間字母是e，意思是用針（needle）和線縫（thread）。

Sow	中間字母是 o，意思是播種粟 (corn) 或麥 (oats)。
Slay	這是個古舊的動詞，但小報的編輯們卻把它在某種程度上賦予了新的用途。
Spit	意思是吐唾沫，其過去式形式為 spat.
Spit	意思是把肉放置在烤肉叉上，是一個規則動詞，其過去時形式為 spitted.
Strike	其比較古舊的過去時形式 striken 一般只用於像 grief-striken 和 panic-striken 一類的表達方法中。

◆ 主要動詞

主要動詞 (Main Verbs) 通常是指一個單獨的單詞，如下面句子中斜體字所示：

Some authors *write* book reviews for newspapers.

Few novelists *earn* a living from their books alone.

Many journalists now *use* word processors.

這三個句子中的限定動詞 write, earn 和 use 都是主要動詞，都是一個單獨的詞，具有明確的意義和連接句子中主語和賓語的語法功能。以第一句話為例，動詞的主語是 some authors，賓語是 book reviews for newspapers。

◆ 助動詞

助動詞 (Auxiliary Verbs)，口語中也稱為幫助動詞 (Helping Verbs)，是放在主要動詞之前的動詞，用來延伸主要動詞的意義或功能，或使主要動詞的意義或功能更加完整。最常用的助動詞是 be, have 和 do，如：

Some authors *are writing* book reviews for newspapers.

Few novelists *have earned* a living from their books alone.

The old journalist *does not use* a word processor.

正由於助動詞延伸了主要動詞的語法功能和意義，所以完整的語法功能就由助動詞和主要動詞來共同實現。當助動詞和主要動詞以這種方式結合在一起時，它們就被視為一個動詞。上面第三個例子中的 does not use 這個短語表明，在助動詞和主要動詞之間可以插入副詞（這裏是 not）。再如：

Journalists *are* now（副詞）*using* word processors.

主要動詞之前也可以有一個以上的助動詞出現，但仍然視為一個動詞，如：

Some authors *may have written* book reviews for newspapers.

Few novelists *can have earned* a living from their books alone.

Many journalists *will have been using* word processors for years.

上面這幾句中的動詞短語 may have written, can have earned 和 will have been using 都被視為起到一個動詞的語法作用。

◆ 及物動詞

及物動詞（Transitive Verbs）中的 transitive 這個詞帶有通過或穿過的意思。一個動詞是及物的，就是說句子的意思可以從主語經由動詞直接傳遞給句子的賓語。看下面的例子：

Matthew Ray *contested* the Grantown South by-election.

Positron, the rock band, *produced* a new album.

Archaeologists *excavated* an Iron Age settlement.

及物動詞可以作為主要動詞,它的意義在缺少賓語的情況時是不完整的。如果我們把上面三句話中的賓語去掉,就會感到所餘的部分在意思上明顯不完整:

Matthew Ray contested

Positron, the rock band, produced

Archaeologists excavated

由此,我們可以判斷出 contested, produced 和 excavated 這三個動詞是及物動詞。

當一個及物的主要動詞前面加上一個助動詞(實際上往往如此),所得到的**複合動詞**仍然是及物的,如:

Matthew Ray *will contest* the Grantown south by-election.

Positron, the rock band, *has produced* a new album.

Archaeologists *have excavated* an Iron Age settlement.

◆ 不及物動詞

不及物動詞 (Intransitive Verbs) 不需把意義傳遞給賓語,它本身在無賓語的情況下就可以使句子的意思完整,如:

Darkness *fell* but the police *persevered*. Stars *glittered* and the moon *shone* as the search *continued*. The chief inspector *shivered*, a sergeant *yawned* and a constable *grumbled*. Their hopes *faded*. Just as dawn *broke* the reinforcements *arrived*. Minutes later the lost child *re-appeared* and the search *ended*.

下面列出了一些其他的不及物動詞，它們不是按照字母順序排列，而是按意思分組放在一起，這樣能夠更清楚地表明某些動作或存在狀態的性質：

> appear, disappear, seem; emerge, arise, occur; hope, aspire; die, expire, live, exist; dive, fall, slide, slip; laugh, smile, rejoice; giggle, snigger, guffaw; amble, linger, loiter, saunter, stroll; look, gaze, peer, stare; cease, desist; persist, remain; meditate, reflect, philosophize, reminisce, wonder, speculate, hallucinate; retreat; flourish, prosper, succeed, thrive; mutiny, rebel, revolt.

不及物動詞的規則，像英語語法中許多其他規則一樣，有著較大的靈活性。有些不及物動詞可以變成及物動詞，如look這個不及物動詞，如果加上不同的副詞和介詞，就可以變成幾個不同的及物動詞，例如給它加上 after, into, down on 或 up to，添加上去的這些詞就變成了一個新的複合動詞或短語動詞 (Phrasal Verb) 中的一部分。

　　複合動詞是指由兩個或兩個以上的詞合在一起構成的動詞；它的另一種說法「短語動詞」，意思是指由一個短語構成的動詞，其實包含兩個或兩個以上的詞，而不是僅僅一個詞。給不及物動詞look加上一些介詞或介詞性副詞，就可以得到很多及物性複合動詞，如：

> look after (care for), look at, look back at; look back on (remember), look down on (literally and figuratively to despise), look for, look forward to, look in on (visit), look into (investigate), look out (items for a jumble sale), look out for (await; beware of), look out on, look over (examine), look through (a lens, or to scan), look to (attend to), look up (a dictionary or an old friend), look up at, look up to (admire).

以上這些複合動詞都是及物動詞，後面必須帶有賓語才能使其意思完整：

> When his neighbour went into hospital, Silas Ramsden *looked after* her cat.

> Children *look forward to* their next birthday; old men *look back on* their past.

◆ 限定動詞

限定動詞（Finite Verbs）是有主語的動詞，動詞的主語，亦即該動詞所在的從句或句子的主語，是該動詞所表明動作或行為的實施者：

> Rock bands（主語）/ attract（動詞）/ big audiences.

> You（主語）/ believe（動詞）/ her.

> Members of the committee（主語）/ consider（動詞）/ the planning proposal.

限定動詞也可用於過去時態和將來時態當中：

> Anxiety（主語）/ undermined（動詞，過去時態）/ the performance.

> Students（主語）/ will write（動詞，將來時態）/ applications for jobs.

限定動詞的主語，即該動詞所在從句或句子的主語是動作的實施者或發起者，以上的例子還表明動詞的主語一般具有名詞性：

> 名　　　詞：*Anxiety, Students*
> 名詞短語：*Rock bands, Members of the committee*
> 代　　　詞：*You*

◆ 指令動詞

　　當一個動詞或動詞加上副詞單獨使用而表示命令時，就打破了通常的 主語 + 限定動詞 + 賓語 這種句子模式。命令的語氣有時常由一個感歎號來表明：

　　　　Stop!　Wait!　Listen!　Get lost!　Go away!　Stand clear!

用以上這種方式來表示直接命令的動詞叫作祈使動詞，帶有祈使語氣。使用祈使語氣時，一般認為動詞的主語是不言自明的：

　　[You] (主語) stop!

　　[You] (主語) stand clear!

◆ 動詞的非限定形式

　　動詞的某些形式，不受主語的人稱、數等語法屬性的限定，因此稱為動詞的 **非限定形式** (Non-finite Forms of Verbs)。它們是動詞的不定式、現在分詞和過去分詞。

　　動詞的不定式可以是其最基本的原形，即只有一個動詞，如：

　　　　attract, believe, consider

也可以在動詞原形式前加上 to：

　　　　to attract, to believe, to consider.

動詞的現在分詞總是以 -ing 結尾：

　　　　attracting, believing, considering.

動詞的過去分詞就是跟在 have 或 had 之後的動詞形式，正如前文所述，規則動詞的過去分詞均以 -ed 結尾：

　　　　attracted, believed, considered.

而不規則動詞的過去分詞形式則變化多樣：

drunk, eaten, gone, held, struck, swum, taught.

◆ 分裂不定式

分裂不定式 (Split Infinitives) 是指在 to 和動詞之間放上一個詞 (通常為副詞) 的情況，例如在科幻小說《星球旅行》(*Star Trek*) 介紹中的一句話：“*To boldly go* where no man has gone before.”。許多普通讀者和一些語法學家都認為這種用法是不符合語法的，然而也有不少語言學家和語法學家認為這在標準英語中是可以接受的，並且從莎士比亞至今的作家們一直在使用分裂不定式。我們認為分裂不定式是可以接受的，而且在有些句子中甚至是必要的，如：

If you want to fully achieve your ambition you must quickly change your attitude and begin to really work.

這個句子中就使用了分裂不定式 to fully achieve 和 to really work.

反對分裂不定式用法的人認為這句話「正確」的形式應該是這樣的：

If you want fully to achieve your ambition you must quickly change your attitude and begin really to work.

但是這個句子的寫法可能造成歧義，因為 fully 既可以修飾動詞 want，也可以修飾動詞 achieve，而 really 既可以修飾 begin，也可以修飾 work。這樣，作者就面臨一種兩難的選擇：分裂不定式在標準英語可以接受，而許多受過教育的讀者卻會認為這種用法是不正確的。為了避免陷入這種尷尬的境地，可以儘量避免使用分裂不定式，以免造成爭拗。

　　限定動詞在標準英語句子中的重要性從下面的例子可見一斑：

> Free tape of Positron's ten best hits to the winner of the competition.

> Last-minute Christmas spending spree by Saturday shoppers.

> Effort and artistry from Australian XV in a high-scoring match.

以上這些敘述雖然傳達了一些資訊，但由於沒有動詞，就造成語法上的不完整，因而在標準書面英語中是不能接受的。第一個敘述讀起來像一則零售廣告的廣告詞，似乎默認了讀者能夠把限定動詞這一句子中丟失的部分補充完整，像下面這樣：

> The winner of the competition *will receive* a free tape of Positron's ten best hits.

其他兩個敘述則像是報紙上的圖片標題，如果它們出現在用標準英語撰寫的報導之中，就要添加限定動詞，改寫為：

> Saturday shoppers *went* on a last-minute Christmas spending spree.

還可以像下面這樣改寫，雖然句子稍欠些想像力，卻也符合語法規範：

> There *was* a last-minute Christmas spending spree by Saturday.

用 There was 或 It was 作句子的開頭，這樣的用法可以舉一反三：

> *There was* effort and artistry from the Australian XV in a high-scoring match.

但下面這樣的寫法似乎更好：

> The Australian XV *showed* effort and artistry in a high-scoring match.

這一寫法中的主語和動詞使句子的意思更加精細，而且也使寫作風格富於變化，形象生動。

下面三個敘述中雖都包含有動詞，但由於使用的是非限定動詞形式，因而語法上不完整，在標準英語中也是不能接受的：

> Amateur archaeologists *to excavate* an Iron Age settlement.

> A marina development *proposed* for Cradle Bay.

> Light engineering factories *competing* for new orders.

給它們各加上一個限定動詞之後，就變成了既符合語法又符合標準英語規範的句子了：

> Amateur archaeologists *are to excavate* an Iron Age settlement. 或：

> Amateur archaeologists *will excavate* an Iron Age settlement.

> A marina development *is proposed* for Cradle Bay.

> Light engineering factories *are competing* for new orders.

上面句子中的非限定動詞通過添加一個助動詞之後，就變成了限定動詞。

以上的每個句子中都只有一個限定動詞，這樣的句子在語法上稱為簡單句。在標準書面英語中，典型的簡單句句型為：主語＋動詞＋賓語。把動詞和賓語放在一起有時稱為句子的**謂語**，意思是所敘述或所論及的事物。這樣的話，句子結構就可表示為：

主語＋動詞＋賓語　或　主語＋謂語　如：

Anxiety（主語）/ undermined the performance（謂語）.

◆ 動詞的主動語態和被動語態

　　動詞的**語態**（Voice）這個概念聽起來有些抽象，不妨作這樣一種想像，假設一個人在一個集會上有發言權，即他有權表達自己的意見並且有權投票，如果他行使了這些權力，那麼他的發言權就是主動的（active）或積極的（肯定的）。相反，如果他被剝奪了發言權，那麼他就是被動的（passive）。雖然語態的概念比較抽象，但動詞的主動語態和被動語態在別人寫的文章中的實例很容易辨別，我們自己使用起來也不難。

　　再來看本章中出現過的幾個句子：

Matthew Ray *contested* the Grantown South by-election.

Positron, the rock band, *produced* a new album.

Archaeologists *excavated* an Iron Age settlement.

以上每句話中的動詞都是限定性主要動詞，語態也都是主動語態。句子中的主語Matthew Ray, Positron, the rock band和Archaeologists是句子中動作的發出者，它們就像前面那個假設的例子中有發言權的人，通過限定性的主要動詞，以一種積極主動的方式統領整個句子的意思。從這種意義上來說，整個句子是主動語態，而不僅僅是句子中的動詞。

　　這些句子也可重新結構成如下的形式：

The Grantown South by-election *was contested* by Matthew Ray.

A new album *was produced* by Positron, the rock band.

> An Iron Age settlement *was excavated* by archaeologists.

其中的主語 The Grantown South by-election, A new album 及 An Iron Age settlement 不是主動者而只是動作的對象，而且每個主語的被動性由動詞的被動語態表示出來，整個句子也因而變成了被動語態。

以上兩組句子有三點不同。第一，主語和賓語的位置互換，如，當 Matthew Ray 是主動者時，它就是句子的主語，the Grantown South by-election 是句子的賓語；當 Matthew Ray 是被動者時，它就變成了句子的賓語，而 the Grantown South by-election 就成了句子的主語。換言之，就是主動語態句子中的主語變成了被動語態句子中的賓語，而主動語態句子中的賓語則變成了被動語態句子中的主語。

第二，被動語態句中的限定性主要動詞之前總有一個助動詞，且該助動詞總是動詞 be 的某種適當形式。在上面的例子中，主動語態動詞 contested, produced 和 excavated 分別變成了被動語態的 was contested, was produced 和 was excavated。當動詞的時態是現在時態或將來時態時也是同樣，例如主動語態動詞 contests (現在時) 變成被動語態就是 is contested。如果是現在時的其他形式，變成被動語態時仍然需要加上動詞 to be 的適當形式，如 is contesting 變成被動語態就應該是 is being contested。如果主動語態動詞是將來時，如 will produce，那麼被動語態就是 will be produced。依此類推，will excavate 就應變成 will be excavated。

第三，在被動句中介詞 by 一般緊跟在主要動詞之後，如 contested by, produced by 和 excavated by。在動作的發出者或施事者不很明確的句子中，介詞 by 就可省略掉：

The lost child has been found and the police search
has been called off.

從寫作手法上來講，以上這些被動語態句的結構方式都是把動作的執行者這一重要資訊放置在句子最後。通過這種手法把資訊後置，有時可以使句子造成一種懸念的效果，同時也使寫作風格富於變化。

　被動語態中的動詞總是及物動詞，也就是動詞後要跟(或者能夠跟)一個直接賓語。不及物動詞不能用作被動語態。前面用到過的關於不及物動詞的例子中有下面幾句話：

Darkness fell. Stars glittered and the moon shone. Just
as dawn broke the reinforcements arrived. Minutes later
the lost child reappeared.

這些句子中的主語和賓語的位置是不能互換的，因為根本就沒有賓語存在。正因如此，也就不能在動詞後加介詞 by：

Darkness was fallen by ...　Dawn was broken by ...

前面有些例句中的不及物動詞也可用作被動語態，但原句的句子結構、風格和部分意義都會發生改變，如：

The chief inspector *shivered*, a sergeant *yawned* and a
constable *grumbled*; their hopes *faded*.

這句話變為被動語態就成為：

A shiver *was experienced* by the chief inspector, a yawn
was emitted by a sergeant and a grumble *was expressed*
by a constable; their hopes *were faded* [by lack of
success]

但這句話卻變得既呆板又不合規範。

　祈使語氣的指令動詞如果從主動語態變為被動語態，即使

該祈使動詞帶有直接賓語，原句的意思也會大大改變，原因在於祈使性的陳述相當於一個直接引語，即從說話者口中直接說出的話，而被動語態的陳述卻相當於間接的或轉述性的引語，例如：

　　[You] Stop the car!

這句話的意思並不是：

　　The car was stopped by him.

而是：

　　He was ordered to stop the car.

使用祈使句的目的在於造成一種權威性的語氣，強令別人執行某個動作或顯示權威，而被動形式的祈使句所取得的效果卻恰恰相反。

◆ 單數動詞和複數動詞

　　我們已經知道，語法上的數分為單數和複數。限定動詞的現在時和過去時也要表明語法上的數的特性，並且要與構成動詞主語的名詞或代詞的數相一致。如：

　　Greenpeace *is*（單數）an international pressure group.

　　Some pressure groups *are*（複數）also registered charities.

第一句中的主語Greenpeace是單數，所跟動詞is也因此是單數；第二句中的主語Some pressure groups是複數，因此動詞are也相應是複數。

　　這一規則同樣適用於限定動詞為過去時和被動語態的情況：

Oxfam *was founded* to feed the hungry.

Millions of lives *were saved* by Oxfam.

Both Oxfam and Amnesty *have been accused* of political bias.

在第一句話中，主語Oxfam是單數，被動語態的動詞was founded也相應是單數，其餘兩句的主語Millions of lives和Both Oxfam and Amnesty均為複數，其相應的被動語態動詞were saved和have been accused也就必須是複數。

• Either ... or 與 Neither ... nor

用either ... or和neither ... nor這樣的結構引出的主語中包括兩個名詞或兩個代詞，這時動詞要用單數，因為either的意思是一個或兩者之一，而neither是either的否定形式。例如：

Either Greenpeace or Friends of the Earth *is* to receive a £50,000 donation.

Neither Oxfam nor Amnesty *sees* an end to injustice.

• 集合名詞

一個從句或句子中主語和動詞之間的數要相一致的關係稱為一致或呼應。語法上所要求的這種一致性，不管是單數還是複數，一般是容易鑒別的；但當句子的主語為集合名詞時，動詞可以是單數也可以是複數。雖然集合名詞本身在語法上來講是單數。如：

an archipelago, a constellation, a shoal

上述的名詞包含兩個或以上的人或物。標準英語中接受這一類含單/複兩重性質的名詞，並且容許用單數或複數動詞，如

A school of whales *has been/have been* stranded in the bay all week, and an armada of small boats *is trying/are trying* to drive the whales back to the open sea.

到底用單數動詞還是用複數動詞，主要看所要強調是集合名詞的整體性和單一性，還是強調其多樣性和多數性。在下面的例子中，所用的單數動詞表明的是把集合名詞看作一個單一的整體：

An *anthology* of war poems *has* just *been* published.

A *collection* of electronic gadgets *was lying* on the bench.

Every Wednesday evening *the choir rehearses* for three hours.

與此相比較，下面句子中的動詞複數形式表明了主語的多數性：

A *string* of race-houses *were galloping* across the downs.

The team, after six home defeats, *are feeling* demoralized.

A *group* of first-year students *live* in the same hall of residence.

從上述兩種情況看來，一致性原則似乎具有一定靈活性；但下述不定代詞的情況卻顯示，一致性原則不能隨意使用，而且有時還會造成混淆。

• 不定代詞

在語法上，不定代詞everyone, everybody, anyone, anybody和no one是單數，因為one和body是單數。從前，標準語法不僅要求不定代詞與單數動詞相一致，還要求同一從句或句子中

的不定代詞跟與其相呼應的人稱代詞相一致。例如，標準英語
語法中曾規定如下的句子才是正確的：

> Everyone *has* a right to *his* privacy.
>
> *Is* everybody ready for *his* lunch?

如果不定代詞僅指女性，人稱代詞就要用 her，如：

> *Does* anyone hope to see *her* words in print?

以上這些情況可稱為雙重一致，即既要注意有不定代詞與單數
動詞的一致，還要注意到不定代詞與相應單數人稱代詞的一
致。

　　在口語語法和非標準語法中，無論是過去還是現在都使用
複數人稱代詞。如：

> Everyone *has* a right to *their* privacy.
>
> *Does* anyone *hope* to see *their* words in print?

不定代詞 none 是以上規則的一個例外。none 的意思是「一個也
不」，它在語法上是單數，卻常常被當作複數，後面跟的動詞和
代詞也都是複數。如：

> The chef looked for his set of knives but none *was* /
> *were* where he had left *it / them* and none *was / were*
> on *its / their hook / hooks*.

　　在六十年代和七十年代，語言學家們開始意識到性別歧視
問題及社會上關於性別問題的爭論，於是就開始用兩個代詞，
一個陽性、一個陰性，來分別指代不同性別的人，如：

> *Does* anyone hope to see *his or her* words in print?
>
> Everyone *has* a right to *his or her* privacy.

但是 his or her 這種用法顯得十分彆扭，也更表明英語中缺乏一

個男女兩性通用的單數代詞，因此語言學家們就開始使用標準
語法中none/their的模式和口語語法中everyone/their的模式。
目前在標準英語中，不定代詞everyone, everybody, anyone,
anybody, no one 也像none一樣，可以在後面跟their，並且已經
廣為人們所接受。例如：

> Everyone *has* a right to *their* privacy.

儘管不定代詞後可跟複數代詞their，但與其搭配的動詞卻不能
是複數：

> *Are* everybody ready for his/their lunch?

> Everybody *have* a right to his/their privacy.

> *Do* anyone hope to see her/their words in print?

動詞必須為單數：

> *Is* everybody ready for their lunch?

> Everybody *has* a right to their privacy.

> *Does* anyone hope to see their words in print?

◆ 動詞的時態

時態 (Tense) 這個詞來自古法語的tens，現代法語相應的詞
是temps (time)。

英語動詞能讓我們在三個主要的時間狀態 (時態) 下表達不
同的時間概念，即現在時、過去時和將來時。每一種時間狀態
都可以由語法上的一般動詞時態來表達。所謂一般動詞時態，
是指每種時態的最簡單語法形式，如下所示：

> 一般現在時：I/you/we/they *write*; he/she *writes*

> 一般過去時：I/you/he/she/they *wrote*

　　　　　一般將來時：I/we *shall write*; you/he/she/they *will write.*

標準英語仍然要求跟在I和we這兩個人稱代詞後面的一般將來時用shall，而其他代詞則用will。

● 現在時

　　每一種時間狀態還可以通過在主要動詞的現在分詞 (-ing形式) 前加上 to be 的適當形式作為主要動詞來表達。用這種方法構成的時態稱為進行時，因為 -ing 形式表明動詞所表達的動作正在進行之中：

　　　　　現在進行時：I *am writing*; he/she *is writing*; we/ you/ they *are writing*

　　　　　過去進行時：I/he/she *was writing*; we/you/they *were writing*

　　　　　將來進行時：I/we *shall be writing*; you/he/she/they *will be writing.*

● 過去時

　　過去時當中還有其他四種時態，前兩種是**現在完成時** (Perfect) 和**過去完成時** (Pluperfect)。雖然有時也用其他語法術語來命名這兩種時態，但 Perfect 和 Pluperfect 最簡單和最清晰。這裏，Perfect 的意思是完成；Pluperfect 這個詞來自於拉丁語的 *plus perfectum*，意思是指某個動作在比現在完成時之前更早的時間裏已經實施。現在完成時由助動詞 has 或 have 加上主要動詞構成，過去完成時由助動詞 had 加上主要動詞構成。如：

　　　　　現在完成時：I/you/we/they *have written*; he/she *has written*

過去完成時：I/you/he/she/we/they *had written.*

過去時的另外兩個時態為**現在完成進行時**和**過去完成進行時**。現在完成進行時由助動詞 has been/have been 加上主要動詞的 -ing 形式構成；過去完成進行時由 had been 加上主要動詞的 -ing 形式構成。如：

現在完成進行時：I/you/we/they *have been writing*；
he/she *has been writing*

過去完成進行時：I/you/he/she/we/they *had been writing.*

• 將來時

英語動詞沒有自身的變化形式來構成將來時，而是通過在主要動詞前加上助動詞 shall 或 will 來構成。前面已經提到，shall 與人稱代詞 I 和 we 一起使用，will 則與其他幾個人稱代詞一起使用。像過去時一樣，將來時也有好幾種時態形式：

一般將來時：I/we *shall write*; you/he/she/they *will write*

將來進行時：I/we *shall be writing*; you/he/she/they *will be writing.*

將來完成時：I/we *shall have written*; you/he/she/they *will have written*

將來完成進行時：I/we *shall have been writing*; you/he/she/they *will have been writing.*

標準英語的將來時還有一些更加細密的表達方式，動詞現在時態的三種形式可以用以表示將來的概念，以下是前兩種形式：

一般現在時用作將來時：I *write* the next chapter tonight.

現在進行時用作將來時：I *am writing* the next chapter tonight.

第三種形式實際上是現在進行時用作將來時的變體，由going加上主要動詞的不定式構成，如：

I *am going to write* the next chapter tonight.

此外還有一種間接表達將來時的方法，即用主要動詞的祈使語氣來表達，如：

Write the next chapter tonight.

● 小結

　　眾多的時態可以使我們更精確或更微妙地表達時間概念，下表是英語動詞時態的一個小結：

動詞時態序列表

現在時態	
一般現在時：	I/you/we/they write; he/she writes
現在進行時：	I am writing; he/she is writing; we/you/they are writing
過去時態	
一般過去時：	I/you/he/she/they wrote
過去進行時：	I/he/she was writing; we/you/they were writing
現在完成時：	I/you/we/they have written; he/she has written

現在完成進行 時：	I/you/we/they have been writing; he/she/ has been writing
過去完成時：	I/you/he/she/we/they had written
過去完成進行 時：	I/you/he/she/we/they had been writing
將來時態	
一般將來時：	I/we shall write; you/he/she/they will write
將來進行時：	I/we shall be writing; you/he/she/they will be writing
將來完成時：	I/we shall have written; you/he/she/they will have written
將來完成進行 時：	I/we shall have been writing; you/he/she/ they will have been writing
其他將來時態	
一般現在時用作 將來時：	I write the next chapter tonight.
現在進行時用作 將來時：	I am writing the next chapter tonight.
to be + going + 不定式	I am going to write the next chapter tonight.
祈使句表示將來 時：	Write the next chapter tonight.

◆ 動詞的語氣

語氣 (Mood) 這個詞是指行為的方式或態度。過去的語法認為動詞有三種語氣，即陳述語氣、祈使語氣和虛擬語氣。

　　陳述語氣中包括了動詞的及物、不及物和主動、被動等所有的普通限定形式。

　　祈使語氣，如前所述，是指動詞的命令形式。

　　虛擬語氣長久以來受到人們的忽視，甚至被很多受過教育的作者所拋棄。虛擬語氣的動詞用來表示條件、假設或願望等。如：

> The chairman demanded that no decision *be taken* without his agreement. Members of the committee would be happier if the chairman *were to resign*. If that *should happen*, [或者用If that *were to happen*] his depute would take the chair.

這段話正是由於表達了條件和願望，才使用了虛擬語氣。虛擬語氣的be taken代替了陳述語氣的was taken，虛擬語氣的were to resign代替了陳述語氣的resigned，should happen或were to happen代替了陳述語氣的happened。下面使用陳述語氣的情形也是人們所認可的：

> The chairman demanded that no decision *was taken* without his agreement. Members of the committee would be happier if the chairman *resigned*. If that *happened*, his depute would take the chair.

即使像I wish I were和If only I were這樣的虛擬語氣形式現在也認為是可有可無的，而Would that I were這樣的形式就更顯得陳腐了，只有在下面的情形下才必須使用虛擬語氣：

> God *bless* this ship and all who sail in her.
>
> Long *live* the King of Comedy.
>
> Let it *be done*. May it *stop* soon.

實際上，虛擬語氣作為一種規範的、帶有修辭色彩的、正式的

語言形式，至今仍在英語中使用；用於目前的行動，虛擬語氣與祈使語氣是完全相同的：

> Bless this ship, God.　Be done.　Stop soon.

◆ 情態助動詞

虛擬語氣已經在很大程度上被陳述語氣所取代，一方面是因為虛擬語氣在日益變得不甚拘泥於正規形式的社會環境中顯得過於呆板，另一方面，由於早在六十年代，對古舊、正規語法的系統教學已經被放棄。然而，我們仍然需要表達諸如條件、假設和願望等語氣。這種功能就由少量被稱為**情態助動詞**（Modal Auxiliary Verbs）的詞來完成。

顧名思義，這些助動詞是放在主要動詞前，來表達主要動詞所包含的語氣，同時它們還可以用來表達作者或說話者的態度或思想狀態。情態助動詞有如下一些：

> shall/should, will/would, can/could, may/might, must/ought.

情態助動詞與其他動詞有幾點不同，首先，它們僅以最基本的原形形式存在，不能在詞尾加上-s構成第三人稱單數的現在時，也不能加上-ing構成現在分詞，以及不能加上-ed構成過去時。也就是說，標準英語中不容許出現shalls, mighting或oughted這樣的形式。will這個詞有些例外，當它用來強調希望的意思時，有詞形變化，如：

> The exhausted athlete *willed* himself to complete the marathon.

情態動詞只能用做助動詞，絕對不能用作主要動詞或單獨使用。雖然有時會看似可以單獨使用，如：

I can, you should, he might, they ought

其實，在這樣的情況下（will 除外），主要動詞是可以從上下文中推測出來的，如：

'Are you coming to the cinema tonight?'

'Do you think I should?'

'Yes, of course. You must.'

很明顯，這個對話中出現的情態助動詞 should 和 must 所帶出的主要動詞是 come，即 should come 和 must come。

除 ought 之外，其他所有情態動詞一般要跟主要動詞的原形，也就是不帶 to 的不定式，如：

Emma *can go* to the cinema tonight.

Tim White *must finish* the marathon.

但 ought 就不同了，如：

You *ought to write* that essay.

下文我們還會講到，在某種特殊情況下，情態助動詞 should, would, could 和 might 可以用作情態動詞 shall, will, can 和 may 的過去時形式。

• Shall 和 Will

Shall 和 will 這兩個情態助動詞主要是用來構成與它們同時出現的主要動詞的將來時。Shall 一般用於人稱代詞 I 和 we 之後，而 will 用於 you, he, she 和 they 這幾個人稱代詞之後，如：

I *shall visit* London this year.

Emma *will return* from holiday next week.

上面的第一個句子中的情態助動詞shall跟在第一人稱代詞I之後，改變了主要動詞visit的時態，從而也改變了它的意思。第二個例子中，情態助動詞will跟在表示第三人稱的名詞Emma之後，改變了主要動詞return的時態和意思。

I/we shall和you/he/she/they will這兩種搭配形式有時可以互換來表達決心或強調之意，以下用黑體突出，以示區別，如：

> I **will** *keep* my promise to write to you.

> You **shall** *travel* with us next year.

Shall和will的用法區別已經逐漸變得不甚明顯，在受過教育的人的談話和寫作中正趨於對所有的人稱都使用情態助動詞will。

Shall放在句子開頭，後緊跟代詞I和we及主要動詞的原形，用來表達將來的動作，既是表示建議，又表示疑問：

> *Shall* I *end* the meeting now?

> *Shall* we *meet* again tomorrow?

同樣用於這種情況下，如果代詞是you，那麼句子開頭就要用will：

> *Will* you *follow* me?

Shall放在代詞I或we之後，還可在以表示條件及其結果的情況下表示將來時態：

> If we search long enough we *shall find* the key.

> We *shall freeze* out here in the cold unless we find the key.

如果條件及其結果是與第二人稱代詞you或第三人稱代詞he, she或they有關，就要用助動詞will，如：

If she drives carefully she *will arrive* safely.

They *will* not *get* the money unless they sign the contract.

• Should 和 Would

Should 主要用來表達三種有細微差別的將來可能性。下面的例子中，should 與代詞 I 或 we 連用、would 與代詞 you, he, she, they 連用都是表示條件：

> I *should be* grateful if you *would remind* him of tomorrow's meeting.

下面的例子中，should 用來表示將來可能出現的結果：

> If she takes the by-pass road she *should avoid* the town-centre traffic and she *should arrive* before noon.

下面的例子則用 should 來表示一種不太可能出現的結果：

> If you *should see* her before I do, please remind her of tomorrow's meeting.

Should 還可以用來表示責任或義務：

> Since you are a member of the society you *should attend* tomorrow's meeting.

當一個人沒有很好地履行職責，should 還可用來表達不滿情緒：

> They *should have warned* us that they would be late.

Should 還有一種用法，就是能夠使陳述的語氣更委婉而不生硬，並且能幫助更加精確地表達出社交中的禮貌及對他人的關懷：

> I *should like* to begin by thanking the organizers of the meeting.

I *should think* that every member of the society would agree with these proposals.

情態助動詞would可用來表示一些意思上有細微差別的條件，如：

Jack *would like* to practise bowling but he has a part-time job in the supermarket.

If Jack *would* only *agree* to open the bowling it *would strengthen* the team.

It *would* be a waste of talent if he gave up cricket now.

像should一樣，would也可以使生硬的陳述變得婉轉：

Since Jack never attends training sessions it *would appear* that [或 it *would seem* that] he has lost interest in cricket.

• Can 和 Could

Can 和 could 用來表示做某事的能力或可能性：

Emma *can speak* French fluently now, but on her first visit to France she *could speak* only a few words of the language.

Could和should及would一樣，可以表示條件或某種將來的可能性，如：

Emma *could learn* to speak Spanish if she wished.

也如should一樣，could還可以用來表示委婉的指責，如：

She *could have told* us she was going to France again. She *could* at least *have sent* us a postcard when she was there.

Can 和 could 有時在非正式的用法中也可表示允許，如：

> *Can* I *borrow* the car on Saturday night?
>
> You *could have borrowed* it last Saturday but we shall need it this week.

但是在較正規的標準英語中，是用情態助動詞 may 來表示允許，如：

> *May* I *borrow* the car on Saturday night?
>
> You *may have* the car if we ourselves don't need it.

May 也可用來表示願望和詛咒，如：

> *May* the saints *preserve* you.
>
> Long *may* this fine weather *continue*.
>
> *May* you *rot* in hell!

May 和 might 都可用來表示簡單的可能性，如：

> We *may/might* need the car ourselves on Saturday.
>
> The weather *may/might* change in the afternoon.

在某些情況下，might 所表達的假設程度或不確定性比 may 更甚，如：

> Civil engineers *might be* able to reinforce the bridge.

這句話就比下面這句話的不確定性更強一些：

> Civil engineers *may be* able to reinforce the bridge.

Might 像 should 和 could 一樣，有時也用來表示不贊成或憤怒的語氣，如：

> Jack *might attend* a training session at least once a month. He *might have* told us about his part-time job in the supermarket.

• Ought 和 Must

責任、義務及要求等可以用情態助動詞 ought 和 must 來表達。Ought 這個詞一般表明所作的陳述帶有某種程度上的約束性或強制性,如:

> Jack *ought to practise* bowling now that he is in the first XI.

前面我們提到過,ought 是惟一需要在其之後跟帶 to 的主要動詞的不定式的情態助動詞。Ought 還可用在一些慣用法當中,表示實現某種期望的可能性或就某兩個事物是否相當作出判斷,如:

> Ten litres of petrol *ought to be* enough for the journey.
>
> We *ought to arrive* before noon.

情態動詞 must 則表明的是一種嚴格的或完全的必要性,如:

> Jack *must attend* the next training session or he will be dropped from the team.
>
> Drivers *must fasten* their seat-belts.

Must 也像 ought 一樣,可以用在習慣表達法中表示一種很可能實現的期望或對某事作出總結,如:

> Anyone who cross the desert alone *must be* very brave or very foolish.
>
> Drivers *must have seen* the burned-out car at the roadside.

此外,上述情態動詞中還有一項特殊的功能。當一個直接引語被改寫成間接引語或被引述時,直接引語中的動詞時態就要在時間上向前推移,變成適當的過去時態。這樣,現在時態

的情態動詞shall, will, can和may就要變成過去時的should, would, could和might，如下面這段話所示：

> The Secretary of State said, 'We *may* find it necessary to introduce new legislation on illicit drugs. The advisory committee *will* report next month. I *can* assure the House that I *shall* study the report carefully before I reach a decision.'

在經轉述之後，這段話就變成：

> The Secretary of State said that they *might* find it necessary to introduce new legislation on illicit drugs. The advisory committee *would* report next month. He *could* assure the House that he *would* study the report carefully before he reached a decision.

副 詞

　　副詞 (Adverbs) 是詞類中的一個大類，用法靈活，形式多樣，可用來修飾動詞、形容詞或其他副詞，使這些詞的意思更加精確。

◆ 副詞與動詞

　　副詞可以直接跟在它所修飾的動詞之後，如：

> Miriam Levy played *confidently* in rehearsal but she performed *nervously* in public.

在這句話中，副詞confidently修飾動詞played，副詞nervously修飾動詞performed。

　　副詞也可以放在動詞後離動詞較遠的位置對它進行修飾，如：

Miriam played the first Chopin sonata *hesitantly*.

這裏，副詞hesitantly修飾動詞played。

有些副詞也可放在緊挨動詞之前的位置，如：

Miriam *always practised* two hours a day.

也可放在動詞之前離所修飾的動詞較遠的位置，如：

Gradually, as she played the second sonata, she *over-came* her nerves and *enjoyed* the occasion.

在上面這個例子中，副詞gradually修飾的是overcame和enjoyed兩個動詞。

當主要動詞帶有助動詞時，副詞一般放在主要動詞與助動詞之間，如：

Miriam had *finally* overcome her nerves and was *actually* enjoying the performance.

在這個例子裏，副詞finally出現在助動詞had和主要動詞overcome之間；助動詞actually出現在助動詞was和主要動詞enjoying之間。

◆ **副詞與形容詞**

副詞的第二個功能是修飾形容詞，在這種情況下，副詞總是放在緊挨形容詞之前的位置。在下面的例子中，副詞exceptionally緊挨形容詞sensitive並放在它前面；副詞hauntingly也是這樣放在形容詞beautiful的前面：

Anna Desai gave an *exceptionally* sensitive performance of the *hauntingly* beautiful clarinet solo.

這個例子還表明，副詞可以通過在其相應的形容詞exceptional和haunting後面加上尾碼-ly來構成。絕大多數副詞確實都是以

-ly結尾，但有些以-ly結尾的詞可以是副詞也可以是形容詞，這要視它們在句子中的功能而定，例如：

> The concert started *late* because of the *late* arrival of the conductor.

> The *high* notes seemed to soar *high* above the audience.

第一句中的前一個late是副詞，修飾動詞started，後一個late是形容詞，修飾名詞arrival；第二句中的前一個high是形容詞，修飾名詞notes，後一個high是副詞，修飾動詞soar。下面這些詞也可以既作副詞又作形容詞：

> early, daily, fast, hard, little, long, only, wide.

這些詞作形容詞和副詞的區別在於，作形容詞時是用來描述或更準確地定義所修飾的名詞，試看下面的例子：

> *late* arrival, *high* notes, *daily* practice, *fast* tempo

然而，作副詞時則是用來修飾或限定動詞：

> He arrived *late*. The note sounded *too high*. She practiced *daily*. They played *very fast*.

◆ 副詞修飾其他副詞

副詞的第三個功能就是修飾其他副詞。當一個副詞修飾另外一個副詞時，第一個副詞往往表明的是大小、頻率或強度，如：

> Miriam plays *supremely confidently* in rehearsal but sometimes performs *remarkably badly* in public. Anna's temperament allows her to behave *sublimely calmly*, so that she seems to play *quite naturally*.

這種用來表明程度的副詞有時也叫做強化副詞 (Intensifiers)，因

為它們可以加強跟在它們後面的形容詞或其他副詞的意義。其他強化副詞還有：

> always, often, frequently, usually, sometimes, occasionally, seldom, rarely, never, normally, fairly, rather, completely, very, highly, extremely, really, truly, immensely, intensely, largely, particularly, peculiarly, amazingly, astonishingly, surprisingly.

這種表示程度的副詞像其他副詞一樣，也可以修飾形容詞。下面是這種副詞的例子：

> *often* anxious, *never* successful, *very* hesitant, *largely* useless, *intensely* angry, *amazingly* fit

◆ 副詞短語

副詞的功能有時可以由一個**副詞短語** (Adverbial Phrases) 來完成。這樣的短語通常是一組不包括限定動詞的詞，如下面句子中所示：

> *Immediately after the concert* the director decided, *quite spontaneously*, that she would take the musicians for a late supper in an Italian restaurant.

Immediately after the concert 是一個時間副詞短語，修飾動詞 decided，説明了導演 (director) 做決定的時間；quite spontaneously 是一個表示方式的副詞短語，修飾動詞 decided，説明了導演如何做出的決定。這個句子中的最後兩個短語，for a late supper 和 in a Italian restaurant，也可以看作是修飾動詞 take，for a late supper 表明了原因和目的，in a Italian restaurant 表明了地點。

◆ 狀語從句

副詞功能也可以由從句(見第275–83頁)來實現，同時，從下面這一小段話語中可以看出，**狀語從句**(Adverbial Clauses)還有一些使主句的內容得到擴展的功能：

> Leonard Vedley was astonished *when he saw his yacht lying in the car park*. The boat looked *as if a giant had hurled it from the marina*, and Mr Vedley stood there gaping *until Len Masters, manager of the marina, arrived*.
>
> 'You won't have heard about the storm *because you were out of town last night*,' said Mr Masters. 'The force of the storm was so strong *that it blew dozens of craft ashore*. It lifted them out of the water *although they had all been firmly moored*. I'm afraid your yacht will have to lie *where it is*,' he added, '*while we wait for a heavy crane*.'

從句when he saw his yacht lying in the car park是一個時間狀語從句，是用來修飾主句Leonard Vedley was astonished，或增加主句細節，説明他(Leonard Vedley)什麼時候感到吃驚。從句as if a giant had hurled it from the marina是一個方式狀語從句，描述了船看起來是什麼樣子。時間狀語從句until Len Masters, manager of the marina, arrived則描述了Leonard Vedley呆呆站在那裏的時間。

上面兩段話的第二段中，because you were out of town last night是一個原因狀語從句，解釋了Leonard Vedley將不會聽到風暴消息的原因；that it blew dozens of craft ashore則是一個表示因果關係的狀語從句，因為它指出了主句The force of the storm was so strong的結果；表示轉折或讓步的從句although they had all been firmly moored 與主句 It lifted them out of the water 的意思形成對比；where it is 是一個地點狀語從句，修飾或解釋主句 your yacht will have to lie；而 while we wait for a heavy crane 是一個時間狀語從句，修飾的是主句 your yacht will have to lie。

上面這些狀語從句都是以一個具有副詞作用的詞開頭，這些詞通過表明時間、方式 (方法)、原因、因果關係、地點或轉折等來使從句對主句起到修飾作用。這裏用到的從句的引導詞為：

when, as if, until, because, that, although, where, while.

副詞同時還起到連詞的功能，即把主句與從句相連接。正由於這些詞的這一雙重功能 —— 既作副詞又作連詞 —— 所以它們又被叫做**狀語連詞** (Adverbial Conjunctions)，同時也再次證明了英語語法的靈活性。

◆ 副詞的辨別

由於副詞的用途廣泛，詞形變化多樣，辨別起來就有一定難度。但我們不要糾纏於那些難解的語法術語上面，最重要是學會利用上述英語語言的靈活性和富於變化的特點。即使如此，有時準確掌握一些詞的功能或句子中詞與詞之間的關係還是非常必要的，因為這樣可以使我們更好地選擇使用最恰當的詞，寫出結構最完美的句子。

有很多指導原則可以幫助我們對副詞加以鑒別。「副詞與形容詞」一節 (見第75頁) 已經告訴我們如何區分副詞與形容詞；一個更為常用的鑒別方法是使用 "Wh?" 詞進行檢驗，也就是看該詞能否回答如何 (how)、何時 (when)、何地 (where) 或者為什麼 (why) 這樣的提問。

　　能回答how的提問的詞一般是表示方式或方法的副詞，包括絕大多數表示程度的副詞，即前文指出的強調副詞，以及其他許多表示行為方式的副詞，如：

　　　　alphabetically, badly, genetically, madly.

能回答when的提問的詞能夠告訴我們某事發生的時間或時間段，這類詞往往是表示時間的副詞，如：

　　　　after, before, currently, historically, lately, never, now,
　　　　previously, soon, suddenly, today, yesterday.

When的提問有時並不是用一個單獨的副詞來回答而是用一個副詞短語來回答。表示時間的副詞短語常以介詞開頭，而介詞屬於功能詞中的一個小類，如in和on等，一般出現在名詞之前指明名詞的位置。下面是一些時間副詞短語的例子：

　　　　at midnight, before daylight, in the afternoon, last June,
　　　　on a certain date, in 1998, much too late.

有些語法學家認為，由於強調時間的副詞，如always, often, frequently和sometimes等可以回答how的提問，應被示為表示方式的副詞。但是把這些詞看作時間副詞似乎更簡單、更符合邏輯。

　　能回答where的提問的詞一般是地點副詞，如：

　　　　in, out, roundabout, here, there, everywhere.

如同時間副詞短語一樣，表示地點的副詞短語也是常以介詞開頭，如：

　　　　inside a prison cell, *outside* the Grand Hotel, *across*
　　　　the Arabian Sea, *under* an apple tree.

當回答why的提問時，我們在這裏所遇到的情況與前面的英語

語法的描述有些前後相左，因為 why 的提問與其他 "Wh?" 詞的提問不同，它不能用表示原因或目的的單個副詞來回答。看下面的詞：

> as, because, for, since, so, consequently, therefore

這些詞只能作為描述某種原因的開始，而不能回答提問。要想對問題作出回答，必須用一個副詞短語或狀語從句來解釋某個動詞發生的原因或目的。下面是兩個副詞短語的例子：

> Musicians from the National Youth Orchestra went to the restaurant *for a late supper*.

> Flights had to be cancelled *because of the strike by air traffic controllers*.

關於原因狀語從句和目的狀語從句會在第六章有更為詳細的講述。下面我們可以先看兩個例子：

> Oscar worked longer hours *so that he could send money home to his family*.

> *Because he was homeless*, he slept in the park.

◆ 副詞的比較

　　副詞形式與其相應的形容詞形式同形的詞，其比較級的變化形式也與形容詞的比較級變化完全一樣。下面是規則副詞的比較級和最高級的變化形式：

原級	比較級	最高級
fast	faster	fastest
high	higher	highest
slow	slower	slowest

下面是一些不規則副詞的變化形式：

badly/ill	worse	worst
well	better	best
little	less/lesser	least
much	more	most

其他副詞，包括所有以 -ly 結尾的副詞按照下面的形式變化：

curiously	more curiously	most curiously
furiously	more furiously	most furiously
luxuriously	more luxuriously	most luxuriously

介　詞

　　介詞 (Prepositions) 是一個相對較小的詞類，是一種常用的功能詞。介詞 preposition 這個詞的字首 pre- 的意思是「在……之前」，而且介詞一般是放在名詞、名詞短語或代詞之前。介詞與其後面的名詞、名詞短語或代詞的意思直接相關並對其產生影響，正是在這種意義上，語法稱介詞對其後面的名詞、名詞短語或代詞起「管轄」作用。看下面的句子：

　　Spectators stood *around the boundary.*

其中的 around 是介詞，是對名詞 boundary 的詳細描述，around the boundary 就構成一個介詞短語。再看下面的例子：

　　Batsmen struggled *against the accurate fast bowler.*

這句話裏的介詞 against 直接與名詞短語 the accurate fast bowler

相連，這個名詞短語就構成了介詞短語 against the accurate fast bowler 的一部分。再如：

> *Between them*, the two batsmen made only ten runs.
> *With the bright sunlight behind him*, the bowler's deliveries were unplayable.

在第一個句子中，介詞 between 引入代詞 them，介詞 behind 引入代詞 him。上面舉例中的第二個句子以兩個介詞短語 with the bright sunlight 和 behind him 開頭，形成了一個擴展的介詞短語 with the bright sunlight behind him。

此例說明，介詞在語法上對代詞的管轄作用表現在代詞必須使用賓格形式，即用 them 和 him 而不用 they 和 he。

有些介詞可以對地點或位置作進一步詳細的說明，如：

> *from* the city shops, *to* the mountain tops, *through* the open door, *on* the pebbled shore.

屬於這種用法的介詞還有：

> across, along, above, among, at, behind, below, beside, between, beyond, down, in, inside, into, near, off, out, outside, over, towards, under, up, upon, with.

有些介詞表示方向或運動：

> *from* Penzance, *across to* France, *through* the spray, *against* the swell, *round* the Bay, *towards* La Rochelle

介詞還可以表示時間：

> *Before* the match *on* the last Friday *in* June he felt nervous but *after* the first over he relaxed. *By* the tenth over he had scored twenty-seven runs and *at* the end of the innings he was not-out for fifty-three. *Until* that game his highest score had been forty-one.

上面這些例子說明，典型的介詞短語具有如下的結構模式：

　　介詞 + 限定詞 + 名詞

或

　　介詞 + 限定詞 + 名詞短語

或

　　介詞 + 限定詞 + 代詞

這種模式有兩種變體。一種是介詞部分不是一個單獨的詞而是兩個以上詞的組合，如：

out into the monsoon rain; *up above* the flooded plain.

這種複合介詞的例子有很多，如：

along with, at the head of, at/to the rear of, away from, in advance of, in front of, in from, in out of (the rain), in through, away from, on top of, out from, out from under, out in, out into (the garden), out of, out through, over and above, up above.

另一種變體是介詞出現在從句或句子的末尾。以介詞結尾的句子曾被認為是不規範的英語用法，但人們似乎並不反對這樣的句子結構，如：

What do you want this hammer *for*?

Which channel is the programme *on*?

This is the town I was born *in*.

Who was that student you were talking *to*?

當然，這些例子可以改寫成不以介詞結尾的句子，但經過改寫的句子並不一定更合乎語法要求，也不見得比原來的句子更好。看看下面這些改寫之後的句子就可以體會到這一點：

For what do you want this hammer?

On which channel is the programme?

This is the town *in which* I was born.

Who was that student *to whom* you were talking?

介詞有時也有副詞的功能。雖然只有語法學家們才對介詞和**副詞性介詞** (Adverbial Prepositions) 這兩個詞類的區別更感興趣，但實際上這兩個詞類的區分並不困難：介詞與名詞、名詞短語或代詞連用，而副詞性介詞與動詞連用。看下面這兩句童謠：

Jack fell *down* and broke his crown

And Jill came tumbling *after*

這裏，down 用來直接修飾動詞 fell，after 用來修飾 came tumbling，因此 down 和 after 在這裏就都是副詞性介詞。

這兩種詞類的區別可以通過下面三對句子更明顯地表示出來，其中每對中的 (a) 句裏用的是介詞，(b) 句裏用的是副詞性介詞：

1. (a) Jenny the news-girl sets off *before* dawn.
   (b) She delivers fifty newspapers *before* she goes to school.

2. (a) Jenny whistles as she walks *along* the deserted streets.
   (b) On most mornings she sees Freddies's milk-float purring *along*.

3. (a) Jenny waves as the milk-float sails *past* her.
   (b) Freddie shouts 'Good morning' as he drives *past*.

在 1 (a) 中，介詞 before 管轄名詞 dawn；在 2 (a) 中，介詞 along 管轄名詞短語 the deserted streets；在 3 (a) 中，介詞 past 管轄代詞 her。在 1 (b) 中，before 是一個副詞性介詞，修飾動詞 delivers；

在2 (b) 中，副詞性介詞along修飾現在分詞purring；在3 (b)中，副詞性介詞past修飾動詞drives。

正如形容詞可以變為副詞、連詞可以變為連接副詞一樣，介詞變為副詞性介詞的現象再一次向我們展示了英語語法的靈活性，這種變化同時還突出了副詞在英語中的獨特地位。有些副詞，尤其是一些以-ly結尾的副詞，很容易辨別，但其他類型副詞的功能就不易確定。對於學生和作者來說，只要能準確有效地運用英語詞彙就可以了，不用過於考究語法上的分類。

連　詞

連詞 (Conjunctions) 是功能詞中的一個小類。對於功能詞來說，其所起的語法作用與其自身所具有的意義同樣重要。

有些連詞被稱為**並列連詞** (Coordinating Conjunctions)，因為它們是用來連接或並置兩個或者更多的語言單位。下面是一些並列連詞的例子：

> and, but, or, both ... and, either ... or, neither ... nor, not only ... but also.

由連詞所連接的語言單位可以是單個的詞，如：

> Neither *Upper* nor *Lower* Sallow has tourist accommodation.

也可以是短語，如：

> The nearby village of Parsemer has not only *a country house hotel, Curtminster Grange,* but also *an eighteenth-century coaching inn, The Bullyard.*

從句也可以由並列連詞來連接，經過這樣連接的從句之間沒有

從屬關係，地位相等。這樣的句子在語法上稱為複合句。下面的例子中用斜線把兩個從句分開：

> Either you stay overnight at Parsemer/or you drive on to the city of Grantown.

> Aldridge Tower at Upper Sallow is derelict/but Thornham Hall in Lower Sallow is still inhabited.

並列連詞可以用來表達相似、比較和對照的概念。用成對出現的連詞，如 both ... and, either ... or, neither ... nor 和 not only ... but also 等，可以把一個或一組事物和其他事物相對比，從而可以使句子取得一種平衡的效果。

我們在狀語從句一節 (頁78) 中還提到過另一種連詞，即狀語連詞或從屬連詞。這一類連詞的語法功能與並列連詞是不同的，它們主要是用來連接一個句子當中兩個或兩個以上的分句，並且其中的一個或一個以上的分句是從屬於句子中某個主句的。這種由一個主句和一個或多個從句構成的句子稱為複雜句。關於複雜句將在第六章中討論。

感歎詞

感歎詞 (Interjections) 是所有詞類中最小的一類，具有表達情感的感歎功能。Interjection 一詞具有插入的意思，即突然在上下文中出現。這種詞一般出現在口語或書面語言裏描述談話的對話中，而很少出現在標準書面英語中。正由於此，感歎詞所表達的與其說是外在情況，還不如說是說話者內心激動的思想狀態。它們出現在書面英語時，會使語言顯得不甚連貫，並給行文增添一種誇張的效果。下面是一些感歎詞：

ah, aha, aargh, golly, gosh, hey, hoy, huh, hurrah, och, oh, ooh, oops, oi, ouch, ow, wow.

感歎詞往往是某個更長的感歎語中的一部分，如：

Ah, the concert was wonderful!

Hey, switch it off!

Oh, I've deleted the wrong file.

值得注意的是，像Wait! Stop it! Jump! Go. Hold on等這樣的表達方式，不管有無感歎號出現，都不能視作感歎詞，而只是具有祈使語氣的動詞。

標點符號

　　標點符號 (Punctuation) 不僅關係到一篇文章的結構、韻律、語氣以及風格，還關係到句子意思的表達。雖然標點符號的使用比標準英語的其他成分，諸如拼寫、語義和語法等更加靈活多變，但也有很明確的規則。這些規則使得標點符號的使用有章可循，成為標準書面英語規範的一部分。如果不遵守標點符號的使用規範，寫出的文章就不會被讀者接受，甚至造成讀者的誤解。

標點與意義

　　標點符號的主要作用是使書寫的東西的意義表達得更清楚。下面這個例子是一個看上去自相矛盾的句子：

> I understood everything he said but I didn't understand a word.

在這句句子當中除了一個撇號 (') 用來表示 didn't 這個詞中省略的 o 這個字母，以及一個連字號 (-) 表示 understand 為一個字之外，再沒有其他的標點符號。這句話如果改寫成兩句話，就會大不一樣了，請看：

> 'I understood everything,' he said. But I didn't understand a word.

我們可以看到，這句話與上一句的句型及詞序完全相同，但句

子中出現的兩個人的身份和關係發生了變化。understood every-thing (全都明白了) 的是說話者 he，而 didn't understand a word (什麼都不明白) 的是句子當中的陳述者 I。雖然在結構上把原來的一個句子分成兩個可以解決原句的矛盾，但主要還是所增加的標點符號，尤其是用來標出直接引語的單引號起到了關鍵作用。

　　在下面的例子中，標點符號的作用更是不可忽視：

　　The *Clarion* editor said the designer is a fool.

　　The *Clarion* editor, said the designer, is a fool.

有了標點符號之後，這兩個在用詞和語序方面完全相同的句子的意思就完全相反了。在第一句中，編輯 (editor) 指責版面設計師 (designer) 是個愚蠢的傢伙；在第二句中，增加了兩個逗號，就變成了版面設計師指責編輯。如果使用引號的話，這兩句話的區別就更加明顯了：

　　The *Clarion* editor said, 'The designer is a fool.'

　　'The *Clarion* editor,' said the designer, 'is a fool.'

　　可見，標點符號可以用來明確文章中所涉及到的人物的身份和角色，它甚至還可以決定具體事物的次序，如：

　　Below, the city lights were shining.

　　Below the city, lights were shining.

以上兩個句子所使用的詞和詞序完全相同，但它們的意思卻迥然各異。第一句的意思是，從高處往下看，例如從飛機上或從山上往下看，城市的燈光閃耀；而第二句的意思是指燈光在城市的下面閃耀，例如在礦井裏或是其他地下建築裏。這兩句話意思上如此大的區別只是由於逗號位置的改變而造成的。

使用標點符號改變句子的意思還有另一種方式，如：

> Vitesse Bordeaux Football Club spent £7 million, more than any other club, on transfer fees last year.

> Vitesse Bordeaux Football Club spent £7 million more than any other club on transfer fees last year.

第一句話的意思是俱樂部花了總共七百萬英磅的轉會費，而其他俱樂部花的沒有這麼多；第二句話的意思是花在轉會費上的錢比其他俱樂部多七百萬英磅，而具體總額是多少卻沒有表明。

標點符號的錯誤使用不僅會使句子意思含混不清，甚至荒謬可笑，還會使讀者的注意力更集中到作者的錯誤上而不是他要表達的意思上，從而降低了作者的權威性和可信性。例如，a little-used car（一輛沒開過多長時間的車）與a little used car（一輛小型舊車）的意思是不同的；同樣，long-suffering specta-tors at a low-scoring match（觀看一場低比分比賽的忍耐已久的觀眾）與long suffering spectators at a low scoring match（觀看一場低水平高比分比賽的長長的飽受折磨的觀眾隊伍）的意思也有差異。下面這個句子可以說是標點符號的不當使用使句子的意思荒謬到了極至：

> The Australian athlete won the marathon one minute after he collapsed.（澳大利亞運動員在因體力不支而暈倒之後一分鐘贏得了馬拉松比賽。）

只要加上標點符號就可以消除句子的歧義，使其意思明白無誤：

> The Australian athlete won the marathon. One minute

after — he collapsed.(澳大利亞運動員贏得了馬拉松比賽，一分鐘之後他就暈倒了。)

這個例子雖然是我們特意設計的，並不是真實的語言，但它卻證明標點對意義的表達往往起到關鍵作用，正因如此，我們有必要更詳細地討論一下使用標點的問題。

標點與文章的節奏和風格

標點影響到文章的節律和意思的表達。在下面討論段落結構，尤其是敘述的節奏時，我們將看到文章的韻律對於節奏、語氣以及整個風格的影響。

文章的節律主要來自於句子的長短和內在結構，以及所用詞彙的長短和發音，因為每個包含兩個或兩個以上音節的詞都可自成一個節律單位。但是，節奏還受到標點的直接影響，因為每個標點符號(連字號除外)都會造成文章中語流的一個停頓。由此我們可以得出這樣的結論，即每一篇文章都有其節律，標點少的文章比標點多的文章讀起來會更加順暢。文章的節律有時在每一段與每一段之間會有不同，每句話之間也有變化，有時甚至顯得雜亂無章，讓人摸不著規律，被認為是「節律紊亂」。即使如此，不管你寫什麼東西，節律也都是其中的一個不可或缺的特性。

節律確實非常重要，有時一段文章的語義(可以大致理解為該段文章中所使用的詞所表達的意思)甚至可以完全由標點和句型結構來支配和操縱。下面這段話就說明了這一點：

> The man, who walked with a limp, jumped into the front passenger seat, and, before he had time to fasten his seat-belt, or time even to close the door, the driver

> of the car, which was a black Ford saloon, accelerated fiercely, sped along the High Street, screeched round the corner into Edward Street, and then, with a noisy gear change, raced out of town.

這段話雖然使用了 jumped, before he had time, accelerated fiercely, sped, screeched 和 raced 等詞，但這一系列詞並沒能表達出快速、緊急的意思，因為這句話讀起來錯綜複雜，讓人覺得非常費解，還使用了多重嵌入式的結構，而且短短的一句話總共使用了十三個逗號，這就大大影響了句子的流暢性。這樣非但沒有給人一種緊急快速的感覺，反而讓人覺得是在慢吞吞地走走停停。

如果減少一下這段話當中的標點數量，同時減少句子中的停頓，這段話的節奏就會加快並更為流暢。如果把這段話再改寫一下，把帶有很多從句的很瞥腳一個長句變成一系列的短句，句子的節奏就會更快。看下面經過改造的句子：

> The limping man jumped into the front passenger seat of the black Ford saloon. Before he had time to fasten his seat-belt or even close the door, the driver accelerated fiercely. The car sped along the High Street and screeched round the corner into Edward Street. With a noisy gear change, the car raced out of town.

這樣，一個長而拗口的句子變成了四個短句，並且只用了不多的標點。這個段落經過這番修改之後，不僅在用詞上表達了一種緊迫感，而且減少標點以及簡化句型都對取得這一效果起到了重要的作用。

我們寫的文章總會創造出某種節奏感。上面的例子說明，節奏可以增強文章意思的表達，而節奏主要是通過句法和標點

來取得的。因此，我們要在對句法和標點充分理解的基礎上來把握文章的節奏。下面我們再用兩個例子來說明這種節奏感的把握方法。

第一個例子是一個冗長而且標點很多的句子：

> Experienced archaeologists, all of them members of the National Archaeological Society, which was founded — after vigorous campaigning — thirty years ago by Dr Jenny Somerford (who is still, despite her other commitments, president of the society), will excavate the site, thought to be an Iron Age burial mound, provided, that is, the site owner gives permission.

這個句子的用詞並不難懂，但它大量使用的標點符號（用法完全正確）卻使句子的語氣沈悶，節律斷斷續續、緩慢拖遝。一個句子中被塞進了太多的資訊，使用了嵌入式分句，像現在這個句子一樣，一個陳述中插入另一個陳述，使句子變得重疊；而且大量使用標點符號的做法非但沒有修飾，反而突出了這種分句結構的重複感以及資訊過於蕪雜的現象。儘管原句中的信息量很大，但如果少用一些標點，句子的意思反而會更加清楚明白。試看下面經過改寫的句子：

> Experienced archaeologists, all of them members of the National Archaeological Society, which was founded after vigorous campaigning thirty years ago by Dr Jenny Somerford, who is still, despite her other commitments, president of the society, will excavate the site thought to be an Iron Age burial mound provided, that is, the site owner gives permission.

這句話雖然使用的標點減少了許多，但比較零散的嵌入式句子結構，仍然使句子不夠流暢，也很令人費解。而且這結構還使句子的前一部分拖得過長，影響了意思的表達。

更好的作法是把原句中的大量資訊拆分成更短的表意單位，也就是更短的句子，並把它們按照一定的邏輯順序排列，這樣就能讓讀者更容易理解了。試看下面重新改寫後的句子：

> Experienced archaeologists, all of them members of the National Archaeological Society, will excavate the site provided the site owner gives permission. The site is thought to be an Iron Age burial mound. The society was founded thirty years ago after vigorous campaigning by Dr Jenny Somerford, who is still president of the society despite her other commitments.

第二個例子在長度和信息量上與第一個例子相仿，但它的做法是儘量少用標點符號：

> Farmers in the Northwest say that the fall in livestock prices could force them out of business. Prices for cattle and sheep have been falling for some months but last week's 15 per cent drop is the biggest single fall. Some farmers are turning to tourism and letting their fields as caravan parks. A few have approached property developers with proposals for out-of-town shopping centres and housing estates.

由於分成四個句子，使得大量的資訊比較容易被讀者接受。加上句子中沒有多餘的標點符號來打斷詞彙與意義的連貫性，使得句子的節奏變得輕快，風格流暢，像一篇寫得不錯的新聞報導。

很少讀者會注意到形成文章風格的這些技能，原因之一是大多數讀者對這些寫作的技巧並不特別感興趣，或者並不真正理解。另一個原因是作者們常常把簡潔，或者對簡潔的追求，做為文章總體設計中的一部分。當作者具有了這種簡潔的寫作風格，他們所要傳達的資訊彷彿會毫不費力地從紙面上傳送到

讀者的心靈或思想中去。正是這種寫作技巧使得作者的技能或寫作藝術對於一般讀者來説神秘莫測。讀者對此也許不能做出解釋，但直覺會告訴他們一個東西在對他們發生作用，而且感到作家、音樂家或畫家們正在向他們施展一種魔力。

　　下面我們要從難以捉摸的寫作技巧轉到標點符號的具體用法。從一個看似高深的話題突然轉到一個現實的話題，這似乎讓人覺得有些掃興，但標點符號確實是形成文章風格的要素之一。因此若要想寫出得體的文章，看一看下述關於標點符號使用的指導原則還是有必要的。

句　號

　　句號 (Full Stop) 的主要功能之一是用來標誌句子的結束，二是用在縮略詞之後。由於第一個功能在這本書裏，尤其在講句子結構的幾章裏都有論述，這裏就不給出具體例子了。

◆ 句號與縮略詞

　　句號的第二個功能，即用來標明縮略詞，只被一些編輯和出版商所使用，其他人很少用到。例如，一些出版商常在表示人的頭銜的縮略語之後加上一個句號：

> V.C. (Victoria Cross)，O.M. (Order of Merit)，Rt. Rev.
> (Right Reverend)，Rt. Hon. (Right Honourable)，
> F.R.S. (Fellow of the Royal Society)，M.A. (Master of
> Arts)

有些編輯和出版商甚至堅持要在像Mr. (Mister) 和M.P. (Member of Parliament) 這類人所共知的縮略語後面加上句號。但也有些編輯和出版商在遇到這類或其他情況時不用縮略語。

不久以前，人們還習慣於在人名的首字母後加上句號，如：

T.S. Eliot, H.W. Fowler, R.S. Thomas

但這一規則已被打破，有些出版商已經不再在這種情況下使用句號了。

大多數出版商現在已經把句號從一些非常著名的機構縮略語中取消，如：

BBC, BP, NATO, RAC, RSPCA, UN

當然有些出版商仍然在這些縮略詞中保留著句號。

過去曾經有這樣一個簡單原則，當縮略詞的結尾字母與該詞的完整形式的結尾字母相同時，縮略詞中的句號就省略掉，例如，Mr, Mrs, Dr 和 vols 等。但是人們並沒有嚴格遵守這一原則。現在英國的編輯和出版商們惟一達成的一致是，省略倫敦郵政區劃中使用的 N (north)、S (south)、E (east)、W (west) 和 C (central) 等幾個縮略語中的句號。

由於沒有就句號在縮略詞中的使用達成一致的意見，所以用不用句號以及縮略語採取什麼樣的形式都不是對與錯的問題，而是出版社的印刷風格 (見第159頁) 或個人喜好的問題。

逗 號

逗號 (Comma) 在標準英語中現在是一個有多種用途的標點符號。它目前的用法不僅表明了標點使用上的變化，還表明了人們對於標準英語句子的看法的改變。直到十九世紀末，按照我們現在的標準應該使用逗號的地方，當時的作者們卻使用的

是分號，而在現在不需要標點的地方使用逗號。'Markheim'是十九世紀英國作家斯蒂文森的作品，是對一個殺人犯進行的略帶傳奇色彩的心理研究，他在文章中寫道：

> The face was robbed of all expression; but it was as pale as wax, and shockingly smeared with blood about one temple.

雖然標點對文章意義的表達起到重要的輔助作用，但標點的使用模式，也就是作者對標點符號的實際使用情況，卻隨時間發生著變化。與上個世紀相比，雖然目前所推崇的做法是使用簡潔的標點模式，但逗號在很多情況下仍然對句子意思的表達起著關鍵作用。

◆ 逗號與副詞

當一個句子以副詞、副詞短語，或者表示相反、時間或地點、原因或目的、方式或方法以及表示因果等的狀語從句開頭時，都要使用逗號。本章的開頭部分就包括兩個這樣的例子：

> Below, the city lights were shining.
> Below the city, lights were shining.

這裏的Below和Below the city都是狀語，因為他們描述或修飾的是動詞were shining，說明了燈光閃耀的地點。在第一個句子中，一個逗號把Below與句子的其他部分隔開，意思是從高處鳥瞰城市；在第二個句子中，經過逗號的分隔，Below the city就成了一個意義單位，而不是Below the city lights。此外還有很多其他用作句子開頭的詞後面必須跟一個逗號，才能使句子的意思表達清楚，如：

Normally, spoken English is less formal than written English.

上面這個句子中，Normally這個詞是一個副詞，用來修飾動詞is，這句話的意思是，「一般情況下，英語口語比英語書面語稍欠正規。」如果去掉Normally之後的逗號，變成：

Normally spoken English is less formal than written English.

這裏Normally修飾的就是spoken，它是動詞speak的過去分詞，這句話的意思是，「一般情況下說出的英語要比英語書面語稍欠規範。」可見這句話與上一句話的意思是不一樣的。

　　有些作句子開頭的副詞短語，尤其是那些表示時間和地點、原因和目的以及因果的短語，如果後面不用逗號隔開就會造成誤解，如：

At the weekend matches were postponed players were disappointed and supporters frustrated.

由於在weekend和postponed之後沒有用逗號，句子前半部分的意思就是「被延期參賽的運動員參加了周末的比賽。」下面是兩個類似的例子：

Shortly after the snow[,] warning, lights suddenly went out.

In the morning, milk[,] was frozen in the bottles.

用方括號標出的錯誤使用的逗號表明這些短語會怎樣被誤讀。還有些用作句子開頭的略帶口語化的短語也要在後面加上逗號，如Above all和Curiously enough等。在下面句子中，錯誤使用的逗號也用方括號標出：

Curiously[,] enough, highly trained athletes are subject to injury and viral infection.

有些作句子開頭的短語中包含有非限定形式的動詞，這時，後面必須要跟逗號。一種非限定形式就是不定式，如 to show 這個不定式就包含在下面這個句子中的開頭短語 to show good will 中，後面就要跟一個逗號：

To show good will, the chairman bought a round of drinks.

其他包括動詞不定式的句子開頭的短語還有 To begin with, To start with 和 To end with 等，後面都要跟一個逗號，如：

To begin with, the sprinters tested their starting-blocks.

開頭短語中的另一種非限定動詞是以 -ing 結尾的現在分詞，這時，該用逗號的地方沒有用或者逗號放置的位置不對都會歪曲句子意思，如下面的句子裏方括號中的逗號就使用有誤：

After eating, some directors[,] began to smoke cigars.

According to 這個短語用在句子開頭，與現在分詞似乎又不大相同，例如：

According to the *Clarion*, supporters[,] agree with the directors' decision.

開頭短語中的第三種非限定動詞形式是現在分詞加過去分詞的組合形式，如 having（現在分詞）won（過去分詞），如：

Having won[,] the race, the sprinter felt elated.

Having won, the sprinter[,] felt elated.

也就是說，這兩個句子中的短語 Having won the race 和 Having won 要分別作為一個整體，後面跟逗號。

　　一般用在句子開頭的狀語從句後的逗號可有可無，但當該狀語從句是以動詞結尾並且動詞後面緊跟主句中的名詞時，這個狀語從句後面就必須跟逗號。此時，逗號也成了句子意思的一部分，如：

> Since Barbara left (從句), /her house has been a melancholy place (主句).

這句話中的狀語從句以動詞left結尾，而主句以代詞和名詞her house開頭，如果把逗號去掉，這句話的開頭就可能被讀作 Since Barbara left her house，這就與原意大相徑庭了。再看下面的例子：

> If she does not return (從句), /her family and friends will be distressed (主句).

這句話的狀語從句以動詞return結尾，主句的開頭是代詞her及名詞family和friends。如果逗號被省略掉或者放置的位置不對，那裏開頭的狀語從句就有可能被讀為 If she does not return her family and friends，這樣的話句子的意思就變得滑稽可笑了。

　　使用逗號最容易犯錯誤的還是當出現如As you know, As I said和As we can see這樣的狀語從句時，因為它們會導致下面這樣的錯誤理解：

> As you know the President of France[,] is in London today.

而這句話正確的說法應該是：

> As you know, the President of France is in London today.

像As you know這樣的結構還會導致句子的歧義，如：

As you know the people object to the marina proposal.

如果逗號放在people之後，從句就變成了As you know the people，主句就成了一個命令句，即 [you] object to the marina proposal；如果逗號放在know之後，從句就是As you know，主句就變成了一種陳述，即the people object to the marina proposal。

◆ 逗號與描述性從句

還有其他兩種從句後也要跟逗號。逗號有時用來指定從句所描述或修飾的對象，這一點我們將在討論複雜句中的從句時涉及到 (第265–69頁)。先看一個例子：

The Sri Lanka bowler who took six wickets was named the man of the match.

在這句話裏，名詞bowler (保齡球手) 是幾個保齡球手中的一個。如果把從句用逗號分開，變成：

The Sri Lanka bowler, who took six wickets, was named the man of the match.

那麼這句話裏，名詞bowler就是惟一的一個保齡球手。

另外一種必須使用逗號的描述性從句是用來修飾限定整個主句的從句，如：

Cradle Bay Sea Angling Club has a new club-house, which is welcome news to the members.

Members of the Sea Angling Club agreed to a higher subscription fee, which pleased the club treasurer.

有時在稍微口語化的説法中，這類從句中的which和動詞is可以省略，但逗號還是必要的，如：

Cradle Bay Sea Angling Club has a new club-house,
[which is] welcome news to the members.

◆ 逗號用於複合句

在複合句的兩個主句之間有時需要用逗號。我們在第六章
會講到，所謂複合句就是由連詞把兩個主句連接起來的句子，
而連詞往往是 **and** 或 **but**。

當兩個分句由 and 連接，並且兩個分句的主語相同或開頭
的短語相同時，一般不需要逗號，如：

Cradle Bay Sea Angling Club was established fifty years
ago and [Cradle Bay Sea Angling Club] has over 300
members.

At midnight the alarm was raised and [at midnight]
the lifeboat was launched.

當用 and 連接的兩個分句的主語不同，或者兩個分句表示對比
的意思時，逗號的使用就可以產生一個停頓，從而更突出了這
種不同或對比，如：

All through the night the search continued, and in the
morning an upturned boat was found.

其他有些用 and 連接的句子也需要用逗號才能使句子的意思更
清楚，如：

Four young anglers applied to the club secretary, and
the committee approved their applications.

The four anglers received their membership cards on
Tuesday, and on Friday they set out for a day's fishing.

如果沒有逗號，上面第一個句子中的一部分就可能被錯讀為

applied to the club secretary and the committee，第二句的一部分就可能被錯讀為 received their membership cards on Tuesday and on Friday。

以連詞but連接的分句往往表示前後兩個分句的不同或對比，這種意思上的對立性會因逗號的使用所造成的輕微停頓而突顯出來，如：

> The four young anglers were enthusiastic, but they had little experience of sea angling.
>
> Older members of the angling club warned them of bad weather, but the young men merely laughed.

◆ 逗號與稱呼用語

當稱呼別人或對某人進行描述時，必須用逗號。

稱呼的一種形式是直呼其名，如：

> Ah, Miller, you are just the man I'm looking for.
>
> Please telephone or write to us, Barbara.

有時稱呼可能是很籠統的形式，如：

> All aboard, ladies and gentlemen, for the *Skylark* Cruise.
>
> Gather round, my friends, and hear the news.

名詞或代詞you的這種使用方法在語法上稱為**呼格**，意思是表示呼喚或稱呼。為了記住呼格以及出現呼格時要使用逗號的規則，可以假想被稱呼的名稱前有一個標誌詞Oh或者Ah。如果不用逗號，被稱呼的名詞就由呼格變成了賓格，這樣會導致歧義的產生，如：

> Keep moving Emily. Give up Fred. Hang on Jack.

正確的寫法應該是：

Keep moving, Emily. Give up, Fred. Hang on, Jack.

另一種對人的指稱方法是使用一個與該人的名字相當的描述性的短語。這樣在一個句子中就有兩種對人加以辨別的方法，例如：

Mr Godfrey Pendleton, editor of the *Daily Clarion*, still takes part in the annual fun run.

在這個句子中，Mr Godfrey先是用名字稱呼，再用一個描述性的短語editor of the *Daily Clarion*，表明了他的職業身份。這種短語與最直接表明該人身份的詞或短語，兩者為同位元關係。在行文中，同位詞並列在一起。

對於動物以及無生命的事物可以用同樣的方法加以指稱，如：

Malus Sylvestris, a three-year-old grey, won the two o'clock race at Doncaster.

Mill House, the Hughes family's holiday cottage, was vandalized.

逗號還用來把諸如said和replied表示講述的動詞隔離開來，以辨明句子中的說話者，並且不管這樣的動詞是引出直接引語還是間接引語，都要用逗號隔開。關於直接引語的討論，請見第121–25頁。下面是一些間接引語的例子：

Miller was just the man he was looking for, he said.

Miller, he insisted, was ideal for the task.

After all, he added, Miller was an expert.

◆ 逗號與插入語

在對人或物的主要描述之外，都可以再加上一些附加的描

述。這些附加的資訊一般以**插入語**(Parenthesis)的形式出現，作為主要資訊的補充。插入語可以用逗號、括弧或者破折號來表明。

插入語在結構和功能上都與上面提到的同位語相似，二者的主要區別在於，同位語總是一個與所指對象意思相同的一個描述性短語，即是所指稱的人的另外一種説法，而插入語可以是任何類型的資訊。再看看我們上面用過的一個例子：

> Mr Godfrey Pendleton, editor of the *Daily Clarion*,
> still takes part in the annual fun run.

這句話裏的短語editor of the *Daily Clarion*是作為人物指稱的一個部分，與Mr Godfrey這個名字是同位元關係。如果把這句話改寫成如下的句子：

> Mr Godfrey Pendleton, who still takes part in the an-
> nual fun run, is editor of the *Daily Clarion*.

這裏用逗號分隔開的從句who still takes part in the annual fun run就不是人物指稱的一個部分，因而屬於插入語。下面的句子與此相似：

> Mr Leonard Vedley, who has just bought a new yacht,
> is the developer of the Cradle Bay Marina.

這裏的從句who has just bought a new yacht是一個插入語，提供了一些有用的附加資訊，也不是用來對人加以辨別和指稱。

◆ 逗號與專案羅列

逗號的最簡單用法之一就是用來分隔兩個或兩個以上的列舉專案(lists)。這些專案可以是單個的單詞，如：

A strike by air traffic controllers affected flights to France, Portugal, Spain and Italy.

Students yawned, coughed, grimaced, writhed and squirmed with boredom.

列舉中的專案還可以是短語，如：

As they drew up outside their holiday cottage, the Hughes family saw the signs of vandalism: uprooted plants, broken windows, a smashed door panel and black paint daubed on white-washed walls.

在所列舉的倒數第二個專案和單詞and之間的逗號可有可無，但有時如果加上一個逗號可以使句子的意思更清楚，如：

She wrote cheques payable to Bayne & Duckett, Marks & Spencer, and Martin & Frost.

句子當中的最後一個逗號把表示and的符號&與and這個單詞區分開來。

分 號

分號 (Semicolon) 在現在語法中的主要功能是用來分隔複合句中的兩個分句，特別是用在複合句中不使用連詞and或but的情況下。下面出自斯威夫特 (Swift) 的《格列佛遊記》(*Gulliver's Travels*) 的這段話，向我們展示了自從1726年這本書面世以來標點和句法所發生的變化：

That he had once, by way of Experiment, privately removed a Heap of these Stones from the Place where one of his Yahoos had buried it: Whereupon, the sordid Animal missing his Treasure, by his loud lamenting brought the whole Herd to the Place, then miserably howled, then fell to biting and tearing the rest; began to pine away, would neither eat nor sleep, nor work, till he ordered a Servant privately to convey the Stones into the same Hole, and hide them as before; which when his Yahoo had found, he presently recovered his Spirits and good Humour; but took Care to remove them to a better hiding Place; and hath ever since been a serviceable Brute.

實際上這段話中只有一個句子，但它包含了一系列完整的敘述，如果寫成現代英語，就會是包括幾個句子的一段話。斯威夫特在本該使用逗號、冒號甚至句號的地方卻使用了分號。我們在當今的英語中更喜歡用較短的句子，少而又有系統性地使用標點符號，包括對分號的使用亦是如此，例如：

Jean-Paul Chambery is manager of Vitesse Bordeaux Football Club; Jerzy Novak is manager of Cracow Solidarnoz.

這句話用分號來代替連詞就打破了句子的連貫性，產生一個停頓，這樣就凸顯出一種並列，造成兩個分句的直接對比或產生一種句子的平衡感。再如：

Vitesse is one of the richest clubs in France; Solidarnoz is one of the poorest clubs in Poland.

當一個句子中有三個分句時，就會出現另一種平衡，如：

Jean-Paul Chambery's career as a player was cut short by injury; Jerzy Novak won fifty-three caps for Poland; both men are expert football strategists.

選擇分號和特定的句型結合起來使用就達到了一種使句子中的分句相區分的效果，如果使用其他的標點和句型就會達到不同

的效果。例如，如果在句子中使用連詞and或but而不用分號，得到的句子在語法上和風格上也是可以接受的，如：

Jean-Paul Chambery is manager of Vitesse Bordeaux Football Club, and Jerzy Novak is manager of Cracow Solidarnoz.

但這樣就不如用分號時產生的對比效果那樣明顯。

此外，還有一種句型結構可以選擇，就是把複合句改寫為複雜句，即把複合句中的一個分句變成從句，再加上適當的關聯詞。下面這個句子中加入的關聯詞是whereas：

Vitesse is one of the richest clubs in France whereas Solidarnoz is one of the poorest clubs in Poland.

這個句子當然也是可以成立的，但這樣就失去了使用分號來分隔兩個分句時造成的突然感，而代之以一個平穩連貫的句子。

在使用分號的複合句中，其中的每個分句一般起到一個獨立句子的作用，但不同分句所表達的意思是緊密相關的，這樣就會讓人感到幾個分句所討論的是同一個主題，因而需要用一個句子來表達。被分號分隔開的幾個分句卻由各分句意思上的連貫性連接起來，這樣就會給人一種節奏緊湊的感覺。相反，如果使各個分句都獨立成句，就會得到一連串不連貫的短句子，顯得極不自然，如：

Chambery's career as a player was cut short by injury. Novak won fifty-three caps for Poland. Both men are expert football strategists.

可見，使用分號來使句子產生平衡感可以取得一種獨特的寫作

效果。除此之外，分號用在僅僅敘述過程的句子中也有其作用，如：

> In the last minute of the game Eddy Tissac tackled hard and won the ball; he struck an inch-perfect pass to Claude Montereau, the Vitesse striker; Montereau's fiercely driven shot went head-high past the Solidarnoz goalkeeper.

這段話如果寫成三個短句，就會顯得更加有力，並使敘述的節奏加快；如果寫成由分號分隔開的一個句子，從一個事件迅速轉移到下一個事件，也能取得相似的較快的敘述節奏，這樣就使每一個單獨敘述的事件成為一系列事件中的一部分，從而也使句子取得一種整體感。

分號的另一個功能就是用來分隔逐一羅列的專案，而且這些專案當中已經有逗號存在，例如：

> Vitesse Bordeaux's board of directors is dominated by three men: Charles Auriol, Chairman, and chairman of three other companies in and around Bordeaux; Henri de Loches, great-grandson of a founding director of the club; and Jacques Cateraggio, the Corsican-born banker.

上面這句話中所羅列的專案都是一些擴展的短語。分號還可以用來分隔句子中的分句，如：

> A large area outside Wembley, the neutral ground chosen for the final, was like a street market. One man was selling scarves, rosettes, pennants, and balloons in Vitesse Bordeaux colours; thirty yards away another salesman had the same items in Cracow Solidarnoz colours; mobile snack bars offered tea, coffee, Bovril, hamburgers, hot dogs, pies and crisps; the man in the Automobile

Association caravan was conducting a half-hearted membership drive; ticket touts were testing the laws of supply and demand.

從 One man was 到 supply and demand，一系列的羅列條目構成了一個長句子，其中包括五個擴展條目，每一個都是一個單獨的分句，每一句就像畫面的一部分，放在一起就構成了一個完整的畫面，從而取得了句子的完整性。

　　上面這五個分句的結構非常有效，但它並不是組織句子資訊的惟一方式。如果在所寫的文章中已經使用了分號把分句隔開的句式，我們可能就會想改換一種句型來使文章的寫法富於變化。例如，在上面所例舉的這段話中，五個分句的前兩個就可以改寫成由一個主句和一個從句組成的複雜句：

One man was selling scarves, rosettes, pennants, and balloons in Vitesse Bordeaux colours, while thirty yards away another salesman had the same items in Cracow Solidarnoz colours.

第三個分句可以寫成一個簡短的簡單句：

Mobile snack bars offered tea, coffee, Bovril, hamburgers, hot dogs, pies and crisps.

而第四、五兩個分句則可以加上一個連詞 and 而變成一個複合句：

The man in the Automobile Association caravan was conducting a half-hearted membership drive, and ticket touts were testing the laws of supply and demand.

以上這些變化表明，標點以及句型的微小改變都會在節奏上和結構上產生不同的效果。正是這些變化才使我們所寫的文章語言多樣，既能增加文章的活力，又能增加文章的感染力。

冒 號

　　冒號 (Colon) 的主要功能，就是用來引導說明或解釋性的文字，如一段引言、一系列的羅列條目或者某種解釋。在句子開始部分先預告資訊，然後用冒號，以示在引出具體資訊前稍作停頓。

　　按照英國報刊的標準，在表示發言的動詞與真正的說話內容之間應使用冒號。表示發言的動詞可以引出一個陳述、一個問題、一個命令或者一個感歎語，如：

　　　　The sports editor of the *Daily Clarion* demanded: 'Why didn't you interview Chambery after the match?'

　　　　Pete Gardelli, the young sports reporter, said: 'There wasn't time for an interview because I had to meet the deadline for the first edition of the *Clarion*.'

在報刊文章中，冒號不必緊跟在表示講述的動詞之後，但必須緊挨著放在真正的說話內容之前，如：

　　　　Jean-Paul Chambery, manager of Vitesse Bordeaux, roared as he entered the dressing room: 'Magnifique! Merveilleux! Parfait!'

出現在冒號前面的部分是間接引語，而緊跟在冒號後面的部分是直接引語。關於直接引語的標點問題請見第121–25頁。

　　冒號上面這種用法的一種變化形式是，冒號前是概括性的敘述，冒號後是一系列的條目或例子，如：

　　　　For the next test match, the selectors have named a squad of twelve: Wyatt (captain) , Alder, Aylmer, Butts, Earnshaw, Flaxman, Fry, Jowett, Loveridge, Otway, Pullman and Wilkes.

就像我們前面講到的逗號用法一樣，跟在冒號後面的一系列條目可以是單個的單詞，也可以是短語，如：

> As they drew up outside their holiday cottage, the Hughes family saw the signs of vandalism: uprooted plants, broken windows, a smashed door panel and black paint daubed on the white-washed walls.

冒號常常用來表示句子中較強的結構上的劃分，造成一個停頓並強調冒號之後所引出的內容。如果把上面的兩個例子改寫一下，不用冒號進行分隔，得到的句子就顯得不像原來那麼有力：

> The selectors have named Wyatt (captain), Alder, Aylmer, Butts, Earnshaw, Flaxman, Fry, Jowett, Loveridge, Otway, Pullman and Wilkes in the twelve-man squad.

> As they drew up outside their holiday cottage the Hughes family saw that the signs of vandalism were uprooted plants, broken windows, a smashed door panel and black paint daubed on the white-washed walls.

冒號的第三種用法是用來引出表示目的或意圖的陳述，以及對該陳述的解釋，如：

> Fran Prasana had to face the facts: with so slight an artistic talent she could never be a successful painter.

> Fran's choice was clear: she could complete her course at art college or join Upstart Genes.

在這種用法中，冒號在句子中起到一個承上起下的作用，使句子人為地分為兩部分。通過這樣把句子中冒號前後兩部分故意地並置起來，就造成一種懸念 (tension)，因此而產生諷刺、滑稽或者警示的效果，例如：

You needn't sell your soul to the devil in order to play this piece: you could try practising instead.

I won't visit the dentist: I'll wait for the tooth fairy.

A little humility can be charming: too much is sickening.

應該指出的是，這種句子結構必須謹慎使用，因為這種修辭手法容易讓讀者做更進一步的縝密思考來理解句子的含義。所以如果使用這樣的句子結構，所寫出的句子就要非常有力才能經得起讀者的推敲。

問 號

書面標準英語中有各種各樣表示疑問的方法，而不管用哪種方法，都要把問號 (Question Mark) 放在疑問句的末尾。

最簡單的疑問方法是用直接疑問句，如：

Have you seen the Camera Club's annual exhibition?

有時在較長或較具體的問句的末尾，作者會把問號遺漏掉，這可能是因為句子太長，寫到句子結尾時作者的思想已經跟剛開始時的想法相去甚遠，以至於作者已經忘記了要寫的句子是問句，如：

Have you had a chance to see the Camera Club's annual exhibition, which was formally opened by the picture editor of *The Times* last Friday and which runs for the next three weeks in Wellington Hall?

上面這些句子必須要用問號，因為它們是直接提出的疑問。這些句子如果是直接引語，句子內容不用改變，只要加上引號就可以了。同樣是這些句子，如果是間接引語，不以疑問的口氣

說出而是以簡單的陳述語氣說出的話，就不必用問號。再看一些例子：

> Cherry Greville asked her colleague Margot Salles if she had seen the Camera Club's annual show.
>
> Margot Salles questioned the standard of some of the portrait photographs in the exhibition.
>
> Cherry demanded to know why Margot was criticizing something she had not seen.

上面每個句子中都有一個表示疑問的動詞，也就是用來提問的動詞，如 asked, questioned 和 demanded，但它們都出現在陳述語氣的句子中。上面三個句子都是用來提供資訊而不是尋問資訊，而只有當句子用來尋問資訊時才使用問號。為了說明提供資訊與尋問資訊的區別，以及陳述語氣與疑問語氣的區別，我們把上面的三個句子改寫成疑問句，並使用引號表明直接疑問的特點：

> Cherry Greville asked her colleague Margot Salles, 'Have you seen the Camera Club's annual show?'
>
> 'Do you think the portrait photographs are up to standard?' Margot Salles asked.
>
> 'Why are you criticizing something you haven't seen?' Cherry demanded.

疑問句，尤其在英語口語中，還有一種常用的表達方法，就是在陳述句後跟一個**附加疑問句**。所謂附加疑問句就是指添加在普通陳述句後的簡短問句，如：

> You haven't seen the exhibition, have you?
>
> The portraits are rather weak this year, don't you think?
>
> Some of the landscapes are beautiful, are they not?

上面的每個附加疑問句都是一個Yes/No問句，也就是可以直接用Yes或No來回答的問句。

Yes/No問句是一種特殊的**限制性問句**(Closed Question)，對這種問句必須作出嚴格限定的真實回答，如：

> Who took the photograph of the River Nile at dusk?
>
> How many of his own photographs is the president exhibiting this year?

與限制性問句相對的是**開放性問句**(Open Question)，對這種問句的回答往往要作出較詳細的陳述，如：

> How did Cherry Greville shoot her sports photographs?
>
> Why did the committee restrict each club member to a maximum of six prints this year?

開放性問句也叫"Wh"問句。"Wh"問句這種命名雖然稍嫌口語化，但它卻無誤地概括出了以Who, What, Why, Where, When和How開頭的疑問句。"Wh"問句往往是開放性問句，因為對它們的回答是需要詳細說明理由或細節。

◆ 反問句

反問句(Rhetorical Questions)與前面討論過的問句不同，因為它並不是用來尋問資訊，因而不需要作出回答。反問句可以是簡單的社交用語，如：

> How do you do? Isn't it a lovely day?

或表示責問，如：

> Do you think I'm doing this for my health?
>
> Just who do you think you are?

這兩個反問句如果變成較口語化、較通俗的說法就是：

> What's it all about?（我作這一切到底是為了誰？）

> Who would have thought it?（有誰會關心你算老幾呢？）

在較高雅 (heightened) 的文字表達中，反問句有時會顯得富有哲理或詩意，如：

> How did we fall so far from the bright morning?

雖然反問句一般無需回答，但句末一定要加上問號。有些從語法上講屬於陳述句的句子常常用來表示疑問，這時也要用問號，如：

> Margot finally went to the Camera Club exhibition last night?

> She said she liked the portraits? Surely not?

> You mean to say she wasn't impressed by any of those strange, haunting landscapes?

就像感歎號用於某些陳述句之後一樣，問號的使用取決於語境 (context，上下文)、對話的性質、思想狀態、以及語氣 (當然這裏指作者所使用的修辭性語氣) 等。問號表明書面文字語調的升降，表示疑問、懷疑或反對等，而表示這些思想感情的語調在口語中是不言自明的。

感歎號

在書面標準英語中，感歎號 (Exclamation Mark) 的作用是用來表明說話時的強烈感情。感歎號的書寫符號（！）本身說明了

在憤怒、驚奇、喜悅或是自憐時所說的話的音調和聲音大小。另一方面，在諸如私人信件或明信片等非正式書面語中，感歎號常用來代替書面文字，相當於口語中的 You know what I mean? 或 Just imagine 等表達方式。這就造成了感歎號在標準英語中的正式用法與在非標準英語中的非正式用法上的明顯差別。

　　在標準英語中，感歎號當然是用來表示感歎，如：

　　What a farce! How stupid! You're fired!

驚歎有時以命令句的形式出現，如：

　　Wait for me! Don't jump! Get out!

有時，在作出起始的感歎之後還可以再跟一個更長的感歎，如：

　　What a farce! Hamlet split his tights and Ophelia lost a false tooth in a fit of the giggles!

感歎還可以用祈禱語的形式出現，即真正地或象徵性地向某人祈求或求助，如：

　　Oh, God! Let this be a comedy!

祈禱與發誓在情感上有相似之處，如：

　　I swear by all the saints that this is true!

在上面這種莊重的誓言中，感歎號可有可無，但詛咒語中，感歎號卻必不可少，如：

　　May you rot for ever!

有些編輯堅持認為感歎號只能用於上面提到的幾種情況之下，但實際上，有時也可用於表達強烈感情的陳述句中，這些陳述句中使用的是一般的普通限定性動詞，如：

He was covered in blood!

Vitesse Bordeaux won the cup!

I've just seen the ghost of Rose de Silva!

還有一種情況也應該使用感歎號，就是所說的話雖普通，但裏面卻包含了如惱怒、不解等複雜的感情色彩，這樣的表達既是一種陳述，又是一種疑問，同時還是一種感歎，如：

The match begins in ten minutes and you've left the tickets at home!

Anna Desai won the national scholarship and turned it down!

再看下面這樣的句子：

You can imagine what the musical director will say to Anna at the next rehearsal!

這句話中感歎號的用法就介於標準與非標準、正式與非正式之間。雖然標準英語與非標準英語的區分有時並不明顯，但有兩種方法可以用來檢驗感歎號的用法是否正確。

首先是一種非常主觀的方法，就是問問自己那些相關的書面文字如果讀出來會是什麼樣的語調。如果能夠確信這些字讀出來的語調比正常語調要加重，音量也提高的話，那麼這句話用感歎號就是正確的。第二種方法更客觀、更可靠一些，就是看所用的感歎號是僅僅作為標點符號呢，還是用來代替了某些文字。看下面的例子：

You can imagine how embarrassed Anna Desai will feel when she has to explain!

Just after midnight, and ten miles from the nearest town, we ran out of petrol!

Sam did his usual demolition job on the sherry trifle!

上面每句話中的感歎號都要求讀者把不足的資訊補充完整，也就是說，這些句子中，僅憑文字本身只傳達了一種意思，感歎號的使用就像是向讀者發出一個信號，讓他們去想像沒有寫出的內容。這種給讀者留出想像空間的作法是向讀者表示友好的一種方式，但標準英語的作者認為讀者不一定會接受這番好意，因此就不指望著本該由作者去完成的工作卻會由讀者來完成，（因此還是把句子寫完整比較妥當）。

即使在非正式的寫作中，過多使用口語化的感歎號也會使文章顯得空洞無物、矯揉造作，使人更加注意文章中的標點而不是實質內容。使用雙重或三重感歎號(即"！！"或"！！！")則給人一種黔驢技窮的感覺，也使文章的風格極不自然又略顯神經質。

引　號

引號 (Inverted Commas) 是較寬泛的標點符號規則中的一個次規則，因為引號的用法以及規定這些用法的規則要比其他標點符號更加詳細。之所以稱之為引號，是因為用它標出的話語都是直接引自他人說的話或書面材料，這也是引號的主要功能。當口語或書面語經這樣引用之後，放在引號中的文字就稱為直接引語。

引號的第二個功能是表明所引用的文字只是把原文照搬，不一定是正確的陳述，或者表明所引用的部分並非作者本人的觀點。引號的第三個功能是用在文章、詩歌或短篇小說的題目中。

◆ 引用語

　　在引用別人說過的話或書面語時，圖書出版商的通常作法是使用單引號，而報紙出版商則使用雙引號。只要保持前後一致，這兩種方法中的任何一種都是可取的。這種前後一致性關係到在 **引用語** (Quotations) 中用什麼標點符號來區分間接引語和直接引語：圖書出版商一般使用逗號，而報紙出版商則用分號。

　　正如本書中的例子所示，如果引文中所使用的文字的字體和大小與上下文的字體和大小不同，並且頁邊的空白也較大的話，就可以不用引號，因為一般僅憑排版印刷上的區別就足以把引文區分出來。但在本書這一節的例子裏，我們還是保留引號。

　　當第一次引用別人的講話或書面材料時，應注意在引述前要先說明講話者的身份。看下面的例子：

> 'The students in question, all ten of them, are members of Central University Literary Society. They say they were following the Wordsworth Trail but got lost in the dark. They parked their minibus in a lay-by and took to the fells, but only two of the students had any experience of fell-walking and none of the party had the right equipment,' said Don Stanton, leader of the Fells Rescue Unit.

這段話把表明說話者身份及權威性的重要資訊放在了長長的引文之後，這樣容易使讀者失去耐心。所以應改寫成：

> Don Stanton, leader of the Fells Rescue Unit, said, 'The students in question ... the right equipment.'

上面的例子表明，當引用語是一個完整的句子或是句子的主要

部分，引號中的第一個詞的開頭字母要大寫，並且句子最後的標點符號(句號、問號或感歎號等)要放在關引號之內。這裏有一個典型的例子，它同時還表明了句子中引用語前面部分的標點用法：

> A spokesman for Central University said, 'We apologize for the foolish behaviour of the men students.'

當引用語是一個長句子的一部分時，如直接引語放在間接引語當中時，在緊接引號之後需要一個標點符號，並且句子末尾要用句號，如：

> What the university spokesman actually said was, 'We apologize for the foolhardy behaviour of the men students', in his statement.

雖然引用語部分本身是一個完整的句子，但它後面不能用句號，因為它只構成一個較長的句子中的一部分，而一個句子中只能有一個句號。students這個詞之後的逗號放到了引號之外，這樣就使引用語部分成了整個句子的一個嵌入部分。

　　當使用其他可以用在句子末尾的標點符號，如問號和感歎號時，情況又有所不同，如：

> The reporter asked, 'Will the university take disciplinary action against the students?' when he interviewed the university spokesman.

由於這裏的問號只與引用語有關，而並不與整個句子相關，所以必須放在引號之內。同樣，再看下面的例子：

> 'Disciplinary action? Don't talk such rot!' snapped the spokesman.

這句話裏的感歎號也是只與引用語有關而與整個句子無關，所

以感歎號也是放在了引號之內。這幾個例子表明當引用語是一個較長句子的一部分時，這個引用語的關引號之中可以用問號或感歎號，而不能用句號，句號只能用在整個句子的結尾。

一個句子只能有一個句號，但可以有多個問號，如：

> Why did the reporter ask, 'Will the university take disciplinary action against the students?' when he telephoned the university spokesman?

這句話裏使用了兩個問號，因為共有兩個問題，一個是直接引語中的問題，一個是直接引語之外的部分提出的問題，也就是整個句子的問題。

◆ 引語中的引語

當某個直接引語之外的部分也是直接引語，也就是説整個句子是引語中套引語的情況下，也可以用兩個問號，如：

> 'Why did the reporter ask, "Will the university take disciplinary action against the students?" when he spoke to me this morning?' the spokesman wondered.

但當被套入整個句子引語中的引語的結尾與所套入的引語的結尾相同時，問號該怎樣處理呢？再看下面的例子：

> The Vice-Chancellor of Central University said, 'When that reporter spoke to you are you sure that he asked, "Will the university take disciplinary action against the students?"'

也就是説，問號可以放在雙引號之內，或者放在單引號之內，而不能既放在雙引號之內又放在單引號之內。兩個問號不能緊挨在一起同時出現，因為按照標準英語的慣例，同一個標點符

號不能在句尾同時出現兩次。就像在句末用兩個感歎號或者兩個句號一樣，句末出現像...?"?'這樣兩個問號的情況同樣讓人感到很不可思議。

當兩個引語都在整個句子的末尾結束時，並且兩個引語都是陳述句而不是疑問句或感歎句的話，句號應放在單引號與雙引號之間，因為這正是整個句子結束的地方，如：

> The *Clarion* reporter said, 'I'll use that first quote you gave me, "We apologize for the foolhardy behaviour of the ten students".'

上面三個例子告訴了我們怎樣在出現雙引語的情況下使用單引號和雙引號。由於本書傾向於多使用單引號，所以我們就給第一層引語用單引號，給引語中的引語用雙引號。再看一個例子：

> Godfrey Pendleton, editor of the *Clarion*, said, 'I like your whiff of irony, "They wandered lonely as a cloud", in your piece on the lost students.'

由於整個句子是以students結尾，句號就放在了students之後、單引號之內。編輯Godfrey Pendleton所說的話的全部內容是這樣的：

> 'I like your whiff of irony, "They wandered lonely as a cloud", in your piece on the lost students.'

由於They wandered lonely as a cloud這句話出自英國詩人華茲華斯(Wordsworth)的詩，屬於引語中的引語，所以必須用雙引號標出，以區別於編輯所說的話，I like your whiff of irony in your piece on the lost students，這樣，華茲華斯這句引語中的引語就在irony和cloud兩個詞之後用標點符號區分了出來。

◆ 引語與段落

當某人的話或某些書面材料被第一次引用時，都要另起一段。當所引用的某人的直接引語有數段時，要在每一段的開頭重複使用開引號，直到引用完畢的一段結尾才使用關引號。如：

Don Stanton, leader of the Fells Rescue Unit, said, 'Around midnight last night a hill farmer telephoned the police to say that he could hear the sound of chanting and bursts of wild laughter drifting across the fells. He told the police he thought it sounded like a coven of witches and warlocks at some midnight ritual.

'The police called me and asked if I could guide them over the fells. It's a tricky route at the best of times and dangerous in the dark.

'We heard the noise from half a mile away: rhythmic chanting and bursts of wild laughter, just as the farmer said. Nearer, the chanting seemed somehow familiar. And then we realized ... Poetry! The students were reciting poetry!'

當所引用的是幾個人的對話，或當有新的引用時，每個人的話都要另起一段，如：

Police Sergeant Harry Mercer said, 'Right, lads. What's the celebration?'

' "Bliss was it in that dawn to be alive, But to be young was very heaven!" ' a student recited in a loud and slightly slurred voice.

'Wordsworth?' said Don Stanton. 'Wordsworth never set foot on these fells.'

'But we thought ...' said a second student. 'I mean, we thought ...'

The first student said to the second, 'You dozy daffodil! I told you we should have turned left at Cockermouth.'

◆ 引號、引證與諷刺

引號的第二種用法是從它的第一種用法發展而來，目的使作者與所引用的話之間產生距離感，而不像第一種用法中的那樣，用來表明是從某人或某書面材料中的直接引語。換句話說，就是作者用引號來表明所引用的部分是別人所說或所想，而不是作者自己的觀點，如：

Don Stanton's favourite 'leisure' activity is climbing mountains on his own in midwinter.

這裏把leisure這個詞加上引號，就說明作者本人認為登山並不是真正意義上的休閒活動，而只是所謂的休閒活動。

有時用引號在作者與所引用的話之間造成一定的距離是有意譏諷被引用的人，使引號的使用達到一種諷刺的效果，如：

He feels 'crowded' if he sees as much as another set of footprints in the snow.

這裏，作者也有意讓讀者感覺到被描寫的人物的滑稽可笑。

引號的使用還有一種變化形式，一些小報的編輯們用它在文章的標題中來標明綽號、引人注目的妙語或者故意使用不當的雙關語。看下面的例子：

Don 'Mr Snowman' Stanton leads midnight rescue

It's 'snow' joke when Don takes to the hills

Have an 'ice' day, Mr Stanton

'Freeze' a jolly good fellow

這幾個例子同時也暴露了引號的這種用法的危險性，它使得文章的風格一下子就變得極不自然，原因在於它會使讀者的注意力集中到作者自作聰明的語言使用技巧上，這正像前面提到過的感歎號的誤用所產生的效果一樣。有的讀者會認為作者是利用標點來掩蓋其內容的空洞無物，同時還會覺得文章的意思模棱兩可。綽號可以表示對一個人的蔑視也可以表示親切；即使對於讀書時非常專心的讀者來說，諷刺這種寫作手法有時也難以讓人理解，甚至會被誤認為是挖苦或嘲笑，而挖苦別人的作法容易引起讀者的反感。所以對於引號的這種功能，使用起來要格外小心。

◆ 引號與標題

大多數英國圖書出版商和編輯習慣用單引號來標明文章、詩歌、短篇小說或雜誌中文章的標題，而對於像書籍、戲劇、雜誌、報紙和電影等較長的或較完整的著作的標題，則用斜體字來表示，如：

Edwin Muir's 'Sick Caliban' in *One Foot in Eden*

'Sick Caliban'是一首詩的題目，*One Foot in Eden*是刊載'Sick Caliban'這首詩的詩集的標題。我們需要一套標準的規範來規定較短小的作品的標點方法，否則就會造成混亂。這裏有幾個沒有按照規範來使用標點來標注標題的例子：Philip Larkin's Coming, W.H. Auden's Missing, Norman Cameron's In the Queen's Room, Stevie Smith's Not Waving but Drowning以及Siegfried Sassoon's Falling Asleep等。

對於較短小作品用單引號來進行標注已經成為常規。此外，它還可以用來把現實生活與藝術形式區分開來，如在英語

文章的行文中看到 Raymond Carver's Venice 與 'Venice' 兩個表達方法，它們是不同的，後面帶單引號的一個是指 Carver 的一首詩，詩名為 'Venice'。再如：

Edward Thomas's Sussex in the South Country

Edward Thomas's 'Sussex' in *The South Country*

前面一個 "Sussex" 是指一個地名，後面一個是指作品 *The South Country* 中的一個章節。當一部短篇小說、短文或者詩歌的作品集的名稱是出自集中某一篇作品的標題時，單引號也是非常好的一種區分方法，如：

the essay 'Fires' in the collection *Fires* by Raymond Carver

the short story 'May We Borrow Your Husband?' in the collection *May We Borrow Your Husband?* by Graham Greene

通過把有的字不加標點、較短小的作品用單引號和較長的作品用斜體這幾種方法結合在一起使用，還可以把用人物的名字命名的小說、詩歌、戲劇或電影的標題與出現在作品中的該人物區分開來，如：

Lispeth in Rudyard Kipling's short story 'Lispeth' in the collection *Plain Tales from the Hills*

The secret agent in Joseph Conrad's *The Secret Agent*

Hamlet in *Hamlet*

音樂作品也可以用這種方法來標注，較短小的作品標題用單引號，較長的或較完整的作品標題用斜體字，如：

Elgar's 'Nimrod' is one of the most popular portraits in his *Enigma Variations*.

Trick Fraser plays a long drum solo in 'Parallax' on *Lunar Landscapes*, the new compact disc by Upstart Genes.

撇 號

　　撇號 (Apostrophe) 帶來的問題是差異的問題。撇號似乎造成詞義上非常細微的差別，並且需要特別注意才能夠加以區分，因此有些作者認為撇號的用法近乎吹毛求疵，沒有必要使用，而有些作者認為撇號帶來的麻煩很小，不必太在意。但是撇號給詞彙及句子所帶來的意義上的不同是確實存在的。如：

　　The band's on stage. (相當於 The band is on stage. 說明舞臺上只有一個樂隊)

這句話就不同於下面這個短語：

　　the bands on stage (舞臺上有兩個或更多個樂隊)

也與下面這個句子的意思不同：

　　The band's live performance on stage is more exciting than its tapes.

有一些詞，如果加上一個撇號，以及加上一個大寫字母，詞義就會改變，如：

　　cant, hell, ill, its, shell, well, were

這幾個詞加上撇號 (或大寫字母) 之後就變成：

　　can't, he'll, I'll (ill 中的 i 變成了大寫字母 I), it's, she'll, we'll, we're

以上這些不同可以從撇號兩種用法的指導原則中得到解釋。第

一是用來表示縮略 (Contractions) 或省略 (Omissions)，如用 can't 來代替 cannot，he'll 代替 he will, we're 代替 we are；第二是用來標明名詞的所有格 (見第132–39頁)。

◆ 撇號表示縮略或省略

許多常用的縮略詞都是代詞與動詞的組合，如：

I'm/I am, you're/you are, he's/he is, she's/she is, we're/ we are, they're/they are.

上面例子中帶撇號的表達方式代表的是口語形式。英語口語是以一串連續發音的單詞為一個標準單位，每個單詞間沒有時間間隔 (停頓)，停頓只發生在不同的單詞串之間。上面這些帶撇號的縮略表達形式正反映了英語口語發音的連貫性，因此這種形式一般不用在書面英語中。雖然目前書面標準英語的規範性已經不如五十年以前，但縮略形式的詞彙仍然讓人難以接受，除非作者想有意創造一種隨意的、口語化的語調。我們用下面這段話來做一下語調上的對比：

Leonard Vedley's a persuasive businessman. Some councillors said they'd oppose the plan for the Cradle Bay Marina, but now they've changed their views. They'll support the plan because they're sure it's a sound investment that'll improve the town.

如果把上面這段話中的縮略詞寫成完整形式，那麼這段話的語調，加之其表達的意思都會變得更加正式，試比較：

Leonard Vedley is a persuasive businessman. Some councillors said they would oppose the plan for the Cradle Bay Marina, but now they have changed their views. They will support the plan because they are sure it is a sound investment that will improve the town.

有時還可以見到下面這種撇號的用法：

> Britain enjoyed an economic surge in the late 1980's
> but suffered a recession in the early 1990's.

雖然1980's和1990's這兩個詞中的撇號可以接受，但並無必要，
還可能引起混淆。説它沒必要是因為這種情況下並無縮略也無
省略，説它易引起混淆是因為這裏的撇號可能被誤認為是所有
格形式中的撇號。1980s和1990s這兩個沒有撇號的形式是簡單
的複數形式，只是按照變複數的常規變法在單數的1980和1990
後加上字母s，而不必使用撇號。

但在下面這句話中，撇號的使用是正確的，它用來表示所
有格：

> The Austin Mini was a 1960s' success story.

短語a 1960s' success story相當於a success story of或belonging
to the 1960s.

撇號用來表明縮略或省略的用法可以在下面的表達方式中
出現：

> House prices soared in the '80s.

> By the early '60s television was the most popular me-
> dium of mass communication in Britain.

這裏，撇號是用來代替年份當中表示世紀的數位19，而如果寫
成in the 1980s或in the 1960s，就不必加撇號了。

下面是撇號的另一種類似用法：

> There are two c's and two m's in 'accommodation',
> and there are two i's in 'liaison'.

這句話中的c's, m's和i's既非縮略形式亦非所有格形式，而只是
簡單的複數形式。這裏之所以要在表示複數的字母s之前加上撇

號，是因為如果寫成cs, ms或is這些形式就容易產生混亂。另外，還有兩種其他的方法來表示單個字母的複數，一種是把字母放在單引號中，而把表示複數的字母s放在引號外，如：

There are two 'c's and two 'm's in 'accommodation'.

另一種方法是把字母印刷成斜體或者粗體字，而表示複數的字母s印刷成正常的字體，如：

There are two *c*s and two *m*s in *accommodation*. (用斜體表示)

There are two **c**s and two **m**s in **accommodation**. (用粗體表示)

◆ 撇號與名詞所有格

用來表示名詞所有格的撇號是名詞的格詞尾的惟一保留形式。我們前文已經提到過，在古英語中，名詞和代詞要按照它們在句子中的語法功能來改變其詞形，有許多陽性和中性名詞表示所有或屬於意思的所有格單數形式都以-es結尾，如：

cyninges	of the king/the king's
weres	of the man/the man's
scipes	of the ship/the ship's
huses	of the house/the house's

在喬叟 (Chaucer，約1345–1400) 時代的中古英語中，其他格的詞尾開始消失，但所有格詞尾-es卻保留下來，並且不僅用於陽性和中性名詞，還開始用於陰性名詞。例如，在喬叟的《坎特伯雷故事》(*Canterbury Tales*) 中就有兩個故事分別叫做"The Prioresses Tale"和"The Seconde Nonnes Tale"，其中的名詞在現代英語中就要寫成Prioress's和Nun's。

到了莎士比亞 (Shakespeare, 1564–1616) 時代又發生了一些變化。在1623年出版的莎士比亞的《冬天的故事》(*The Winter's Tale*) 裏，所有格的詞尾 -es 一般用於女性，如Ladyes 和 Ladies (lady's)，以及 Queenes (queen's) 等；有時也用於孩子，如 Boyes (boy's) 和 Sonnes (son's)，但不再用於指男性的名詞，如 my Lords tricks, my Fathers honour'd friend 和 the Kings Brother in Law 等 (這些例子還表明，當時幾乎所有名詞的開頭字母都要大寫，並且當時還沒有出現現代英語在合成詞中使用的連字號，如 brother-in-law)。在《冬天的故事》裏，用來表示縮略和省略的撇號的用法非常系統而有規律，如 honour'd, Hee'le (he will)，You'le (you will) 以及 let me have't (let me have it) 等。與此相反，當時表示所有格的撇號卻很少使用，甚至1623年版的《冬天的故事》這個劇的英文標題也寫做 A Winters Tale。

到十七世紀，曾經出現過像 my Master his table (my master's table)，Mr Heminges his word (Mr Heminges's word) 這樣的所有格形式，但並沒有流傳下來，這大概是由於印刷商們已經在十七世紀開始使用表示所有格的撇號了。

到十八世紀初，用撇號表示所有格已經成為常規。在約翰·德萊頓 (John Dryden, 1631–1700) 的1721年版的《古今神話》(*Fables, Ancient and Modern*) 一書中，過去的所有格詞尾 -es 已經不存在了，單數名詞的所有格已經和今天的形式完全相同，都是在名詞尾加上撇號和字母 s，即 's，如 your Grace's accession, the old Gentleman's Excuse 和 Chaucer's Stories。再者，也許是德萊頓本人，也許是他的印刷商，已經開始把標題用斜體字來印刷，如 *The Wife of Bath's Tale*，而早在喬叟時代的出版商們在標題中不用任何標點，如 The Tale of the Wyf of Bathe。

使用撇號表示所有格的關鍵要看名詞是不是要用所有格，也就是看是否有什麼事物是屬於該名詞。判斷好這一點之後，還要看名詞是單數還是複數。下面我們分別就單數和複數名詞所有格中撇號的用法做一介紹。

● 單數名詞

如果用作所有格的名詞是單數，就把撇號和字母 s 加到該名詞的詞尾，如：

> a car's tyres, the manager's tracksuit, a bus's windscreen, a glass's rim, Miriam's piano, Mike's computer, Thomas's ambition, Evans's mortgage, Smith's salary, Jones's overdraft.

名詞的單數形式中可能包括不只一個詞，如 Arms & Armour Press 是一家出版社的名字，Marks & Spencer 則是一家公司的名字。這種情況下仍適用前面講到的單數名詞的所有格變化方法，即在機構名末尾加上 's，如：

> Arms & Armour Press's latest book, Marks & Spencer's chief executive.

用連字號連接的詞的所有格形式也是同樣的變法，如：

> the Attorney-General's ruling, the vice-captain's benefit year, his brother-in-law's party.

當表示兩個人或者兩個物共同擁有某個事物時，變化方法還是同樣，如：

> Miriam and Anna's concert performance

這個短語的意思是由 Miriam 和 Anna 兩個人共同舉辦的音樂會，如單簧管二重奏或鋼琴二重奏等。Miriam and Anna 被當作一個整體，因此 's 就放到了這個整體的末尾。再看下面的例子：

Miriam's and Anna's concert performance

這個短語的意思是Miriam和Anna各自舉辦的音樂會。還有這樣的例子：

the house and the garage's insurance policy

意思是包括房子和車庫在內的一張保險單，而下面的形式就不同了：

the house's and the garage's insurance policy

這樣就變成了房子和車庫分別各有一張保險單。

此外，還有一種值得注意的變化形式，如：

a painting of Winston Churchill

意思是畫的內容是Winston Churchill這個人。如果加上一個's，意思就不同了：

a painting of Winston Churchill's

這樣Winston Churchill就變成了畫的作者，而不再是畫的內容。同樣：

a wild story of Dylan Thomas

意思是關於Dylan Thomas這個人的一些越軌行為的故事，而如果變成下面這種形式：

a wild story of Dylan Thomas's

意思就是由Thomas寫的一個故事。

對於絕大多數單數名詞來說，變成所有格形式只需在詞尾加上's。

這一規則的例外情況，多數發生在某些單數名詞看起來或讀起來像複數名詞的情況下，如：

gallows, measles, scissors, trousers, acoustics, ethics, hysterics, logistics, mathematics, politics.

這些詞看起來和讀起來都讓人感到很彆扭，如果在其詞尾直接加上's，就會引起混亂，如：

gallows's platform, trousers's pockets, hysterics's cure, politics's rewards

因此要儘量避免在這些詞後加's，根據不同的情況把這些詞的所有格用其他方法表達出來，如：

the platform of the gallows, the pockets of the trousers/ the trouser pockets, a cure for hysterics, the rewards of politics/political rewards.

上面這種避免尷尬的方法同樣適用於那些來自希臘語、以 -is結尾的單數名詞，如：

antithesis, basis, diagnosis, hypothesis, paralysis.

這些名詞的所有格也不要寫成下面的形式：

the diagnosis's results, the paralysis's cause

而是要根據上下文靈活變化，如：

the result of the diagnosis, the cause of paralysis

至於-is結尾的字要寫成複數-es時，也應避免使用's，而應該寫成以下形式：

the results of the diagnoses, the causes of paralyses.

　　還有一類值得注意的名詞，就是以字母s結尾的作家的姓，如Burns, Dickens, Graves, Hughes, Keats, Thomas以及Yeats等。對於這種情況，通常的作法是在姓名末尾的s後加's，如：

Burns's songs, Dickens's novels, Robert Graves's

autobiography, Ted Hughes's poems for children, Keats's sonnets, Edward Thomas's essays, Yeats's poems and plays

• 複數名詞

複數名詞如果不以字母 s 結尾，變成所有格形式時依然是在詞尾加上 's，如 child 的複數是 children，所有格就變成 children's；sheep 的複數是 sheep，其所有格就是 sheep's。這一類的例子還有：

children's comics, men's habits, women's rights, aircraft's pilots, deer's habitat, geese's eggs, news media's messages, plateaux's structures.

對於大多數以 s 結尾的複數名詞，變成所有格時只要在詞尾 s 後加上撇號即可，如：

players' entrance, students' grants, nurses' duties, doctors' prescriptions.

當一個複數名詞用來指代兩個或兩個以上的家庭成員時，並且這家的姓不以 s 結尾，變成所有格時也是在詞尾直接加撇號，例如，某一家人的姓是 Smith, Brown 或 Jackson，指代兩個或兩個以上的家庭成員時就變成複數 the Smiths, the Browns 或 the Jacksons，那麼其所有格就如下面的變化形式：

the Smiths' house, the Browns' house, the Jacksons' house.

上述 the Smiths' house 這個短語的意思就是屬於兩個以上的 Smith 家庭成員的房子。

當家庭的姓以 s 結尾，變成複數時要在詞尾再加上 -es，這時要變成所有格形式就要在最後的字母 s 後加上撇號，例如，某

個家庭的姓是Evens, Hughes或者Jones，指該家庭的兩個以上成員時變成複數就是Evenses, Hugheses或者Joneses，其所有格形式如下：

> the Evanses' mortgage, the Hugheses' holiday cottage, the Joneses' overdraft.

有些作者或編輯覺得像Evanses', Hugheses'和Joneses'這種表示家庭名稱的複數名詞所有形式看起來和聽起來都很蹩腳拗口，所以就採用一種變通的方法，使用family這種詞的單數所有格形式，即family's，如：

> the Evans family's mortgage, the Hughes family's holiday cottage, the Jones family's overdraft.

一些維護正統語法規則的學者有時會反對下面這樣的表達方法：

> Edinburgh's Holyrood Park, London's Bloomsbury Square, Australia's Sir Don Bradman, New Zealand's Sir Richard Hadlee

他們認為這些所有格形式都是不正確的，不符合標準英語的規則，應該改寫成如下的正確形式：

> Holyrood Park, Edinburgh; Bloomsbury Square, London; Sir Don Bradman of Australia; Sir Richard Hadlee of New Zealand.

> 或者寫成這樣的形式：

> the Australian, Sir Don Bradman; the New Zealander, Sir Richard Hadlee

但是反對像Edinburgh's Holyrood Park和Australia's Sir Don Bradman這樣表達方式的理由似乎並不充分，因為這些短語的

形式正確，表達的意思也清楚。反對者還會說，從文體的角度
來看，這些表達方式既不正式又稍顯粗俗，但在標準英語中很
久以來一直有這樣的類似用法，如：

> Edinburgh's parks, London's squares, Australia's great-
> est batsman, New Zealand's greatest bowler.

但是這種反對意見似乎來得太遲了，因為這裏提到的名詞複數
所有格的表達方式早已在標準英語的口語和書面語中得到確
認。至於談到文體方面的因素，更不用多說，因為這是標準英
語中的用法，是能夠得到接受的。

◆ 撇號與人稱代詞

在上一章講到代詞時我們提到過，英語中不多的幾條絕對
規則之一就是在人稱代詞的所有格之後從來不跟撇號，如：

> yours, his, hers, ours, theirs, its

同樣，關係代詞who的所有格whose後面也不跟撇號。

然而its和it's以及whose和who's這兩對詞在拼寫上容易混
淆，對於如何區分這兩對詞，我們已經在第24頁上做了說明，
可以參考一下那裏的解釋和例子。為了避免這兩對詞使用時的
拼寫錯誤，可以採用這樣的方法，就是不使用it is和who is的
縮略形式it's和who's，這樣就不會出錯，並且這種完全形式的
寫法也符合標準英語的規則。

下面一段話表明了用來表示所有格的撇號的用法，先看看
下面這一段沒有撇號的情況：

> *Oliver Twist* and *Great Expectations* are cinemas most
> successful adaptations of Dickenss novels. The novels
> effectiveness in the cinema stems from their dramatic

plots, their atmospheric locations, and above all their large casts of contrasting characters. Olivers innocence and vulnerability, for example, contrasts with Sykess brutality and Fagins cunning. The central contrast in *Great Expectations* is between Pips younger and older selves.

這段話應該加上標點。下面是加標點之後的情況：

Oliver Twist and *Great Expectations* are cinema's most successful adaptations of Dickens's novels. The novels' effectiveness in the cinema stems from their dramatic plots, their atmospheric locations, and above all their large casts of contrasting characters. Oliver's innocence and vulnerability, for example, contrasts with Sykes's brutality and Fagin's cunning. The central contrast in *Great Expectations* is between Pip's younger and older selves.

其中Sykes這個詞的所有格形式可以是Sykes'或者Sykes's；另外其他幾個以s結尾的詞，如plots, locations, casts, characters和selves，它們後面沒有加撇號，是因為這幾個詞只是簡單的複數形式，而不是所有格形式。

連字號

　　除了連字號 (Hyphen) 之外，其他所有標點符號都會造成文章的行文在某種程度上的停頓、分隔或者不同部分之間的劃分，而連字號是惟一用來起連接作用的標點符號。

　　連字號的書面形式是一個短橫杠，但它比破折號 (見第149–52頁) 的長度要短，但是有些鍵盤上使用同樣的符號來代表連字號和破折號。區分方法是這樣的，鍵入連字號時就把它當作某

個合成詞中的一個字母，在連字號與構成合成詞的兩個單詞之間不留空格，如low-key就是一個帶加連字號的合成詞。當鍵入破折號時，可以在破折號前後兩端各留出一個空格，這樣橫杠兩端的詞就被分隔開來。

◆ 連字號與構詞

連字號的主要功能是把兩個或兩個以上的單詞連接成一個**合成詞**或**複合詞**。例如，人們習慣於把a man eating tiger寫成a man-eating tiger，把the vice captain寫成the vice-captain，這從一個側面表明了連字號的用法。雖然很少有人會把上面沒有加連字號的兩種表達方式分別理解為「吃老虎的人」和「邪惡的船長」，但很多讀者會無意間產生這種荒謬的理解，前文我們已經提到過，讀者的理解有時會動搖作者的權威性，因此還是選擇意思表達更加明瞭的形式為妙。

由兩個以上的單詞構成的合成詞也是把每個單詞用連字號連接，如：

three-year-old child, *fifty-four-year-old* lecturer, *brother-in-law*, *mother-in-law*, *foot-and-mouth* disease

有些合成詞，如brother-in-law和mother-in-law，還有兩位元數的數位，如fifty-four, twenty-one和ninety-seven等，這些詞永遠都是以連字號連接的形式出現。而一百及大於一百的詞，不管對於讀者還是對於作者都要容易許多，因為它們都用數位形式書寫而不是用英語字母的形式書寫(見第37–38頁)。

以某些字首開頭的單詞，在其字首與後面的單詞部分之間總要有一個連字號，如：

anti-hero, ex-directory, ex-president, neo-Nazi, pan-

American, post-war, Post-Impressionist, pre-Conquest, pre-election, vice-captain, vice-chancellor.

有時一個單詞前也可以用連字號添加兩個字首，但看起來比較彆扭，如：

ex-vice-captain, pre-by-election.

字首ex不能用於像ex-British Prime Minister或者ex-German Chancellor這樣的表達方式中，因為它們可以理解為「不再是英國人的首相」和「不再是德國人的總理」，即職位沒變卻改變了國籍。為免造成誤解，可以寫成a former Prime Minister of Britain和a former Chancellor of Germany。為免使發音或拼寫造成混亂或難以辨認，在字首de或re與它們後面的詞根之間有時就要加一個連字號，如：

de-afforestation, de-ice, re-educate, re-entry.

一個單獨的字母做字首時也要用連字號，如：

T-bone, U-turn, X-ray, Y-chromosome

還有一些永遠要加連字號的詞，如：

Anglo-Saxon, Attorney-General, bee-keeping, cross-examine, double-barrelled, fox-hunting, heart-rending, spine-chilling.

標準英語中也有很多現成的形容詞短語用來表達各種各樣的情況，如：

blow-by-blow, cut-and-dried, door-to-door, down-and-out, down-to-earth, face-to-face, fly-by-night, free-for-all, happy-go-lucky, out-of-the-way, ready-to-wear.

其他一些詞也可以加上連字號用來表達更精確、更獨特的想法，如：

six-wicket victory, two-goal lead, blood-spattered rugby shirt, free-range hens, oven-ready chickens, pre-election promises

利用連字號來幫助表達獨特的思想，這在英語中是一種奇異的語言現象。多種語法組合都可以構成這樣的複合詞，並且可以在很多種語境中使用，這樣便給英語構詞帶來無盡的源泉，使之更加豐富多彩，並且更有活力和創造力。整個複合詞的意義和語法形式及功能都與構成該複合詞的每個成分相異。

可以用 soft-pedal 這個詞來說明一下連字號改變意義及語法功能的作用。當兩個詞單獨使用時，如在 the soft pedal of a piano 這個短語中，soft 是一個形容詞，修飾名詞 pedal。如果把這兩個詞放在一起用連字號連接變成一個複合詞時，其中的 soft 就成了副詞，而 pedal 則變成了動詞，複合動詞 to soft-pedal 的字面意思就是降低鋼琴的音調，比喻義是對某事做低調處理。

從下面所舉的例子可以看出連字號在創造新詞及賦予單詞以新的語法功能方面的作用。把形容詞和名詞用連字號連接可以構成新的名詞，如：

double-bass, half-term, side-show, single-decker;

把副詞 (或介詞) 與名詞用連字號連接也可構成名詞，如：

by-product, off-chance, out-worker, under-manager;

兩個名詞，如表示施事的名詞連接在一起，表示某個人的職業或活動，如：

child-minder, fire-fighter, house-mother, piano-tuner;

還可以把兩個無生命的名詞連接在一起，如：

death-wish, road-map, shelf-life, time-switch;

名詞還可以通過把一個名詞與一個動詞用連字號連接得到，如：

air-drop, face-lift, ski-lift, wind-break;

或者把一個動詞與一個名詞用連字號連接，如：

flick-knife, go-cart/kart, hang-glider, slip-knot;

還可以把一個動詞與一個副詞連接，如：

break-in, change-over, drop-out, flare-up.

把兩個形容詞用連字號連接可以構成一個新的複合形容詞，兩個形容詞中的一個是動詞的過去分詞或現在分詞形式，如：

flat-footed, heavy-handed, fast-talking, high-flying;

複合形容詞還可以由一個名詞加上一個形容詞，其中的形容詞也可以是過去分詞和現在分詞形式，如：

accident-prone, duty-free, goal-hungry, word-blind, beer-stained, grief-stricken, oil-fired, dope-peddling, mind-bending, soul-destroying;

或者可以把上面的情況顛倒一下，由一個形容詞加上一個名詞：

first-rate, second-hand, short-range;

一個副詞加上一個由過去分詞構成的形容詞：

fully-fashioned, hard-bitten, ill-advised, short-lived;

一個介詞加上一個名詞：

in-house, off-peak, on-line, up-country.

複合動詞可以由一個副詞加上一個動詞構成：

cross-examine, quick-freeze, out-think.

用現有的動詞也可生成新的複合動詞：

dive-bomb, freeze-dry, kick-start, shrink-wrap.

還有的複合詞由動詞—連詞—動詞形式構成，如park-and-ride，這是一個複合形容詞，意思是供停車後再換乘公共車輛的地方；再有一種複合詞的形式是動詞—副詞＋動詞—副詞，如roll-on roll-off car ferries這個短語中的roll-on roll-off，也是一個形容詞，意思是(船、渡輪等)滾裝滾卸的，「開上開下」式的(指汽車可以開上開下的)。

複合副詞可以由一個副詞或一個介詞加上一個名詞構成，這樣構成的複合副詞有些可以作形容詞，如：

above-board, off-shore, on-stream, up-market.

目前，有些像index-linked, freeze-dry和shrink-wrap等這樣的詞尚屬於新詞，即新近在語言中出現的詞；而像up-market和roll-on roll-off這樣的詞則是口語或俗語，也就是這些詞在人們的說話或者寫作當中廣泛使用，但尚未成為標準英語。雖然有人譴責這種構詞方法，但它們中的絕大多數都是用來識別或定義某種在不斷變化的世界中出現的新現象。英語語言，就像生活本身一樣，一直處於不斷發展變化之中，標準英語的字典中就包括許多從前的新詞、口語用詞、俚語或是外來詞。複合詞的大致發展過程是這樣的，一旦用連字號連接的複合詞成為標準英語用詞，連字號往往就被去掉而使原來的兩個單詞成為一個單詞。

上面的例子表明大多數的詞類，除了代詞以外，都可以用連字號連接。另外，還有副詞，尤其是以-ly結尾的副詞，也很少用連字號連接。根據標準英語的規則，well這個詞作副詞用時不用連字號，作形容詞時可以用連字號，如：

　　　Arthur Miller's plays are well known.

這句話中的well是副詞，修飾動詞are known。再看下面這句話：

　　　Arthur Miller is a well-known playwright.

這裏的複合詞well-known是一個形容詞，修飾名詞playwright。

　　從上面的講述可以看到，用連字號構成的複合詞有著諸多的形式，這裏需要來小結一下。複合詞可以通過連字號把兩個或更多的詞、或者把一個詞和一個或一個以上的字首連接起來而構成；用連字號連接之後構成的整個複合詞的意思與它的各個組成部分的詞的意思不同，不然的話就沒有必要用這種方法把詞拼湊在一起了。

　　複合詞的語法作用或者詞性(作名詞、動詞、形容詞、副詞)總是與構成複合詞的某一個詞不同，並且可能與其中的每個詞都不同。

　　在大多數由連字號連接的複合詞中，一般都是前一部分限定或修飾後一部分，以income-tax這個詞為例，前一個詞income就限定了後一個詞tax的種類。再如，在high-income tax proposal這個短語中，high修飾income，所以它的意思是針對高收入者的徵稅提案。

　　下面這段話中，錯誤地省略了連字號，可以看到由此而引起的語義上的模糊和混亂：

　　　The long suffering, rain soaked spectators had hoped for an action packed game but the Vitesse Bordeaux Cracow Solidarnoz final was a low scoring match with too much time wasting.

　　　Bordeaux supporters were finally rewarded by a last minute goal by Claude Montereau. The twenty

two year old striker took an inch perfect pass from the
mud spattered Eddy Tissac, the hard working mid field
player. Montereau's fiercely driven shot went head high
past the goalkeeper.

Swiss born Jean Paul Chambery, the Vitesse
manager, was delighted. His pre match plan and his
well chosen words at half time had brought about the
breakthrough and the long awaited victory.

以下是上面這段話加上連字號之後的情況：

The long-suffering, rain-soaked spectators had hoped
for an action-packed game but the Vitesse Bordeaux-
Cracow Solidarnoz final was a low-scoring match with
too much time-wasting.

Bordeaux supporters were finally rewarded by a
last-minute goal by Claude Montereau. The twenty-
two-year-old striker took an inch-perfect pass from the
mud-spattered Eddy Tissac, the hard-working mid-field
player. Montereau's fiercely driven shot went head-
high past the goalkeeper.

Swiss-born Jean-Paul Chambery, the Vitesse
manager, was delighted. His pre-match plan and his
well-chosen words at half-time had brought about the
breakthrough and the long-awaited victory.

應該注意到，其中以 -ly 結尾的副詞 + 動詞 finally rewarded 和
fiercely driven 兩對詞之間沒有用連字號，這一規則已經在前文
講過了。

◆ 連字號與斷字法

連字號的第二個功能是在文章中某一行的結尾處表明某個
單詞被斷開。之所以把單詞用連字號斷開，主要是出於行間距

和文章排版的需要，被斷開的單詞仍然是一個單詞。對於用手書寫的文章，斷字的問題不會出現，因為書寫者一般會把某一行末寫不下的單詞放到下一行；但對於使用文書處理軟體來寫作的人來說，他要是想調整文本的版面，使左右兩邊在垂直方向上對齊，就會遇到斷字的問題，這時應遵守以下一些指導原則。

單音節的單詞不能用連字號拆斷，因為這樣看起來會很不舒服。有的印刷商和出版商也不容許在像人名等的專有名詞中使用連字號把單詞隔斷，一方面是考慮到對人名的尊重，另外也是為了避免引起一些小的混亂，如下面把這些表示人名的單詞拆開後就容易引起誤解：

Arm-/our (Armour), Boy-/den (Boyden), Long-/man (Longman), Man-/sell (Mansell)

在行末對某個多音節詞進行拆分時，要以音節為單位進行拆分和移行。當單詞中有一個或多個音節是字首或尾碼，拆分就容易了，例如雙音節詞 freedom 可以拆分為 free-/dom，三音節詞 disgraceful 拆分為 dis-/graceful 或者 disgrace-/ful。如果單詞中的音節不易區分，就要根據單詞的發音和意義來進行拆分，如 com-/plicate 和 illus-/trate。

Com-/plicate 和 illus-/trate 的拆分移行符合已有的規則。大多數印刷商和出版商認為在能夠避免引起歧義或意思荒謬的情況下，應該在單詞中的某個母音之後和輔音之前進行拆分，如 parti-/ciple, criti-/cism 和 pri-/mary，但是 disconnect 就應拆成 dis-/connect 而不是 disco-/nnect，同樣，minister 要拆成 minis-/ter，而不是 mini-/ster。

還有一條規則，就是有的動詞改寫為現在分詞時要雙寫

其詞尾的輔音字母，如appal/appalling, drop/dropping, grovel/ grovelling和run/running等，這時拆分要把連字號放在雙寫的兩個輔音字母之間，即appal-/ling, drop-/ping, grovel-/ling和 run-/ning。但是，當動詞的詞根本身就是以兩個輔音字母結尾時，拆分就應在兩個輔音字母之後，如add-/ing, bless-/ing, dwell-/ing, purr-/ing和sniff-/ing。

破折號

破折號 (Dash) 能夠提醒讀者有意識地注意到句子的結構和內容，這樣，它就違背了一條文體上的普遍規則，即在表達文章的意思和形成文章的節奏的過程中，標點的作用不應該過於引人注目，然而破折號卻很明顯地打斷了句子的節奏而引起讀者的注意。由於細心的讀者可能對句子的結構有著更強的辨別力，所以作者在使用破折號時就要加倍小心。

破折號的第一個功能是用來區分一段附加或補充的資訊，這與括弧和逗號所具有的附加說明的功能相似。使用破折號的最佳效果是在附加的資訊能令句子的敘述重點發生轉移的時候。下面是一個普通結構的句子：

> Radio Norgate, the independent local station that be-gan to broadcast only last month, repeated the storm and flood warning in hourly news bulletins throughout the night.

其中附加的說明性文字the independent local station that began to broadcast only last month前後是用逗號作了正確的分隔。但是如果變成下面的結構就會不太相同：

> Radio Norgate — the independent local station began to broadcast only last month — repeated the storm and flood warning in hourly news bulletins throughout the night.

改造後的這個句子中，破折號的使用使説明性文字與句子主體的不連貫性凸顯出來。可以説破折號之間的資訊構成了句子中的一個句子。

再看一個例子。在下面這句話中，説明性的附加部分也是用逗號進行了正確的分隔：

> Tenants in sheltered housing in the Seagate area of the city, an unsuitable site for the elderly and infirm, had to be evacuated at midnight.

把這句話變成下面的結構：

> Tenants in sheltered housing in the Seagate area of the city — Why was such an unsuitable site chosen for the elderly and infirm? — had to be evacuated at midnight.

這裏的説明性文字是一個較長的句子中的一個問句，破折號的使用使它與句子主體的不連貫性更加凸顯現來。

破折號的第二個用法，是作為一個單獨的標點符號，引出一個具有輕微戲劇性或諷刺性的停頓，以改變句子的敘述角度或語調。如：

> City councillors held an emergency meeting and agreed to build new flood barriers — when funds allowed.

破折號可以用來達到一種突降的效果（指從有重大意義的精彩內容突然轉入平淡或荒謬內容的一種修辭手法），如：

> On the morning after the storm Mr Leonard Vedley found his new yacht — in the marina car park.

破折號的第三個功能是用來把一系列列舉的條目與隨後的內容分隔開來。前面我們提到過，分號可以用來引出列舉的條目，而這裏，破折號則可以用來作為列舉的結束。如：

> Yachts, cabin cruiser, sailing dinghies, power boats, lobster boats — dozens of craft were torn from their moorings in the marina.

> Seagate, Port Street, Fisherman's Row, Marina Parade, Vedley Close — all were flooded at the height of the storm.

以上是使用破折號的三種僅有的情況，即使在這些情況下，如果破折號用得過多，仍然會使句子顯得不自然並且支離破碎。如果破折號使用不當，就會使一篇連貫的文章變成像一連串匆匆記下的筆記，讀起來就像是未經整理的記錄，而不像是一篇完整的文章。下面是一個錯誤使用破折號的例子：

> Radio Norgate repeated the storm warning — every hour throughout the night. At the height of the storm — around midnight — fifteen-foot waves struck Cradle Bay Marina — and the neighbouring streets. Grantown Fire Brigade — and the police — evacuated elderly tenants, some of whom were dressed for the storm — others wore only their nightclothes.

括 弧

括弧 (Brackets) 分為**圓括號**和**方括號**，都是用來附帶插入語的形式。像旁白、插入語、評價、突然想起的事物、思路的改變或者轉回到原來的思路等這些插入性說明都可以放入圓括號中，或者像前文講到的那樣用逗號或者破折號來分隔。圓括號

和方括號一般用來括出一段資訊，以表明該段資訊與句子中的其他部分有著不同的性質。這兩種括弧都可以表明作者敘述重點的改變。

　　用圓括號括出的資訊一般是文章中的次要部分，但與文章的主體緊密相關或者是主體的補充。由圓括號括入的成分可以是一個單詞，也可以是幾個句子。例如在新聞寫作中，圓括號可以用來指明一個人的年齡：

> Rose de Silva (37), the novelist and critic, was killed in a climbing accident in the Scottish Highlands yesterday.

在文學或歷史研究中，圓括號還用來指明人的生卒年月，如：

> W.H. Auden (1907–73) and Louis MacNeice (1907–63) are joint authors of *Letters from Iceland*.

當括弧中的資訊構成整個句子的一部分時，句子末尾的句號應放在括弧之外，如：

> Brackets indicate that the writer is making a change in narrative focus (see Narrative Viewpoint in Chapter 6).

當括弧中的資訊構成是完整的句子或者是幾個句子時，句號就應放在括弧之內，如：

> One of the first poems Auden wrote after emigrating to the United States in 1939 was 'In Memory of W.B. Yeats'. (MacNeice, who remained in Britain, published a critical study of Yeats in 1941, the year MacNeice joined the BBC as a drama producer.) Auden's elegy marks the end of an era as well as the end of a great writer's life.

方括號用來表明一個更大的、更具體的敘述中心的轉移，它只能用來表示對作者原文的附加部分或注釋部分。例如，某人的

筆記或者日記經過別人編輯，編輯的人就可以把他自己的注釋用下面的方法表示出來：

> I have decided to accept E.P.'s [Edwin Palfrey's] challenge to a race across three Scottish peaks. We have agreed to set off from the MacGregor Arms inn at seven tomorrow morning. [These are the last words Rose de Silva wrote before her death.]

方括號最為通常的用法是用來括住拉丁字 *sic*（如此，這樣），即 [sic]，意思是指[sic]之前的引文部分可能是不正常的情況或者甚至有誤，但所引用的原文就是如此。如：

> A red boy [sic] marked the site of the wreck.

> John Ireland (1879–1962) was a thoroughly English [sic] composer.

對於括弧，尤其是方括號，必須謹慎使用，因為如果文章中出現過多的敘述中心的轉移，書面上出現過多的像（）或 [ ] 這樣的符號，就會給人一種零亂不堪的感覺。出於同樣的文體方面的和為讀者考慮方面的原因，最好不要在括弧中再使用括弧，因為這樣會使句子看起來像多層從句嵌入式的句子結構。下面這段話本來應該是對Auden和MacNeice兩個人進行對比，但由於使用了過多的括弧，主題卻變成了討論W.H. Auden的詩歌，所引述的Auden同時代的人只是作為一種參照：

> One of the first poems Auden wrote after emigrating to the United States (with Christopher Isherwood (1904–86) the novelist) in 1939 was 'In Memory of W.B. Yeats' (first published in the *London Mercury* in April 1939). MacNeice, who remained in Britain, published a critical study of Yeats in 1941, the year MacNeice joined the BBC as a drama producer. MacNeice's own radio

plays (see *The Dark Tower*, 1947) attracted critical
acclaim. Auden's elegy on Yeats marks the end of an
era as well as the end of a great writer's life.

這段話讀起來像是出自一篇拙劣的學術論文的片段。如果減少
其中使用的括弧，並把零散的資訊進行合併調整，就可以使這
段話變得更加通順流暢，也更容易理解。看下面經過變化的情
況：

One of the first poems Auden wrote after emigrating to
the United States in 1939 with the novelist Christopher
Isherwood (1904–86) was 'In Memory of W.B. Yeats',
which was first published in the *London Mercury* in
April 1939. MacNeice remained in Britain and published a critical study of Yeats in 1941, the year
MacNeice took up the post of drama producer with
the BBC, where his own radio plays, published as *The
Dark Tower* in 1947, attracted critical acclaim. Auden's
elegy marks the end of an era as well as the end of a
great writer's life.

省略號

Ellipsis這個字出自希臘語，是省去的意思。省略號 (Ellipis)
的主要功能是用來表示句子或段落中的詞語省略。

省略號可以表示某人所說的話沒有說完，聲音漸小而消
失，如：

'The road to Kiln Acres,' he repeated. 'It's ... Well ... I
mean ...'

與此稍有不同，省略號還可用來表示說話當中的猶豫而不是詞
語的省略，如：

> He said the Kiln Acres issue was ... difficult. He needed time ... to think.

小說作家沒有必要去解釋他們所使用的省略號的功能是表示詞語的省略還是表示語氣上的猶豫，因為在長篇小說或短篇小說中，省略號的功能是不言自明的，如果插入作者的解釋，就會打斷行文的流暢。但在非文學作品中，作者卻可以告訴讀者省略號的作用，如：

> 'The road to Kiln Acres,' he repeated. 'It's ... Well ... I mean...' His words tailed away.

> He said the Kiln Acres issue was ... difficult. He needed time ... He paused again. Time, he said, to think.

讀者有時需要作者就某處省略號的用法加以解釋，因為省略號的用法還有一種情況，就是用來表明一段口頭或書面的敘述的原文已經經過了刪節。在這種用法中，如果省略號用來表示大量的省略，就要放在句子或段落的末尾，而不能放在開頭，如：

> Sarah Harding, Secretary of Kiln Acres Action Group, said that the area was no longer a derelict site. There had been natural regeneration in the three years since the brickworks had been demolished and the rubble cleared ...

> Kiln Acres, Ms Harding continued, was now a habitat for plants and creatures found nowhere else in the area. Two varieties of wild orchid grew there, fritillary and hairstreak butterflies had returned, and pipistrelle bats had begun to colonize the old ash trees.

省略號的排版印刷方式有多種，作者使用時必須前後一致，可以把它當作一個單詞看待，在其前後各留一個空格，像上面的

幾個例子就是這樣；還可以把它當作單詞當中的一個字母來看待，前後不留空格，如：

Well... I mean...

當省略號在句子末出現時，可以像上面所有出現的例子一樣，把它看成是整個句子最後的標點符號；也可以在省略號後面加一個句號，省略號與句號之間留出一個空格，也就是像這樣 (....)。

大寫字母

大寫字母 (Capitals) 的使用有一系列的原則。

每句話的第一個單詞的第一個字母要大寫。我們在講到引號的使用一節時提到過，如果引用的不僅是一個單詞或一個短語，直接引語中的第一個單詞的第一個字母要大寫，例如，下面的引語就必須以大寫字母開頭：

Derek Bly said, 'My brother was astonished when he passed his driving test at the first attempt.'

當引用的內容簡單到只有一個單詞時，這個單詞的開首字母就不用大寫了，如：

Derek Bly said his brother was 'astonished' when he passed his driving test at the first attempt.

前面在講到名詞一節時還提到專有名詞的開頭字母必須要大寫，例如，人名中要用大寫字母，某個人的特有的職位也要用大寫字母：

Maria Riesgal, Director of the National Youth Orchestra

Jean-Paul Chambery, Manager of Vitesse Bordeaux Football Club

這些例子還表明，在表示某個特定機構的名稱中也要用大寫字母。如果文章中已經給出了每個單詞開頭字母大寫的機構名的全稱，再次出現該機構名的縮略形式時就可以不用大寫字母，如：

Maria Riesgal is Director of the National Youth Orchestra. The orchestra will tour Australia and New Zealand next year.

某些表示特殊的地理特徵的詞也屬於專有名詞，像大陸名、國家名、縣名、城市名、河流湖泊名和山脈山谷名等，開頭字母都要大寫，如：

Antarctica, Shropshire, New York, Ben Nevis.

這些地理特徵名稱的全名一經在前文出現過，後面就可以用諸如 the continent, the county, the city 和 the mountain 這樣的小寫單詞來表示。

另外還有兩種專有名詞，一種是一個星期中的七天，一種是一年中的十二個月份，如：

the first Monday in October, every Saturday in August.

一年中的四個季節當作普通名詞，不用大寫字母，即要寫成下面這樣的形式：

spring, summer, autumn, winter.

大多數縮略詞都要用大寫字母來拼寫。如某些機構名：

AA, BBC, NATO, UNESCO, YMCA

還有對人的稱呼、學位或者榮譽稱號等，如：

BSc, Dr, FRC, MP, OBE, VC

化學元素以及化合物的縮寫：

Al, C, H, O, H$_2$O, TNT, ZnCO$_3$

還有一些首字母縮略詞，即由全名中每個單詞的每一個字母組成的詞，如：

AIDS, NAAFI, NATO, UFO, VAT.

有些首字母縮略詞已經被吸收到標準英語中成為了普通名詞，因此只要小寫字母拼寫，如：

radar (radio detection and ranging), laser (light amplification by stimulated emission of radiation), scuba (self-contained underwater breathing apparatus), sonar (sound navigation and ranging)

表示重量和其他度量單位的縮寫一般要寫成小寫字母，如：

m, cm, mm, km, ft, sq yds.

印刷風格

所謂印刷風格 (House Style) 是指由某個出版或印刷公司或機構所制定的一系列指導原則，用來規範英語中可以有多種書寫或印刷、排版方式的用法。就拿簡單的日期的表達方式來說，如果月和年都拼寫完全的話，就有八種不同的寫法：

24 June 1999; 24 June, 1999; 24th June 1999; 24th June, 1999; June 24 1999; June 24, 1999; June 24th 1999; June 24th, 1999

此外還有一種寫法，當月份寫成數位，年份僅用最後的兩位元

數位來表示的話,就寫成24.6.99。按照美國人的習慣,要把月份寫在前面,即6.24.99。

同樣,人名的寫法也有多種形式,如:

Miss Francesca Prasana; Ms Francesca Prasana, Miss Fran Prasana, Ms Fran Prasana, Francesca Prasana, Fran Prasana, Miss F Prasana, Ms F Prasana

如果把Ms和F後加上一個句號,即變成Ms.和F.,就會有更多的變化形式。

圖書、雜誌和報紙的出版社所制定的一系列書面規則,稱為出版體例,它詳細說明了出版社的習慣用法。出版體例的目的就在於把可變因素變為不變因素,從而使出版社的編輯們或者報紙記者們在英語的用法上得到統一,也使個人作者的用法前後一致。有了這種統一性和一致性,作者就可以把那些容易引起誤解和混亂的用法明白無誤地展現給出版社工作人員和讀者。

這種一致性的要求並非僅限於出版社和大的出版發行機構,不管是一封信、一篇短文或是一個報告,任何文章內部像連字號的用法、字母的大小寫以及標點符號的用法等都要前後一致。印刷風格規定一系列規則的目的在於使文章更加清楚明白,這也應該是每個作者所追求的目標。

對於有些縮略詞後面有或沒有句號,很容易引起混亂,如:St既可以表示Saint,也可以表示Street;Dr既可以表示Doctor也可以表示Drive;而大寫字母C則可以表示one hundred, century, Celsius, centigrade,以及音樂中的C大調或碳元素。縮略詞在它所出現的上下文中,一般來說意思是比較明確的,但如果沒有把握的話,最好寫出它的完全形式。

第三章 | 拼寫

到 1755 年塞繆爾・約翰遜的《英語字典》出版時，英語詞彙的拼寫 (Spelling) 方法已經得到確定和規範，並且幾乎所有從那時之前進入英語的詞彙的拼寫也都已固定下來，但也有例外。有些尚未完全英語化的外來詞仍然有不同的拼寫方法，如 amuck, amock, amok; guerilla, guerrilla; harem, hareem, harim; orang-utan, orang-utang, orang-outang 和 veranda, verandah 等。有些很久以來拼寫已經確立的詞彙也打破了固定的模式，出現多種拼寫方式，如 acknowledgement, acknowledgment; connection, connexion; enquire, inquire; inflection, inflexion; jeweler, jeweller, jewelry, jewellery 和 judgement, judgment 等。當然還有一些其他單詞的不同拼寫形式，如 burned, burnt; dreamed, dreamt; spelled, spelt，以及 mis-spelled, mis-spelt, misspelled, misspelt 等。

但上面這些例外情況只佔巨大的英語詞彙量中的很少一部分。詞彙拼寫的嚴格規範化就使得拼寫錯誤很容易發現，比違反書面標準英語的其他規則的錯誤要易於鑒別得多。普通讀者可能對語法、語義、句法和標點等方面的規則不是很清楚，但很多人卻能夠輕易地發現拼寫錯誤，並且任何人都可以通過查字典來檢查拼寫是否正確。

認識單詞並知道單詞的正確拼寫，這是有讀寫能力的人的共同特徵，並且讀者和作者都具有這種能力。鑒於此，加之拼

寫錯誤是可以避免的，所以一旦發生，就容易比犯其他規則方
面的錯誤受到更多的責難。不管是短文、報刊文章還是政府報
告，只要出現幾處拼寫錯誤，就會破壞文章本身、文章的作者
以及作者所代表的機構的權威性。如果讀者的拼寫能力強於作
者，那麼讀者就不僅有權撰文對作者的權威性提出質疑，而且
有權對該作者是否適合從事寫作這一職業提出疑問。

　　英語有著比其他任何語言更多的詞彙，這就使得英語語言
內容豐富並且富於表達。與此同時，也正是由於英語巨大的詞
彙量，使得沒有人能夠記住所有英語單詞的拼寫。但這對懂得
使用字典的人來說並不成為問題。有幾家出版社出版的字典價
廉而且值得信賴，其中還包括一些拼寫字典，給出了單詞的多
種形式，如名詞複數的不規則變化形式、源自名詞的形容詞、
動詞的原形及其現在分詞和過去分詞形式等。我們從拼寫字典
上瞭解到英語單詞的拼寫是以多種多樣的原則為基礎，有時甚
至無原則可言。

　　古英語屬於日爾曼語，是盎格魯—撒克遜人所使用的語
言。它是一種拼音文字的語言，也就是單詞中的每一個字母都
代表一個發音。由於單詞中每個字母都發音，所以單詞的書寫
形式與發音形式之間完全一致。但隨著古英語開始從其他語言
中吸收詞彙，英語詞彙原來那種讀寫形式一致的規律就逐漸打
破了。古英語起初是從拉丁語吸收了少量詞彙，又從北歐海盜
所說的古斯堪的納維亞語吸收了一些，在1066年的諾曼征服之
後，又有數百個古法語詞彙進入了英語中。

　　到1362年，英語以國語的面貌出現時，它已經吸收了很多
的法語單詞，也就不再屬於日爾曼語了。這一同化吸收外來語
的過程一直持續著，最終使得從法語、拉丁語和希臘語中借入
或衍生而來的詞大大超過了古英語原有的詞彙。

　　大多數的外來詞都已經在拼寫和發音方面完全被英語化了，但這一過程並不具有系統性和連貫性，在有些詞彙中還是可以找到些外來語的痕跡。我們從幾個借自法語或仿照法語的造詞方法而來的詞彙，可以瞭解到英語吸收外來詞過程的不系統性。

　　源自法語的名詞尾碼 **-ment** 的發音在數百英語單詞中都已完全英語化，如 announcement（宣告）、employment（雇用）和government（政府），但在 denouement（結局）這個詞中卻仍然保留著法語發音。

　　同樣是來自法語的尾碼 **-age**，在 baggage（行李）和 carriage（馬車、客車廂）兩詞中已經完全英語化，在 garage（車庫）這個詞中只是很大程度上得到英語化而並未完全英語化，而在camouflage（偽裝）、dressage（馴馬技術）、entourage（周圍、環境）、massage（按摩）、sabotage（破壞）這幾個詞中卻明顯保留著法語的發音特徵。來自法語的尾碼 **-ette** 的發音已經英語化，與 **-et** 的發音相同，如 brunette（淺黑膚色的女人）、cassette（盒式磁帶）、etiquette（禮節）、silhouette（輪廓）等，但它的拼寫卻仍然保留著法語的形式，或至少沒有完全使用英語的拼寫形式。

　　現代英語仍在繼續從其他語言中引入新詞，例如，從法語吸收了 au pair（平等的）、discothèque（迪斯可舞廳）、piste（滑雪道）、quiche（乳蛋餅）；從德語中吸收了 delicatessen（熟食店）、diktat（勒令）、gestalt（完全形態），以及軍事用語 blitz（閃電戰，blitzkrieg 的縮略形式）和首字母縮略詞 flak（高射火炮，Fliegerabwehrkanone，英語意思是 pilot defence-gun）、Gestapo（蓋世太保，Geheime Staatspolizei，英語意思是 Secret State-police）；從日語中引入的詞彙有 bonsai（盆景）、karate（空手

道)、kung fu (中國功夫)、origami (折紙手工) 等，由於日本經濟的強大使得人們不能忽視它的文化和語言；還有從俄語中引入的詞彙，如 glasnost (公開化) 和 perestroika (改革) 這兩個詞在二十世紀八十年代末九十年代初時已經在英語中廣泛使用，在當時屬於暫時借用的詞，而現在已經被收入了英語詞彙中。

　　英語還在不斷地從拉丁語和希臘語中衍生出新的科學、醫學和技術方面的詞彙，如 cryogenics (低溫學)、cybernetics (控制論)、microsurgery (顯微外科)、nanometrics (納米技術)、quadriplegia (四肢麻痺) 和 tomography (X線斷層攝影技術) 等。自從瑞典科學家卡爾·林奈 (Carl Linnaeus) 在十八世紀創立了動植物種屬定義原則的「雙名法」之後，科技詞彙的構成就變得非常有系統性。當今，科技語言已經國際化，甚至不再依賴於標準英語而獨立存在。

　　在引入外來詞和派生新詞不斷繼續的過程中，英語的拼寫仍將處於一種難以統一、難以保持前後連貫的狀態，有時可能把一個外來詞完全英語化，有時只是部分地英語化，而有時卻又保持外來語的原貌。這種狀態對英語產生的一個明顯影響之一，就是使越來越多的詞的拼寫與發音相脫離。一個拼音書寫系統可以通過發音判斷並寫出書面的表達形式，但完全的拼音系統卻難以分辨出發音相同或相近的詞，如 cue (暗示)、queue (佇列)、Kew (克佑區，英格蘭東南部大倫敦區的西部一區)；main (主要的)、Maine (緬因州)、mane (鬃毛)，也難以分清拼寫相同而發音不同的詞，如帶有 **ough** 這個字母組合的 bough (大樹枝)、cough (咳嗽)、dough (生麵團)、hiccough (打嗝)、lough (湖、港灣，相當於愛爾蘭語的 loch)、thorough (徹底的)、through (通過) 等。

在不同的歷史階段引入不同語言的詞彙，這又可以說明英語詞彙拼寫的另一特徵。英語中有數百個同音異義詞，也就是發音相似但拼寫和意義不同的字，如palate, pallet, palette，Palate是在中古英語時期借入，源自拉丁語的 *palatum* 這個詞；pallet來自英國法語詞paillete，也是中古英語時期引入，有「稻草」之意；palette是一個古法語詞，直到十七世紀二十年代才成為英語詞。

還有其他原因造成英語單詞的拼寫與發音脫節。英語字母表中有二十六個字母，每一個字母代表一個聲音，但這二十六個字母並不足以用來代表一個人說英語時的所有發音，也不能非常系統而清楚地表示出英語詞彙中所有單詞的發音。

與英語的拼寫不同，英語的發音從來沒有得到規範化，而是隨著地域和時間的不同而有所差別。即使作為英語口語規範的英語標準發音（在英語中稱為received pronunciation, Queen's or King's English, Oxford English或者BBC English）也沒有得到完全的規範化，不同的社會或職業的人群之間以及不同時代的人群之間都有不同。受過正規訓練的演員的標準發音與英國皇室成員的標準發音並不相同，年輕一代演員的標準發音與老一代演員的標準發音也有差異，這一點可以從不同時期英國電影的錄音中得以驗證。

實際上，發音的變化是無窮的。每個人都有他自己特殊的發音方式，其聲音範圍（range of sounds）形成一種特定而複雜的發音模式，而且都有自己的獨特性，就像人的指紋一樣，沒有任何兩個人的指紋看上去是相同的。一方面，所有英語單詞都是由簡單的二十六個字母組成，另一方面，英語的詞彙量巨大而且發音方式又變化無窮。可見，英語拼寫目前的狀況只能作為在這兩個方面之間達成的一種妥協。

拼寫規則

儘管英語單詞的拼寫缺乏統一性，但還是存在一些比較固定的拼寫模式。模式之一就是在把輔音字母加上字母 y 結尾的名詞變成複數時，要去掉 y，加上 ies，如：

> charity/charities, rarity/rarities, biography/biographies, choreography/choreographies.

如果名詞的單數形式是以母音字母加上字母 y 結尾，變為複數時只在詞尾加上字母 s，如：

> holiday/holidays, stowaway/stowaways, jockey/jockeys, turkey/turkeys, convoy/convoys, newsboy/newsboys.

代表字母 e 的長音形式的字母組合 ie 出現在很多單詞中，要想把它拼寫正確，有一條簡單易記的規則：除了跟在字母 c 後之外，其他情況下都是把字母 i 放到字母 e 之前，a piece of pie 這個短語會有助於記憶。下面是一些包括字母組合 ie 的單詞：

> achieve, belief/believe, chief, grief/grieve, hygiene/hygienic, piece, pier, pierce, retrieve, siege, thief.

代表字母 e 的長音形式的字母組合如果緊跟在字母 c 之後，就要拼寫為 ei，如：

> conceit, conceive, deceit/deceive, receipt/receive.

字母組合 ie 的拼寫規則也有例外，如 seize 和 weird。

關於字母 e 的拼寫還有一條規則：當 e 出現在單詞的末尾並且不發音，後面加上一個以母音字母開頭的尾碼時，就要把不發音的 e 去掉，如：

> ache/aching, shake/shaking, adore/adorable, endure/endurable, nerve/nervous, serve/service.

但如果後面加上的是以輔音開頭的尾碼，那麼單詞末尾不發音的 e 就要保留，如：

> boredom, wholesome, looseness, useless, astutely, stately, pavement, basement, tasteful, wasteful.

沒有一條拼寫規則是絕對的，上面這條規則也同樣有例外。當 e 出現在發輕輔音的 c 或 g 之後時，即使後面所添加的尾碼以母音開頭，字母 e 也還是要保留，如：

> manageable, noticeable, courageous, outrageous.

少量以 -inge 結尾的動詞在變成現在分詞時有兩種變法，一種是對於像 singe 和 swinge 這樣的動詞，變成現在分詞時要保留原形詞尾的 e，以區別於動詞 sing 和 swing：

> singe/singeing, sing/singing, swinge/swingeing, swing/swinging

但其他以 -inge 結尾的動詞變為現在分詞時都要去掉 e，如：

> cringe/cringing, impinge/impinging, infringe/infringing, tinge/tinging.

有些拼寫規則還涉及到以輔音字母結尾的單詞。以一個母音加一個輔音字母結尾的單音節單詞，後面添加以母音字母開頭的尾碼時，單詞結尾的輔音要雙寫，如：

> dam/damming, dim/dimming, slam/slamming, slim/slimming, sad/sadder, plod/plodder, grit/gritty, wit/witty.

如果單詞由兩個或兩個以上的音節構成，以一個母音加一個輔音結尾，並且單詞的重音在最後一個音節，那麼在後面添加以母音開頭的尾碼時，單詞最後的輔音字母也要雙寫。這條規則聽起來有些複雜，但實際變化時卻很簡單，如：

abhor/abhorred/abhorrence, occur/occurred/
occurrence, commit/committed/committal, rebut/
rebutted/rebuttal, distil/distilled, compel/compelled,
instal/install/installed, forget/forgettable, regret/
regrettable.

有一些這類動詞只部分遵守上面的規則，如confer, infer, inter
和refer等，變成現在分詞和過去分詞時，要雙寫詞尾的r：

conferring/conferred, inferring/inferred, interring/
interred, referring/referred

但這些動詞變成名詞形式時卻仍然只用詞尾的一個r：

conference, inference, interment, reference.

關於輔音字母l的拼寫規則是這樣的：以一個母音字母加一個輔
音字母l結尾的單詞，後面添加以母音字母開頭的尾碼時，要雙
寫l，如：

criminal/criminally, national/nationally, snivel/snivel-
ling/snivelled, swivel/swivelling/swivelled, patrol/patrol-
ling/patrolled, pencil/pencilling/pencilled, council/
councillor, counsel/counsellor.

與此規則相似，以-ial結尾的形容詞變成副詞時要雙寫詞尾
的l，如：

artificial/artificially, judicial/judicially.

這裏的模式同樣只是指導原則，而非絕對規則，當然也會有例
外產生。以單獨的字母l結尾的形容詞在加上尾碼-ism或ity變
成名詞時，仍然只用一個l，如：

cannibal/cannibalism, symbol/symbolism, national/
nationalism/nationality, sentimental/sentimentality.

以-ful結尾的形容詞為數不少，並且常被拼錯。要注意，形容詞

full 中有兩個 l，但以 -ful 為尾碼結尾的形容詞卻只有一個 l，這些形容詞加上 -ly 變成副詞以後也有兩個 l，如：

artful/artfully, hurtful/hurtfully.

尤其要注意以 -ful 結尾的兩個形容詞 skilful 和 wilful。它們的名詞形式 skill 和 will 中都有兩個 l，但變成形容詞後，原來的兩個 l 就變成了一個，即 skilful 和 wilful；這兩個形容詞在加上 -ly 變成副詞時，原來詞尾的 -ful 中也變成了兩個 l，即 skilfully 和 wilfully：

skill/skilled/skilful/skilfully, will/willed/wilful/wilfully.

我們也應注意動詞 fulfil 的拼寫。這個動詞的原形是 fulfil，而它的現在分詞和過去分詞則分別是 fulfilling 和 fulfilled，名詞是 fulfilment。

有少量以 -our 結尾的抽象名詞有時也會讓我們犯錯誤，因為這些詞在加上 -ous 變為形容詞之後，原來的 -our 就要變成 -or，如：

amour/amorous, clamour/clamorous, humour/humorous, labour/laborious, odour/odorous, rancour/rancorous, rigour/rigorous, valour/valorous, vigour/vigorous.

Laborious 這個詞有些例外，它的詞尾中增加了一個字母 i。

還有一類以 -ice 結尾的名詞也容易引起混淆，它們在變成相應的動詞時要把 -ice 變成 -ise，如：

advice/advise, device/devise, practice/practise;

還有一些詞與此類似：

choice/choose, licence/license, prophecy/prophesy.

下表中列出了一些平時容易發生拼寫錯誤的詞：

abscess	analysis	benefiting
abysmal	annihilate	besiege
accessible	anonymous	bigot
accommodate	antibiotic	bigoted
acknowledge	appal	bourgeois
acoustic	appalling	boutique
acquaintance	apparent	braille
acquire	Arctic	breathalyser
acquisition	argument	brief
acquit	ascend	brochure
acquittal	asphyxiate	Buddhist
address	assassinate	bulletin
adolescent	assessment	buoy/buoyant
advertisement	assignment	bureaucracy
aggravate	attendant	business
aggressive	balloon	by-election
alignment	banana	bypass
allege	bankruptcy	caffeine
a lot (很多)	beautiful	calculator
allot (分配)	beginning	calendar
allotted	behaviour	calibre
allotment	believe	calorie
all right	beneficial	campaign
already	benefit	cannabis
analyse	benefited	carbohydrate

carburettor/ carburetter	coolly	ecstasy
cassette	coronary	effervescent
casualty	correspondence	efficient
ceiling	courageous	eighth
census	cynic	eightieth
changeable	deceive	eligible
character	decipher	embarrass
chauffeur	definite	encyclopedia/ enclyclopaedia
chief	dehydrate	enrol
chrysanthemum	delicatessen	envelop (動詞)
clientele	descendant	envelope (名詞)
colleague	develop	equip
committee	dialogue	equipped
commuter	diarrhoea	escalator
comparative	discipline	espionage
complementary	discreet	exaggerate
complimentary	discrete	excel
concealment	disguise	excellent
conceit	dissatisfied	excite
condemn	dissuade	exercise
conscience	draft	exhilarate
conscientious	draught	existence
conscious	drought	expansive
consensus	dynasty	expensive
consignment	earnest	Fahrenheit
	eccentric	

faithful	glamorous	hemisphere
faithfully	glamour	heroin
fascinate	gnarled	heroine
fatal	goodbye	hierarchy
fatally	gorilla	hi-fi
fatality	guerrilla/guerilla	hijack
fatigue	gossip	hilarious
favourite	gossiping	hindrance
February	gouge	holocaust
ferocious	government	honorary
feud	graffiti	honour
fibre	grammar	humorist
fibreglass	grief	humorous
fiery	grotesque	humour
flammable	gruesome	hygiene
fluorescent	guarantee	hypnotist
foyer	guardian	hypocrisy
freight	haemorrhage	hypocrite
frequent	hallucination	hypodermic
fulfil	hallucinogen	hysterical
fulfilled	harass	icecream
gardener	harassment	icicle
garrulous	haulage	idiosyncrasy
gauge	havoc	idyllic
ghetto	hazardous	illegible
gimmick	height	illicit

imitate	ledger	meter (動詞，如
impasse	legionnaire's disease	測量，計量)
impetuous	leukaemia/leukemia	metre (拍子；長度
impetus	liaise	單位)
imprisonment	liaison	midday
inaccessible	libel	migraine
inaccurate	libellous	millionaire
incognito	licence (名詞)	mimic
incommunicado	license (動詞)	mimicked
inconceivable	licensee	mimicry
incredible	loose (形容詞)	minuscule
incredulous	loosen (動詞)	miscellaneous
independent	loosened	mischief
indictment	lose (動詞)	misdemeanour
ineligible	malign	model
inexhaustible	manageable	modelled
innocent	manoeuvre	monetary
inoculate	marijuana	mortgage
jeopardy	marvel	motorcycle/
juggernaut	marvellous	motor cycle
kaleidoscope	mayonnaise	moustache
kidnap	medieval/	mystify
kidnapped	mediaeval	negligible
lacquer	meteorology	ninetieth
lager	meter (名詞，如	noticeable
launderette	水量計，水錶)	obsession

occasion	pedal（自行車）	privilege
occasionally	peddle（販毒）	profession
occur	penicillin	propaganda
occurred	perceive	prophecy（名詞）
occurrence	permit	prophesy（動詞）
omit	permitted	protein
omitted	personal	pseudo
ophthalmic	personnel	psychiatry
opportunity	physiology	psychology
orthopaedic	physiotherapist	quarrel
oscillate	picnic	quarrelled
oscilloscope	picnicked	queue
outrageous	plaintiff（名詞）	queued
overdraft	plaintive（形容詞）	rabbi
overrate	pneumatic	rabbis（複數）
overreach	pneumonia	rabies
overrun	poltergeist	racial
panacea	polythene	racially
panic/panicked	possess	racketeer
paralysis	practice（名詞）	radios（複數）
parliament	practise（動詞）	ransack
pasteurize	precede	rebel
pastime	precedent	rebelled
patrol	predecessor	rebellious
patrolled	prejudice	receipt
peaceable	prerogative	receive

recipe	rhyme	shield
reconnaissance	rhythm	shriek
reconnoitre	ricochet	shy/shyer/shyest
recur	rigorous	shyly
recurrence	rigour	siege
refer	risotto	sieve
reference	rissole	skilful
referred	rivet	skilfully
refuel	riveted	slay
refuelled	rocket	sleigh
regret	rocketed	sleight-of-hand
regrettable	sabotage	sleuth
regretted	saccharine	slyly
rehearsal	sacrilege	sombre
rehearse	sacrilegious	spaghetti
relief	sadden	squalor
reminisce	safeguard	staccato
rendezvous	satellite	stiletto
repentance	schizophrenia	stilettos
repertoire	seismic	straight
repetitive	seize	strait
reprieve	separate	strait-jacket
reservoir	separation	strait-laced
restaurant	serviceable	stupor
resuscitate	sheikh	subterranean
retrieve	sheriff	successful

suddenness	thief	tycoon
superannuation	thinness	tyranny
superintendent	thorough	tyrant
supersede	threshold	unconscious
surveillance	throughout	underdeveloped
susceptible	tobacco	underprivileged
symmetrical	total	underrate
synchronize	totally	unduly
syndicate	traffic	unequal
synonym	trafficked	unequalled
synthetic	tranquil	unforgettable
syringe	tranquillizer	unfortunately
taboo	tranquilly	uninterrupted
tariff	transcend	unnecessary
tattoo	transmit	vaccinate
taxi	transmitter	vacuum
taxiing	transparent	variegated
technology	traumatic	vegetarian
teetotaller	treacherous	veil
televise	trek	vein
temperature	trekking	vendetta
tenancy	tremor	veneer
tenant	trespass	vengeance
terrestrial	trousers	veto
therapeutic	trousseau	vetoed
therefore	turquoise	vicious

vigorous	welfare	writhe
vigour	whereabouts	wrought-iron
virus	wherewithal	X-ray
viruses	whole	yacht
voluntary	wholly	yield
wagged	wield	yogurt/yoghourt
waive	withhold	zealous
wave	wonderful	zigzag
wallop	wondrous	zigzagged
walloped	woollen	Zionism
warrant	wreak	zoology
weird	wreath (名詞)	
welcome	wreathe (動詞)	

本書讀者的詞彙量可能在十萬至十五萬之間，當然，這裏包括同一單詞的各種變化形式，如walk的變形walking和walked等。一個人的詞彙量是指在他的大腦中所儲備的詞彙，或者叫個人用語，也就是每個人都有與他人不同的詞彙量和對語言的使用。

語言變化

所有活的語言都處在不斷的發展變化之中。在英語語言的發展過程中，變化最為顯著的當屬詞彙。下面是塞繆爾·約翰遜在他1755年出版的《英語詞典》中對幾個詞的定義：

to hack: To hackney; to turn hackney or prostitute（出租馬車；變成苦役或娼妓）

jogger: One who moves heavily and dully（行動笨重的人）

mouse: The smallest of all beasts; a little animal haunting houses and corn fields, destroyed by cats（最小的一種野獸；一種經常出沒於住宅和田間的小動物，常被貓獵殺）

在現代英語字典中，to hack又增加了一條意思：以非法手段獲

取電腦文件；jogger的意思是以娛樂或健身為目的的慢跑者；而mouse則有一種意思是用來輔助或取代電腦鍵盤的一種裝置。我們把這種給業已存在的詞賦予新意的現象稱為**重新定義**。

下面是約翰遜對另外幾個詞的定義：

micher: A lazy loiterer, who skulks about in corners and by-places, and keeps out of sight; a hedge-creeper (終日躲在角落裏和偏僻地方的遊手好閒者，不為人所見；爬越他人籬笆進行偷盜的人)

woundy: Excessive. A low bad word (極度的，是一個低俗粗劣用語)

有些現代英語字典中收錄了這兩個詞，但micher這個詞被注明是屬於方言，也就是非標準用語；woundy是一個廢棄不用的古舊詞，約翰遜把它說成是「低俗粗劣用語」，主要因為它是By Christ's wounds (遭老天報應) 這個褻瀆上帝語的縮寫形式。

有些詞會從當前使用的口語和書面語中消失，而有些詞卻經過重新定義而獲得了新的意義。但是社會的發展變化如此之快，單憑重新定義的方法已經無法滿足用語言來表達新發現、新思想和新習俗的需要了，這樣就需要新詞。在第二章的連字號一節，我們講到把兩個或多個原來已經存在的詞用連字號連在一起構成新詞的方法，這裏我們再看一看生成英語新詞的其他途徑。

英語中的外來詞

我們現在使用的詞大多數都是直接來自其他語言或者從其

他語言派生而來。直接取自其他語言並且在形式上稍有改變或保持原樣的外來詞，有時被稱為**借用詞**，但這個說法並非名副其實，因為雖是借用詞，卻從來都不會再歸還給原來的語言。實際上，大多數的外來詞都已完全英語化，根本看不出其外來語的痕迹。

英語從其他語言中借用詞彙的原因很多。有時是因為外來語所表達的事物或概念是英語中所不存在的，例如，盎格魯・撒克遜人就從拉丁語中借入了如下的詞：

font, pope, school, street, wine

有些外來詞進入英語是文化衝擊與交流的結果，如在公元900年左右盎格魯・撒克遜人與斯堪的納維亞人在英國和平共處的時期，有很多古挪威語詞彙就在那時滲入了英語，如：

dunt, fellow, law, leg, skin, skull.

公元1066年以後，隨著法國人的軍事統治一併而來的是語言和文化上的統治，許多法語詞也就在此期間滲入英語，如：

loyal, royal, voyage, baptism, glory, saviour, mercy, victory.

很多英語中的外來詞，都是借自或派生自法語、拉丁語和希臘語的詞彙，這些詞基本上已經被英語完全同化，看不出它們原來語言的特徵。然而，英語從一些非歐洲語言中借入的許多詞彙，從形式到發音上仍然保持著它們原來語言的特點。英帝國主義曾把英語強加給世界上很多國家，到了後帝國主義時期，英國和美國通過商業、印刷業、通訊業、娛樂業以及旅遊業等，繼續過去那種語言文化的輸出過程。在長達幾個世紀的進程中，英語也從許多各地土語中吸收了大量詞彙，如：

　　來自美洲土著居民用語的詞彙：

　　　　moose, raccoon, skunk, squaw, tomahawk, wigwam;

來自阿拉伯語的詞彙：

　　　　almanac, arsenal, assassin, calibre, harem/hareem/
　　　　harim, hashish, nadir, zenith, zero;

來自印地語的詞彙：

　　　　bungalow, dinghy, dungarees, juggernaut, pyjamas,
　　　　veranda/verandah;

來自波斯語的詞彙：

　　　　azure, bazaar, caravan, shawl, tulip, turban;

來自漢語的詞彙：

　　　　kowtow/kotow, tea, ketchup, mah-jong/mah-jongg;

來自澳大利亞土著語的詞彙：

　　　　boomerang, budgerigar, didgeridoo, kangaroo,
　　　　kookaburra;

來自馬來語的詞彙：

　　　　amuck/amock/amok, kapok, orang-utan/utang/outang,
　　　　sago, sarong.

　　我們衣廚裏衣服的名稱都有可能是外來語，如來自法語的
有：

　　　　beret, blouson, cagoul/cagoule, cravatte/cravat, culottes,
　　　　pants（來自 pantalon 這個詞）.

此外還有來自愛斯基摩語的 anorak 和 parka，來自德語的 dirndl，
來自佛蘭德語的 duffel（duffle，粗呢），來自日語的 kimono

（和服），再有就是上面已經列舉過的來自印地語的 dungarees（工作服）、pyjamas（睡衣）和來自馬來語的 sarong（馬來群島土人所穿的圍裙）等。

外來語名詞的複數

有些外來語名詞的複數形式很不規則，是一種有趣的語言現象。有些外來詞有不只一種拼寫方法，如：

harem/hareem/harim, orang-utan/orang-utang/outang

這說明這些詞尚未完全被英語化，但即使對於一些已經在英語中確立了牢固地位的詞，它們的複數拼寫形式有時也還是讓人摸不著頭腦。

有些來自拉丁語的外來詞，其單數形式的詞尾是 -um，複數形式卻以 -a 結尾，如：

addendum/addenda, erratum/errata, memorandum/memoranda

但這類詞中的有些詞已經被部分地英語化，它們以 -s 結尾的英語複數形式和以 -a 結尾的拉丁語複數形式都在較正規的口語和書面語中使用，如：

gymnasiums/gymnasia, maximums/maxima, mini-mums/minima, referendums/referenda, stadiums/stadia.

同屬於這類詞中的 media 和 data 兩個詞本來是複數形式，卻常被錯誤地當作單數形式使用。其實它們的單數形式應該分別是 medium 和 datum。造成錯誤使用的原因之一，是這兩個詞的複數形式 media 和 data 已經被當作集合名詞，因此被認為是單

數，用media來代表news media，即新聞媒體的總稱，而用data來代表sets of information，也就是各種資訊的總合。現在media甚至有時被錯誤地當成了television的同義語。

以-x結尾的拉丁語單數名詞的複數詞尾是-ices，這類詞也已經被英語化，英語式的複數形式和拉丁語式的複數形式都是正確的。但index這個詞的複數形式在數學中習慣的用法是indices，再看其他例子：

> apex, apexes/apices; appendix, appendixes/appendices; index, indexes/indices.

以-us結尾的拉丁語名詞比較讓人難以掌握，有些已經完全英語化，有些只是部分地英語化，還有一些則根本沒有被英語化，如：

> focus, focuses/foci; nucleus, nuclei; opus, opera; syllabus, syllabuses/syllabi; terminus, termini; virus, viruses.

大多數單數形式以-is結尾的來自希臘語的名詞變成複數時，詞尾變為-es，如：

> analysis, analyses; basis, bases; crisis, crises; emphasis, emphases; synopsis, synopses; thesis, theses.

來自希臘語的criteria和phenomena是兩個複數形式的名詞，卻也像media和data一樣，常被誤用作單數，也是出於它們有時被看作集合性單數名詞的原因。這兩個詞正確的單數形式應該分別是criterion和phenomenon。

單數形式以-o結尾的外來語名詞的複數形式可能以-s, -es或-i結尾，很多這類詞是來自於義大利語，有一些是來自於西班牙語，還有一些來自葡萄牙語，它們的複數形式沒有統一的規則。先看一些來自義大利語的這類名詞：

fresco, frescos/frescoes; graffito, graffiti; inferno, infernos;
manifesto, manifestos/manifestoes; volcano, volcanoes.

甚至同是來自義大利語中的一些音樂方面的名詞都有不同的複
數變化形式：

oratorio, oratorios; piano, pianos; piccolo, piccolos;
tempo, tempos/tempi; virtuoso, virtuosos/virtuosi.

來自西班牙語的名詞複數變化同樣是沒有規律：

cargo, cargoes; lasso, lassos/lassoes; potato, potatoes;
sombrero, sombreros; tornado, tornadoes.

來自葡萄牙語的名詞複數變化同樣是無章可循：

buffalo, buffaloes; commando, commandoes; flamingo,
flamingos/flamingoes.

來自法語的以 -eau 結尾的單數名詞變為複數時也是沒有統
一的規則，有的採取英語化的詞尾 -s，有的則保留法語中這類
名詞複數的結尾 -x，如：

bureau, bureaux/bureaus; gateau, gateaux; plateau,
plateaux/plateaus; tableau, tableaux.

我們普通人都不具備過目不忘的超人記憶力，所以要想正確
使用這些變化多端的名詞複數變化形式，最好經常翻閱一下拼
寫字典。

字首、尾碼與構詞

添加詞綴構成的新詞不如外來詞那樣豐富多彩，也不容易
辨別出是否是新詞。從前文講到的名詞與形容詞的部分中，我
們已經瞭解到詞綴是一個簡短的詞素，尚不足以形成一個完整

的單詞，一般要添加到詞根詞之前或之後，放到詞根詞之前的稱為前綴或字首 (Prefix)，放到詞根詞之後的稱為後綴或尾碼 (Suffix)。由於添加詞綴構成新詞的方法簡單，致使人們往往意識不到這是一個生成新詞的重要來源。因此，我們在這一節中介紹一些通過添加字首和尾碼的方法來構成新詞的主要構詞模式。

◆ 字　首

有少數幾個表示肯定和否定意義的字首構成了大量的動詞、名詞和形容詞。字首 en- 和 in- 表示肯定意義的「使……，使成為……」，如：

動詞	名詞	形容詞
engage	engagement	engaged/engaging
inspire	inspiration	inspired/inspirational

字首 em- 和 im- 與 en- 和 in- 的意思基本一樣，只不過前二者用在以字母 **b**, **p** 和 **m** 開頭的字根字中，如：

embarrass	embarrassment	embarrassed/embarrassing
implant	implantation	implanted

下面是否定字首 de- 和 dis- 的幾個例子：

動詞	名詞	形容詞
derail	derailment	derailed
disobey	disobedience	disobedient

其他否定字首還有 anti-, mis-, non- 和 un-。Anti- 可以用在名

詞、形容詞和副詞中，例如，antibiotics（名詞）、anticlockwise（形容詞和副詞）、antisocially（副詞）。Mis-出現在名詞、形容詞、動詞和少量副詞中，如，mistake（名詞）、mistaken（形容詞）、mistakenly（副詞）。Non-可以放在很多名詞和形容詞前面，如non-payment, non-alcoholic，還可以放在少數副詞前，如non-sensically。Un-，正如我們前面所說的，主要用於形容詞和動詞，如unfair（形容詞）、unfasten（動詞）；也可用於一些名詞，如unconsciousness, unhappiness；還可用於少數副詞，如unconditionally。

來自拉丁語和希臘語的一些字首可以構成與數位有關的詞，如：

前綴	意義	詞彙
mono-, uni-	one, single	monopoly, unison
bi-, di-, duo-	two, twice	bilingual, diagonal, duet
tri-	three	triangle
quad-, tetra-	four	quadruped, tetrameter
quin-	five	quintuplet
hexa-, sex-	six	hexagon, sextet
sept-	seven	septennial
oct-, octa-, octo-	eight	octave, octopus
nona-	nine	nonagenarian
dec-, deci-	ten	decimal
cent-, hec-, hecta-	hundred	century, hectare
kilo-, mil-	thousand	kilometre, millimetre
giga-	billion	gigawatt

有的來自拉丁語和希臘語的字首表示數量、大小和規模，如：

前綴	意義	詞彙
micro-, mini-	small	microscope, miniature
maxi-, mega-	large, great	maximum, megalomaniac
hyper-, super-	over, beyond	hyperbole ('hype'), superhuman
sub-	under, less	submarine, sub-human
ultra-	beyond	ultrasound, ultraviolet

有時候有些字首並不按照其真實的意思來使用，而是為了吸引讀者或聽眾，例如，一個演藝界人士 (entertainer) 可以被稱為一個 megastar (演藝巨星)；一個購物區 (shopping area) 可以被稱為 hypermarket，一個新發明的小器具 (gadget) 可以被說成是 ultramodern (超現代化的，尖端的)。

字首還可以表示地點、位置和關係，如：

前綴	意義	詞彙
ad-, pro-	to, towards	advance, proceed
retro-	back	retrospect, retro-rocket
intra-	inside	intravenous
inter-	between, among	international, intermingle
extra-	outside	extraterrestrial
equi-, iso-	equal	equilibrium, isobar
auto-	self, alone	autobiography
homo-	same	homonym, homosexual
hetero-	other, different	heterodox, heterosexual
dia-, per-, trans-	through, across	diameter, percolate, transport
pan-	all	panorama

前綴	意義	詞彙
para-	alongside	parallel, para-medical
cata-	down, away	catacomb
ante-, pre-	before	antenatal, premeditated
post-	after	posthumous
tele-, telos-	far	telescope

下面這些來自拉丁語和希臘語的字首表示各種學科領域：

前綴	意義	詞彙
aero-	air	aerodynamic, aerosol
anthropo-	man	anthropology
bio-	life	biology, biography
eco-	habitat	ecology
electro-	electricity	electronics
fluor-, fluo-	flow	fluorescent, fluoride
haemo-, hemo-	blood	haemorrhage
neuro-	nerve	neurotic
optic-, opto-	sight	optician
phil-	love of	philanthropy
proto-	first	prototype
psycho-	mind	psychology
pyro-	fire	pyrotechnics
socio-	society	social
spectro-	sight, image	spectrograph
techno-	art, craft	technical, technology
therm-, thermo-	heat	thermometer

其中字首eco-的字面意思是*房屋*，構成了economy這個詞的主幹。economy這個詞以前有「家務管理」的意思。

◆ 尾碼

　　英語中的許多尾碼並不改變詞根詞的意思，而只是對詞根詞的意思加以稍微的調整。例如尾碼-able和-ment可以擴展詞根詞agree的意思，或使其原來意思的表達形式更加多樣化，如agreeable和agreement。與此相對比，如果把字首dis-放在agree的前面，就構成了一個意思相反的詞，disagree。有很多尾碼都有這種稍微調整詞義的作用，如-acy, -ator, -ation, ous, -urgy和-yte等。

　　與醫學有關的尾碼構成了尾碼中的重要一種，如：

後綴	意義	詞彙
-algia	pain	neuralgia
-ectomy	cutting out	appendectomy
-itis	disease, inflammation	appendicitis, tonsillitis
-lysis	loosening	paralysis
-oma	tumour	carcinoma
-osis	condition	thrombosis
-scopy	examination	radioscopy

有些尾碼既可作普通意義的用法，也可用來構成醫學術語。用-phil, -philia, -path, -pathy, -sata等來自希臘語或拉丁語的尾碼的擴展意義構成的詞，有些時候會讓人琢磨不定，看下面的例子：

後綴	意義	詞彙
-arium	place for	aquarium
-cide	kill	homicide
-gram, -graph, -graphy	writing	diagram, autograph geography
-mania	madness, obsession	maniac, kleptomania
-naut, nautic	sailor, voyager	astronaut
-path, -pathos	feeling, disease	empathy, sympathy, pathology
-phil, -philia	lover of	Anglophile
-phobia	dread	agoraphobia
-scope	look, examine	microscope
-sphere	ball, globe	hemisphere
-stat	standing	thermostat

　　最後，還有少量的尾碼出現在數百個英語單詞中。尾碼-ism 就是使用頻率非常高的一個，可以表示信念、理論、過程和特徵等意思，如：

　　baptism, hooliganism, modernism, optimism.

以尾碼-logy 和-ology 結尾的單詞也可以表達與上述類似的表示人類各種活動的概念，這兩個尾碼起初的意思是指「詞彙」，後來慢慢用來表示某種學科，如：

　　archaeology, demonology, mythology, zoology.

與以尾碼-isms 和-ologies 結尾的詞緊密相關的是一些表示某些動作執行者的施事名詞，它們以尾碼-ists 和-ologists 結尾，指那些從事以-ism 和-ology 結尾的詞所表示的事物的人，如：

atheist, bigamist, pacifist, specialist, biologist, pathologist, psychologist, terrorist.

使用字首和尾碼的魅力之一就在於它們可以用來表達新生事物，滿足社會發展的需要。例如，下面就是一些在科學和醫學方面我們正在使用的詞彙：

antibiotics, computer graphics, interferometry, micro-biology, neurosugery, superconductivity, thermonuclear, energy, tomography, ultrasonics.

當我們把來自希臘語和拉丁語的字首和尾碼用於表達社會事件或人類行為的新生事物時，這種應用往往並不十分精確，有些用這種方法造出的新詞甚至是錯誤的或者讓人覺得不可思議。例如，bikeathon（馬拉松式的自行車比賽）和swimathon（馬拉松式的游泳比賽）這兩個詞就很有意思，它們是仿造marathon和pentathlon兩個詞而來；chocoholic和workaholic是模仿alcoholic而來。試想，如果alcoholic的尾碼不是-oholic而變成-ic，那樣就會出現很有意思的結果。

有些由詞綴生成的新詞能夠很貼切地描述一些新生事物，因而能得到廣泛應用。例如，sexism, sexist和ageism, ageist兩對詞就能很好地表達出在性別和年齡兩個方面所存在的歧視現象，這也使這些詞很可能成為標準英語中的正式用語。其他很多每年產生出的新詞也是一樣，這裏再舉一些例子：biohazard, destabilize, disinformation, Eruocurrency, user-friendly, hyper-inflation, megadeath, multi-task, optoelectronics, prequel, superovulation, telemarketing.

人名名詞

　　所謂人名名詞 (Eponyms)，是指用人名來命名的地名或機構名，現在又擴展到用人名來命名的事物或動作名。人名名詞最常用於地名。全世界有無數的街道、建築、城鎮等是以探險家、政治家、將軍和富豪等傑出人物的的名字來命名的。也有一些普通的、日常使用的人名名詞，如cardigan (羊毛衫) 這種服裝的名稱就是以卡迪根 (Cardigan) 的第七代伯爵布魯登諾爾 (James Thomas Brudenell) 命名的，他曾在克里米亞戰爭 (Crimean War) 中統領輕騎兵隊；balaclava (巴拉克拉法帽)，來自克里米亞戰爭中的一個戰場名；wellingtons (高統靴)，得名於惠靈頓 (Wellington) 第一代公爵亞瑟・韋爾茲利 (Arthur Wellesley)；sandwich (三明治)，源自於桑威治 (Sandwich，現為英格蘭東南部一自治市) 第四代伯爵約翰・蒙塔古 (John Montagu)，據說此人沈迷於賭博，常常在他賭博時命人拿夾心麵包來給他吃，這種食物因而得名；mackintosh (膠布雨衣)，也作macintosh，是以查爾斯・麥金托什 (Charles Macintosh) 的名字命名的，這種雨衣就是用他所發明的防水材料製作成的；stetson (斯泰森氈帽)，是約翰・斯泰森 (John Batterson Stetson) 發明的一種寬沿帽，多為美國西部牛仔所戴用，後來澳大利亞人也戴這種帽子。

　　人名名詞在科學技術領域的使用非常普遍，例如在植物學中就有數百種以人名命名的植物，其中人們較熟悉的如bougainvillaea就是用法國探險家路易斯・布幹維爾 (Louis Antoine de Bougainville) 的名字來命名的，還有，如dahlia得名於Anders Dahl，fuchsia得名於Leonhard Fuchs。僅在植物學中楓樹的不同種類就有不少人名名詞，如：

人名名詞	人 名
Miyabe's maple	Kingo Miyabe
Lobel's maple	Mathias de l'Obel
Van Volxem's maple	Van Volxem
Trautvetter's maple	Ernest von Trautvetter
Heldreich's maple	Theodore von Heldreich
Père David's maple	Armand David
Forrest's maple	George Forrest

下面是一些電子學中的人名名詞：

人名名詞	人 名
farad（法拉，電容單位）	Michael Faraday
hertz（赫茲，頻率單位）	Heinrich Hertz
joule（焦耳，功和能量單位）	James Prescott Joule
maxwell（麥克斯韋，磁通量單位）	James Clerk Maxwell
ohm（歐姆，電阻單位）	Georg Simon Ohm
volt（伏特，電壓單位）	Alessandro Volta
watt（瓦特，電力單位）	James Watt

人名名詞說明了人對英語語言的直接影響。當一個人名名詞得到廣泛使用，這個詞就能完全被語言所吸收，這樣人名就變成了普通名詞，甚至還可用作形容詞。例如，geiger counter（蓋革記數管）中的形容詞geiger來自人名Hans Geiger, diesel engine（柴油發動機）和diesel fuel（柴油機燃料）中的形容詞diesel來自人名Rudolf Diesel。但其他一些更具有專業性的人名名詞大都保留一些科技詞彙的特色，不太可能完全被英語語言所同化，

如gauss's law（高斯定律）和gaussmeter（高斯計，磁強計）這兩
個表達中的gauss這個人名名詞多用於電磁學之中，它得名於德
國科學家卡爾・高斯（Karl Friedrich Gauss）。

有些人名名詞只是作為臨時用語，風行一時，一旦這個詞
賴以存在的條件不存在，或者有新的詞彙出現來代替，這個詞
也就會隨之消失。二次大戰中，英國飛行員用Mae West這個俚
語詞來昵稱他們的充氣式救生衣，原來，Mae West在當時是一
個胸部很豐滿的美國舞臺和電影演員。再如，becquerel（貝克
勒爾）是一個放射性活度單位，是用法國物理學家安托・貝克勒
爾（Antoine Henri Becquerel）的名字命名，這個詞曾在新聞媒體
對1979年美國賓夕法尼亞州的三里島（Three Mile Island）的核
泄漏和1986年烏克蘭的切爾諾貝利（Chernobyl）核泄漏的報導中
大量使用。

首字母縮略詞

所謂首字母縮略詞（Acronyms）是指由一個片語中幾個單詞
的起首字母組成的詞。與上面講到的人名名詞相似，首字母縮
略詞使用範圍越廣，尤其是在新聞媒體中使用的頻率越高，就
越有可能被英語吸收為正式用語，並且被當作一個獨立的單詞
進行讀寫。AIDS（有時寫作Aids）就是其中的例子之一，它的全
稱為Acquired Immune Deficiency Syndrome，這個縮略詞在二
十世紀八十年代滲入英語，並且取代了一個原有的縮略詞AID
（Artificial Insemination by Donor）。AIDS進入英語不久就取得
了獨立詞彙的地位，而與之相關的逆轉稱為病毒HIV（Human
Immunodeficiency Virus）卻仍然被按照三個字母的方式進行拼
讀，沒有被當成一個單詞。

　　首字母縮略詞，即 acronym 這個詞，是在二十世紀四十年代隨同與二次大戰有關的幾個首字母縮略詞一同滲入到英語中，如：

首字母縮略詞	全　稱
asdic	**A**llied **S**ubmarine **D**etection **I**nvestigation **C**ommittee
radar	**Ra**dio **d**etection **a**nd **r**anging
sonar	**So**und **n**avigation **a**nd **r**anging

Pluto 也是二次大戰時期出現的一個首字母縮略詞，其全稱為 **Pi**pe **l**ine **u**nder **t**he **o**cean，這個縮略詞是設計海底輸油管的科學家和工程師們的一個聰明的創意，因為非縮略語形式的 Pluto 這個單詞是希臘神話中的地獄之神。同時，人們所熟知的迪士尼卡通片中有一條狗也叫 Pluto，於是就有人把具有「海底輸油管」之意的首字母縮略詞的 Pluto 與名叫 Pluto 的這條狗聯繫起來，卻聯想不到希臘神話。後來還有一條狗成了首字母縮略詞，Fido，全稱為 **F**og **I**nvestigation and **D**ispersal **O**peration，這是一種空中霧氣調查及驅散操作。

　　二十世紀四十年代出現的一些首字母縮略詞，在某種程度上說明了這種詞為什麼會受到人們歡迎，如：

首字母縮略詞	全稱
NAAFI	Navy, Army and Air Force Institutes
WAAF	Women's Auxiliary Air Force
WREN	Women's Royal Naval Service

　　這些首字母縮略詞讀起來和寫起來比它們的全稱要顯得不那麼拘泥，而且更親切、更便於記憶。然而也正是這種更趨人

性化、更加簡化的趨勢，才導致出現了像WREN這樣錯誤的首字母縮略詞，因為它並沒有按照首字母縮略詞的規則取其全稱 Women's Royal Naval Service 中每個單詞的起首字母。其他屬於符合這種簡化趨勢要求的首字母縮略詞的例子有 laser (**l**ight **a**mplification by the **s**timulated **e**mission of **r**adiation)，maser (**m**icrowave **a**mplfication by the **s**timulated **e**mission of **r**adiation)；還有來自天文學的 quasar (**quas**i-stell**ar**，類星體的)。CAT 和 PET 是二十世紀八十年代出現的兩個首字母縮略詞，它們的全稱分別是 **c**omputerized **a**xial **t**omography 和 **p**ositron **e**mission **t**omography，這是兩種可以獲取物體內部三維空間圖像的非介入式掃描技術，也可以用來掃描人體和大腦。CAT 和 PET 這兩個首字母縮略詞會讓使用者或患者都感到親切，不會像它們的全稱那樣多少會讓人產生某種恐懼感。

當今，首字母縮略詞無處不在。如一些國際機構的名稱：

首字母縮略詞	全稱
GATT	General Agreement on Tariffs and Trade
NASA	National Aeronautics and Space Administration
NATO	North Atlantic Treaty Organization
UNO	United Nations Organization

再如一些與電腦有關的術語：

CAD	Computer-aided Design
CAM	Computer-aided Manufacture
RAM	Random Access Memory
ROM	Read Only Memory

此外還有一些口語化的縮略語，其中有些來自於某些特定的社會或政治事件，不太可能在英語中存在下去，例如Nimby (**N**ot **i**n **m**y **b**ack **y**ard)，這個詞曾經為道路或房屋建設計劃的反對者所使用；OMOV (**O**ne **M**ember **O**ne **V**ote)，是指英國工黨掀起的取消工會集團投票的運動；Quango (**Qu**asi-**a**utonomous **n**on-**g**overnment[al] **o**rganization)，用來指那些半獨立性質的實體，如藝術委員會這樣的組織；再者，有些施加社會影響的壓力團體也常選擇一些簡潔易記、容易上口並且讓人感到親切的首字母縮略詞，如ASH (**A**ction on **S**moking and **H**ealth)。

像英語中的其他詞一樣，首字母縮略詞的發展變化也沒有太多的規律可循。正如我們前面提到的像AIDS這樣的詞，它們由兩個或多個單詞的詞首字母組合在一起，但能像獨立的單詞一樣進行讀寫，而像HIV這樣的詞，雖然也簡化成了首字母縮略詞，但只能當作幾個字母來讀。這種不統一性在英國有關金融業的一些首字母縮略語中也可見一斑，如VAT (**v**alue **a**dded **t**ax)和MIRAS (**m**ortgage **i**nterest **r**elief **a**t **s**ource)可以像獨立的單詞一樣進行讀寫，而PAYE (**p**ay **a**s **y**ou **e**arn)卻要按照四個字母的形式來讀。AIDS, VAT和MIRAS這幾個詞通常所有的字母都要大寫，屬於專有名詞；而radar, sonar, laser和scuba等詞中的字母全部小寫，屬於普通名詞。

首字母縮略詞之所以引起了我們的特別關注，一是因為它簡化了，或者至少是看起來簡化了某些複雜的術語；二是因為它作為構詞法的一種，使英語語言的內容更加豐富多彩，並且為之增添了活力。

第二部分

應用篇

如果我們對某方面的事物有特別的興趣，不管是電腦、攝影還是搖滾樂，我們就會很自然地把與這方面相關的詞彙或表達方法納入我們個人的詞彙庫當中，而且興趣越濃厚，就越有可能掌握這方面的詞彙。這樣吸收詞彙的過程有時是無意的或有意無意間的，可能是由於我們對所感興趣的事物的注意力過於投入，使得我們根本意識不到自己已經在慢慢習得與之相關的詞彙了。

一個人的詞彙量與同齡人或具有相似成長經歷及教育背景的人的詞彙水平大致相當，這似乎已經是人所共知的常識，並且可以通過一個簡單的方法加以驗證，例如讀過下面所列的五個簡短敘述之後，很多讀者都會判斷出這些句子可能出自地區性或地方性的報紙：

(a) Two first-half goals by Glasborough Rovers dashed Wallfield United's hopes for the league title.

(b) Prices fell sharply at Deanvale this week. Cattle were down to 102.5p a kg (–6.5 from last week).

(c) Beechmount Players' Christmas revue, *The Icing on the Cake*, had the audience helpless with laughter on opening night last Saturday.

(d) Three Cradle Bay children were seriously injured on Monday when the school bus in which they were travelling overturned on Marina Road.

(e) Upstart Genes' 'Schizophrenia', their controversial follow-up to 'The Beginner's Guide To Death', has been banned by the BBC.

　　上面幾段話都沒有明確給出所討論的主題,但我們還是能夠判斷出每段話所講的主題,因為每段話中都包含有與某一主題相關的詞彙。(a) 講的是一場足球賽或者一場其他類似的比賽;(b) 講的是牲畜市場的事情;(c) 是有關一個業餘劇團的聖誕節演出;(d) 是一則關於道路交通事故的新聞報導;(e) 涉及到的話題是一個搖滾樂隊的新唱片。這五個主題中所使用的每一個詞彙都是具有某一領域或範圍,這種範圍有時也稱為語域 (register)。

　　我們每個人都在不知不覺的過程中掌握很多種語域,掌握的方式也有多種,或者通過讀和聽,或者通過參加或觀看體育比賽,或者通過交談。一旦我們要對某一領域的知識進行正規的學習,那麼掌握該語域的過程就變成有意識的了,尤其當我們在學校或工作中所學的並不是我們所感興趣的科目時,這更是一個有意識的過程。當我們和另外一個人談論某個學科領域的話題,如果這個人對此話題的瞭解比我們自己對該話題的瞭解要少得多或者多得多的情況下,再有就是當我們要寫一篇關於某個學科領域的文章的情況下,我們更能意識到語域的存在,因為此時我們必須把我們對該話題的理解轉換成思想和文字。在這樣的情況下,我們就能意識到我們對詞彙的掌握程度就是我們與他人進行交流的能力的一種體現。如果我們自己或者與我們進行交談的對方所掌握的詞彙量中缺乏足夠的與交談的主題相關語域的詞彙,我們就不能很順利地對該話題進行討論和交流。從廣義來講,我們每個人所掌握的詞彙的多少不僅限制了我們與他人進行交流的能力,而且還限制了我們自身的理解能力。

每個人的詞彙總量在成年時期的絕大部分時間裏一般都保持在一個相當穩定的水平。我們會忘記一些單詞或短語，但同時還會習得另外一些新的；習得的方式正如我們前面所提到的，有正式的方式，如通過在學校學習、接受高等教育或者在工作中學習，還有非正規的方式，如通過閱讀和收聽廣播，通過參加體育或娛樂活動，或者通過交談等。

一個人對詞彙的掌握情況完全是他自己的事情，使用字典可以使我們對詞彙的掌握更輕鬆。但要記住一點，重要的不在於你所能記住的單詞總量的大小，而在於你在說話和寫作中恰當使用詞彙的能力。此外還要特別注意提高我們自己理解別人所使用的詞彙的能力，尤其是對某些政客、廣告詞撰寫者、記者以及教師的用詞，我們要加倍小心，因為這些人的目的往往是要改變我們的想法。

中性詞彙和帶感情色彩的詞彙

想改變別人思想的人有時候會精心選擇一些帶感情色彩的語言及詞彙，目的是激發起人們的情緒或情感以改變人們的思想或行為。例如，慈善機構的廣告商和壓力團體都試圖激起人們的同情心和道德上的正義感，以達到讓人們捐款或加入壓力團體的目的；政客們則從滿足人們的個人利益出發或者激起人們的愛國熱情以贏得更多的選票；有些小報每天通過對一些聳人聽聞的事件的報導來左右我們對所報導人物的愛憎，造成事實與杜撰的混淆；汽車廣告總是想讓人們產生自己就是權力和地位化身的幻想；化妝品廣告則總是使用這樣的技巧，即先讓人感覺自己有些先天的不完美之處，然後推出自己的產品，強調這些不完美可以通過美麗的外表來彌補。

　　使用帶有感情色彩語言的典型例子是對戰爭的報導。一個中立的戰地記者就可能用中性詞guerrilla forces來指代非正規武裝部隊，支持非正規武裝這一方的記者就可能把他們描述成gallant freedom-fighter（勇敢的自由鬥士），而反對這一方的記者就會把他們描述成bloody terrorists（血腥的恐怖分子）。在上述這種情形以及其他許多情形下，能夠識別出帶有感情色彩的詞彙的用法，對於一個讀者來說是至關重要的，因為如果讀者不能辨別出文章中帶有感情色彩的內容，就會很容易受到作者的影響，被其帶有偏見的觀點所左右。

　　如果你是一個作者，注意用詞的感情色彩同樣重要，因為如果你不能控制感情，就會被感情所控制。當你在激動的情緒下表達你的觀點時，你的推理及論述過程就會受到情緒的感染，你所要表達的真實觀點就會被誇張或者歪曲，而說出像'All Conservative politicians are corrupt', 'All Labour politicians are liars', 'Upstart Genes is the best rock band in the world', 'Positron's music is absolute rubbish'等這樣明顯情緒化的語言。

　　情緒的偶爾失控是可以理解的，因為作者不可能在所有時候都能完全控制住自己的感情，但在遇到那些容易引起人的情緒波動的話題時還是要特別注意，如政治、民族、社會問題、體育運動隊以及各式各樣的音樂等。如果對自己的喜好或偏見缺乏瞭解，就會使所寫的文章過於誇張，從而破壞了作者的權威性。當感情不能很好地得到控制時，不僅會出現像上一段中所列舉的那樣令人匪夷所思的過分誇張性描述，還會導致某種形式的語言貶值，使語言本身喪失其真實的意義。例如，如果把體育比賽中的失敗者說成national disaster, tragedy或catastrophe，實際上是把這些詞的意義過於膨脹了，因為當描寫一場導致數千人死亡的戰爭或饑荒時，還是要用到這些已經用來描述體育比賽的詞，那麼從

這種意義上來説，體育比賽的失敗本來都已經被描寫得無以復加，如果描寫比體育比賽的失敗更慘烈的戰爭或饑荒時還用這些詞，這就意味著語言上的一種貶值。

下面是一些中性詞和帶感情色彩用詞的例子：

名詞

中性詞	感情色彩用詞
dissident, non-conformist	deviant, insurgent, rebel, revolutionary
enthusiast, visionary	dreamer, fanatic, zealot
farm worker/labourer	bumpkin, clodhopper, peasant, rustic, yokel
idiosyncrasy	affectation, eccentricity, fetish, oddity, peculiarity
industrialist, businessman	baron (as in *press baron*) magnate, mogul, supremo, tycoon
servant, subordinate	flunkey, lackey, underling
waste, debris, detritus	garbage, refuse, rubbish, trash

形容詞

中性詞	帶感情色彩用詞
adventurous, enterprising	bold, daring, foolhardy, rash, reckless
evasive, elusive	furtive, shifty, sly, stealthy, surreptitious
private, confidential	clandestine, covert, secret, shrouded, veiled
undeveloped	backward, crude, primitive, raw
unusual, uncommon	bizarre, fantastic, mysterious, odd, peculiar, strange

上面的多數形容詞都可以通過在詞尾加上 -ly 變成副詞，如 unusually, uncommonly, bizarrely, fantastically, mysteriously。副詞也有中性用詞和帶感情色彩用詞之分。

動詞

中性詞	帶感情色彩用詞
complain	bewail, bleat, gripe, grouse, grumble, moan, whine, whinge
criticize, appraise, assess, evaluate, judge	attack, blast, lash, slam
debate, dispute	argue, bicker, clash, quarrel, squabble
fall, descend	crash, plummet, plunge, slump, tumble
reduce, contract, diminish, lessen	axe, butcher, chop, cut, slash
rise, ascend, climb, mount	rocket, soar, spiral
weep, lament	blubber, sob, wail, whimper

以上這些例子提醒我們要注意幾個問題。在很多情況下，不管是中性用詞還是帶感情色彩用詞都有多個選擇項，給我們精確地表達出意思上的細微差別和不同的強調重點。一個人可以被說成是 friend, chum, colleague, comrade, confidant 或 crony，雖然人都是同一個人，但用不同的詞來描述給讀者的印象是不同的。這主要是中性詞與帶感情色彩用詞造成的差別以及帶感情色彩用詞中褒義詞與貶義詞之間的差別，例如，在上面所舉的形容詞中與 adventurous 和 enterprising 相關的帶感情色彩用詞中，bold 和 daring 是褒義詞，而 foolhardy, rash 和 reckless 則是貶義詞。表示貶義的詞有時用來作輕蔑語。

　　中性的陳述一般來說應該是表達客觀公平的態度，多數情況下屬於事實性的陳述，其中所使用的關鍵字常為名詞、形容詞、動詞和副詞，用來指明或界定陳述的意義，在這個意義上也是限定其意義。中性的陳述是描述性的，而帶感情色彩的陳述則用來表明觀點而不是事實，其關鍵字也是用來表達一定的隱含意義或相關意義。所以從這種意義上說，帶感情色彩的陳述是帶有含義的。

　　最典型的帶有感情色彩的語言之一是「小報用語」（tabloidese），它是各種以轟動性報導為特點的通俗小報特殊用語。「小報用語」的目的在於強化用詞的感情色彩和煽動效果，有時甚至不顧所用詞彙的詞義是否精確。「小報用語」實際上常常把好幾種相關但不相同的意思縮減成只用一個單詞來表示，例如agony這個詞就可以涵蓋很多種意思，而這些意思本應該用anguish, distress, grief, pain和sorrow等不同的詞來表達。下面是小報的編輯們用一個詞來表示多種意思的一些例子：

感情色彩用詞	所能代表的意思
axe	abandon, cancel, dismiss, drop, omit, remove
blitz	attack, campaign, drive
blow	disappointment, disillusionment, rebuff, setback
boost	encourage(ment), improve(ment), incentive, increase
deal	arrange(ment), contract, exchange, negotiate, negotiation, transact(ion)
dump	abandon, dismiss, drop, omit, reject, throw, out, throw away

感情色彩用詞	所能代表的意思
fury	anger, dissent, opposition, rage
move	attempt, development, initiative, plan, scheme, venture
rap	admonish, caution, discipline, insult, reprimand, warn
set to	could, likely to, may, prepared, ready, will
storm	argument, conflict, controversy, debate, disagreement, discussion
top	distinguished, eminent, important, well-know

如果同一個詞被反復使用來達到同樣的效果 (這些效果往往是不明顯的或讓人摸不透的)，這個詞的用法就會成為一種程式化的東西，人們對它做出的反應也就會變成一種固定模式，成為一種條件反射。

這裏還有一些小報編輯們喜歡用的感情色彩用詞：

> backs, blaze, blunder, bungle, ban, bar, bid, clampdown, clash, crackdown, curb, cut, dash (dash hopes, mercy dash), drama, feud, grab, looms, oust, outrage, probe, quit, quiz, rebel, riddle, rock, row, shake out, shake up, shock, slap, slam, snag, snub, soar, storm out, supreme, swoop, threat, vigil, zap.

這些例子還表明作者使用這些帶感情色彩詞彙的目的在於讓讀者先入為主地接受現成的觀點，而不讓他們做出自己獨立的判斷。有些讀者對於自己被作者們用這種方法所操縱毫無所知；有些讀者要先看作者到底是出於什麼樣的目的用這樣的詞彙，然後就有可能既拒絕接受這些帶感情色彩的用詞，又拒絕接受

作者的整篇文章；還有的讀者則可能把作者的這種用詞看作一種有趣的文字遊戲。

在小報的文章標題中還有一個更為有趣的現象，就是同一個單詞可以被用作不同的詞類，例如，shock這個單詞在Shock Death Sparks Probe這個標題中是一個形容詞，而在Death Probe Sparks Shock這個標題中卻很容易地變成了名詞。正是由於對詞類的使用混亂，才使得小報的文章標題有時顯得含義模糊不清或讓人覺得不可思議，如：

> HP firms up down-payments
> Reinforcements sent to massacre town
> UNO medics lick cholera outbreak
> Euro-climbdown over butter mountain
> Tories face split over arms
> Health heads foot trust bill

最後我們還要注意一點，當談及人的情感時並不一定要涉及到帶感情色彩用詞，像I am angry, She is in love和He is ambitious這樣的句子並沒有任何感情色彩，而只是中立的、事實性的、描述性的陳述。如果把憤怒 (anger) 表述為：

> I am angry with that greedy, lying trickster.

或者把愛表述為：

> She is in love, the naïve, besotted fool.

或者把一個人的野心描寫為：

> He is so ambitious he will cheat, betray or trample
> underfoot anyone who gets in his way.

那麼這幾句話中的關鍵字greedy和lying-trickster, naïve和besotted fool, betray或trample underfoot就明顯地帶有感情色彩，用來激起人們的情感波動。

◆ 感情色彩用詞與語氣

　　感情色彩用詞對所寫文章的語氣有很大影響。文章的語氣大致與說話的語氣相當，它是句子結構、文章節奏以及詞彙之間相互結合所達到的效果，而其中詞彙所起的作用尤為重要。

　　每篇文章都有一定的語氣，我們寫的文章不可能完全中立和客觀，因為即使能夠做到這一點，那麼中立和客觀本身也是一種語氣。如果一篇文章較多地使用具體描述性的單音節詞彙，並且多使用長度較短的句子造成一種緊湊的節奏，這樣的文章多適合描述人體的動作或緊張的心理狀態，但不宜用來創造寧靜的氛圍。要使文章達到創造出寧靜氛圍的效果，就要使用長度較長並且較流暢的句子和較抽象的多音節詞。看下面的兩個例子：

> Bask on sliver sands in golden sunlight by day. Wine and dine beneath velvet skies until midnight.

> Lie on a compound of granulated silica, calcium carbonate and sodium chloride in temperatures of $25\,℃$ to $30\,℃$ from 0900 to 1800 hours. Eat and drink in the open air until 2400 hours.

第一個例子是一則刊登在假日指南上的廣告，其中的名詞 sunlight, skies, midnight，形容詞 sliver, golden, velvet，動詞 bask, wine, dine 都帶有一定的感情內涵，使讀者沈浸於一種溫馨浪漫的氛圍之中。與之相比，第二個例子雖然講述的是同樣的事物，但它的用詞造句就欠恰當，讀來頗似一篇科技文章的文體。

語言的簡約

　　我們應該盡力使自己使用的語言簡潔，這不僅是選詞方面

的要求，造句也是如此，句子結構和段落安排也要簡練。使用長詞和長句不一定使我們所寫的文章顯得更有分量或更具權威性，反而顯得冗長、自負而浮誇。文字簡練卻可以使我們的文章更有力度，更加輕快流暢，使文風剛健而優雅，也只有這樣，我們寫出的句子才能簡練地傳情達意，讓讀者更好地理解文章所要表達的意思。

記者們常使用的一種使語言簡練的方法，是以最少的用詞把細節描寫壓縮為用幾個形容詞修飾一個名詞的結構，如下面這些短語：

> Petite 27-year-old brunette mother-of-two Jane Marsh ...
>
> Prize-winning, best-selling Edinburgh-born author ...
>
> Ex-footballer and keep-fit fanatic Doug Kirk, now a fridge factory assembly-line supervisor ...

這種使語言簡練的方法多用於一些小報，並且已經成為這類報紙經常玩耍的一種文字遊戲。我們不應該像小報的這種作法一樣去刻意強求文章的簡潔，而要做得順理成章，沒有雕琢的痕迹。看下面兩個囉嗦的句子：

> A total of four firefighters, each of whom was wearing breathing apparatus, effected an entry to the warehouse, which was used for the storage of furniture, by means of a door at the side of the warehouse.
>
> Margot Hunter, a soprano who has performed in a considerable number of operatic productions at an amateur level, has no wish to achieve professional status as an operatic soprano.

經過改寫成下面的句子，就可以把上面兩個句子所包含的資訊既簡潔又流暢地表達出來：

Four firefighters wearing breathing apparatus entered the furniture warehouse by a side door.

Margot Hunter has sung soprano parts in many amateur opera productions but she has no wish to turn professional. 或者改寫成：

Opera soprano Margot Hunter has performed in many amateur productions but does not want to sing professionally.

下面再看兩個更長一些的段落，先看第一段：

Leonard Vedley's company, Metropolitan Assets plc, submitted an application for planning permission that would allow the company to demolish the old lifeboat station in Cradle Bay and, on the then vacant site, to construct a hotel with seventy-five units of bedroom accommodation and with car-parking provision for 100 vehicular units. A total in excess of 800 people, which constitutes the majority of the adult residents in the Cradle Bay area, lodged an objection to the application for planning permission on the grounds that the lifeboat station, although no longer being utilized for its original purpose, was nevertheless a structure of considerable social and historical interest. The residents went on to state that at this moment in time there was adequate provision of hotel accommodation in the area. Mr Matthew Ray, the Member of Parliament for the constituency that includes Cradle Bay, stated his willingness to give active consideration to the petition bearing the signatures of the greater proportion of the adult population in Cradle Bay.

在對上文作出修改之前，有幾點需要做一下特別說明。像 submitted an application, lodged an objection 和 tendered his resignation這樣的短語一般可以簡化為一個動詞來表達，即applied, appealed和resigned; that would allow和which would permit可以簡化為allow和permit；有些人習慣寫成seventy-five units of bedroom accommodation和100 vehicalar units的表達方法應簡化為seventy-five bedrooms和100 parking places；A total in excess of應寫成Over或More than；從句which constitutes the majority的用法有些故弄玄虛，寫成which is the majority似乎更好些；utilized也是這樣，應改為used；The residents went on to state可以簡寫為The resident added; at this moment in time也可改為now, at present或currently; adequate provision一般與enough或sufficient同義；對馬修・雷先生 (Mr Matthew Ray) 的過於冗長的稱謂可以簡化為the local constituency（地方議員）；stated his willingness可以簡化為agreed；還有，bearing the signatures of the greater proportion of the adult population in Cradle Bay這個短語也顯得故弄玄虛，應改為signed by most of the adult population in Cradle Bay。下面是上文經過修正後的情況：

> Leonard Vedley's company, Metropolitan Assets plc, **applied** for planning permission to demolish the old lifeboat station in Cradle Bay and in its place to build a **seventy-five bedroom** hotel with **100 parking spaces. Over** 800 people, **the majority of** residents in the Cradle Bay area, objected on the grounds that, although the lifeboat station was no longer **in use**, it was a building of considerable social and historical interest. The residents **added** that **at present** there was **enough** hotel accommodation in the area. Mr Matthew Ray, the **local** Member of Parliament, **agreed** to consider the petition **signed by most of the adult population in Cradle Bay.**

下面是第二個例子：

> A Rovers defender committed a foul on the United striker, who sustained an injury to his left shoulder and was taken to hospital for X-ray purposes. Subsequent to the fouling incident, there was an outbreak of fighting between the supporters of the rival teams. Police succeeded in putting an end to the fight but in doing so three officers suffered injuries of a minor nature; seven supporters were taken into police custody. In court on the morning immediately after the match, the first of the accused tendered a plea of guilty but pointed out that it was the first time he had committed any offence. The magistrates admonished the accused. The magistrates refused, however, to extend a lenient attitude towards the second accused, who had been convicted time and time again for criminal activities involving the use of violence. They decided to impose a custodial sentence of eighteen months' duration.

按照修改第一段時所遵循的原則和使用的技巧，我們可以把這段話變得更加精練，更加流暢。下面是經過修改後的情況：

> A Rovers defender **fouled** the United striker, who **injured** his left shoulder and was taken to hospital for X-ray. **After the foul** there was an outbreak of fighting **by rival fans**. Police **stopped** the fight, **but** three officers **were slightly injured** and seven supporters **were arrested**. In court **the next morning, one of** the accused **pleaded guilty** but **said it was his first offence**. The magistrates admonished **him but they were not lenient with** the second accused, who **had many previous convictions for violent crime**. They **sentenced him to eighteen months in prison**.

誤用及誤解詞彙

　　粗劣浮誇的文章比簡潔優雅的文章寫起來要容易得多,但我們還是要盡力使文章具有後者的風格,因為這樣才能使你所寫的文字、思想及創見有效地深入到讀者心中。要真正做到這一點實際上並不容易,因為英語詞彙的數量非常龐大,沒有一個作者能夠掌握所有詞彙的所有意義。下面我們來討論一下使用詞彙時容易讓人產生疑問的幾個方面。

◆ 同根詞

　　有些詞根或詞素會同樣出現在好幾個單詞中,有時還會出現在多個屬於同一詞類的詞中,令人難以分辨出每個詞的準確意思。例如,來自拉丁語的詞根bene的意思是well或good,它在benediction, benefaction, benefactor, benefice, beneficiary, benefit, benevolence這些詞中都是同樣的意思。

　　下面是一些具有相同詞根的單詞,並且該詞根在所列單詞中的意思是相同的:

administer, administrate	audience, audition
admission, admittance	authoritarian, authoritative
adversary, adversity	biannual, biennial
adverse, averse	captivate, capture
alternately, alternatively	centenarian, centennial
ambiguous, ambivalent	centurion, century
amiable, amicable	childish, childlike
amoral, immoral	coherence, cohesion
artist, artiste	commitment, committal

contemptible, contemptuous	sociable, social
dependant, dependent	stimulant, stimulus
electrify, electrocute	technical, technological
human, humane	union, unity
humanist, humanitarian	variation, variety
imaginary, imaginative	wonderful, wondrous
judicial, judicious	xylograph, xylophone
luxuriant, luxurious	yoga, yogi
negligent, negligible	zoology, zootomy
personal, personnel	

◆ 同音異形詞

英語中有很多**同音異形詞** (homophones)，也就是單詞的發音相同但拼寫不同，如 rain, rein 和 reign，此外還有近似於同音異形的詞，如 flaunt 和 flout。下面給出了一些這兩類詞的例子：

allergy, allegory	conscience, conscious
bazaar, bizarre	demist, demystify
boy, buoy	dinghy, dingy
broach, brooch	disaffected, disinfected
cache, cash	eligible, illegible
calibre, calliper	executioner, executor
cartilage, cartridge	faint, feint
coarse, course	flaunt, flout
chord, cord	gamble, gambol
choral, coral	genius, genus
cymbal, symbol	ghetto, grotto

gorilla, guerrilla	militate, mitigate
gruelling, gruesome	moot, mute
hoard, horde	prodigy, protégé
incognito, incommunicado	right, rite, wright, write
ingenious, ingenuous	stationary, stationery
lama, llama	tycoon, typhoon
lightening, lightning	wrapped, rapped, rapt
magnate, magnet	you, yew, ewe

如果把executioner（劊子手）誤用為executor（執行者），gorilla
（大猩猩）誤用為guerrilla（游擊隊），或者lama（喇嘛）誤用為
llama（美洲駝），就會冒犯別人或者鬧出笑話，同時也會影響作
者的權威性。

◆ 對照片語

有些詞由於意思相對或基本相對而常被放在一起，並且由
於經常成對出現而使它們不易被區分開來。如果想起了其中的
一個詞，就會條件反射地想起另一個詞，雖然我們知道這兩個
詞不同，但有時卻弄不清到底該用哪一個。Concave和convex
可以這樣區分，前者的意思是向內彎曲的凹陷，像cave一
樣。Stalactites（鐘乳石）和stalagmites（石筍）這兩個詞可以這樣
來記憶，c代表ceiling，g代表ground（c和g這兩個字母分別在
兩個詞中出現），鐘乳石是從洞頂往下生長，而石筍則從地面
往上生長。請試著區分下列對照片語：

artist, artiste

centrifugal, centripetal

> critic, critique
> emigrate, immigrate
> fission, fusion
> latitude, longitude
> moral, morale
> rational, rationale
> review, revue

◆ 大詞小用，語義貶值

作者為了給讀者以深刻的印象或者為了使文章適應某種較正式的場合，在選詞時經常犯大詞小用的錯誤，產生不正確的意義，例如把 advance 誤用為 advancement。下面是一些誤用的例子：

> design, designate
> differ, differentiate
> escape, escapement
> form, formulate
> progress, progression
> simple, simplistic

出於同樣的原因，有的人會在該使用 deny 的場合使用 refute，前者的意思是拒絕，後者的意思是證明某事或某人是錯誤的（駁斥），而駁斥比簡單地拒絕似乎在程度上顯得更進一步，所以不應在該使用 deny 的地方使用 refute，因為 refute 的語勢更強，所指的事物也更具重要性。Anticipate 這個詞的誤用與上面的情形相似，有時被誤用來代替 expect，前者的意思是對某事做預先的考慮或對未來的事情做出預測，而後者則是期待或盼望。

　　對decimate這個詞的誤用正好與上面的情況相反，它的意思本來是減少或降低十分之一，但常被誤用作毀滅之意，造成這種混淆的原因大概是由於decimate這個詞讀起來好像是把destroy(毀滅)的第一個音節與eliminate(清除、淘汰)的後兩個音節組合在一起構成的一個詞。

　　Disinterested中的否定字首dis-使很多人都誤以為這個詞與uninterested(不感興趣的)同義，其實前者的意思是不受個人感情因素影響的，或公正的。

　　下面這段話中列舉了一些有時被誤用的詞：

Scientists warn that we are *gambolling/gambling* with our natural *heritage/hermitage*. The problem, they say, is no longer a *moral/morale* question of *personal/ personnel conscience/consciousness* but a question of the survival of the planet.

Toxic *omissions/emissions* from *industrial/industrious sites/sight/cites* are causing *climatic/climactic* changes throughout the world. As a result, we are *loosing/losing* several *species/specious* every year because *their/there habits/habitats* are being destroyed.

Marine/maritime pollution is damaging *coral/ choral* reefs and *fowling/fouling* the world's *beeches/ beaches*. Trees are *dying/dyeing* because of acid *rain/ reign/rein* and *desert/dessert* areas are spreading. In Africa mountain *gorillas/guerrillas* are *prey/pray* to poachers; in South America *luxuriant/luxurious* tropical forests are being felled; in England the *barn/baron/ barren* owl has become rare.

Astronomers/astrologers claim that the *depletion/ deletion* of the ozone *layer/lair* is causing damage on such a *cosmic/cosmopolitan* scale that the entire *echo- system/eco-system* could be *affected/effected*.

以下是對上面這段文章中斜體詞的正確用法的解釋：

Scientists warn that we are gambling [gamble 的意思是冒險或投機，而 gambol 的意思是跳躍或雀躍] with our natural heritage. [heritage 的意思是我們所繼承的或從前輩手中流傳下來的東西，hermitage 是指隱士的隱居之所] The problem, they say, is no longer a moral question [a moral question 是指關係到對與錯、正義與邪惡的問題，morale 則含有自信心或士氣的意思] of personal [personal 的意思是個人的或私人的，personnel 的意思是人員] conscience [conscience 是指一個人的道德感，consciousness 是指意識、知覺，它不含任何道德意味] but a question of the survival of the planet.

Toxic emissions [emissions 這裏是指從工場或生產過程中散發出來的物質，omissions 是省略或遺漏的東西] from industrial sites [industrial sites 是指進行工業生產的地方，如發電場或化學工場等；industrious 的意思是勤勉的、刻苦的；sights 是指所看到的東西；cites 是動詞 cite 的第三人稱單數現在時形式，意思是引用、引述] are causing climatic [climatic 是指與氣候有關的，而 climactic 是名詞 climax 的形容詞形式] changes throughout the world. As a result, we are losing [lose 的意思是損失、丟失，loose 的是意思是使寬鬆或釋放] several species [species 用於生物學中，這個詞的單、複數同形，指植物或動物的一個種類；specious 是形容詞，意思是美好的、令人喜愛的，徒有其表的] every year because their [their 是所有格限定詞，意思是它們的或屬於它們

的，there是一個表示地點的副詞] habitats [habitats 是指動物的棲息地或植物的自生地，habits是指行為習慣] are being destroyed.

Marine [marine是指與海洋有關的或屬於海洋的，maritime是指經由海洋的商貿或運輸活動，它作地理名詞時的意思是指沿海的，在這個意義上，這裏使用maritime pollution也是可取的] pollution is damaging coral [coral是一種很小的海洋生物，珊瑚，大量的珊瑚殘骸可以形成島嶼或珊瑚礁；choral是形容詞，指與合唱或歌唱有關的] reefs and fouling [fouling的意思是愚弄或弄髒，fowling的意思是捕捉野禽、捕鳥] the world's beaches. [beach這個單詞中的母音字母是ea，可理解為beside the sea，意思是海灘，而beech中的母音字母是ee，與tree有關，是一種叫作山毛櫸的樹。這樣可以幫助我們記憶] Trees are dying [dying是指生命的結束，dyeing的意思是染色] because of acid rain [rain是雨的意思；reign是指帝王或君主的統治；rein的意思是駕馭、控制，就像馬的韁繩所起的作用] and desert [desert是指沙漠，dessert的意思是布丁或甜食] areas are spreading. In Africa mountain gorillas [gorillas是指大猩猩，guerrillas是指參與小規模戰爭的非正規武裝，即游擊隊] are prey [prey是指獵物，這個詞的動詞與名詞同形；pray的意思是懇求] to poachers; in South America luxuriant [luxuriant的意思是茂盛的，多指植物；luxurious是名詞luxury的形容詞形式，意思是豪華的、奢侈的] tropical forests are being felled; in England the barn [the barn owl是指習慣在穀倉建巢的貓頭鷹；

baron 的意思是男爵；barren 的意思是貧瘠的] owl had become rare.

　　Astronomers [astronomers 指天文學家，astrologers 是指占星家或算命者] claim that the depletion [depletion 的意思是減少或耗盡，deletion 的意思是刪除] of the ozone layer [layer 的意思是指一個層面，這裏指大氣層；lair 指動物棲居的地點，尤指獸穴] is causing damage on such a cosmic [cosmic 的意思是宇宙的或世界的，cosmopolitan 既是名詞又可作形容詞，意思是世界各地的 (人)] scale that the entire eco-system [eco 是 ecology 的縮略形式，它是生物學的一個分支，叫做生態學，專門研究關於動物和植物以及它們的習性和關係；echo 的意思是回聲] could be affected. [affected 的意思是受到影響或受到改變的，effected 的意思是帶來的或產生的]

使用正確的詞彙

　　用標準英語寫成的文章的任何一個段落中，都會既有具體名詞又有抽象名詞，就像文章中既有單音節名詞(只有一個音節構成的詞，如 noun)；又有多音節名詞(由兩個或兩個以上的音節構成的名詞，如 monosyllabic 和 polysyllabic) 一樣。單音詞往往給人以迫切感並使文章顯得簡潔，而與之相對的多音節詞則讓人感覺很正規，看下面的例子：

單音節詞	多音節詞
work, job, trade	employment, occupation, profession, vocation
pay	remuneration
play	recreation
car	automobile
bus, coach	omnibus, charabanc
train	railway locomotive
school	educational institution
home	residence
shop	retail premises

雖然具體名詞和單音節名詞比抽象名詞和多音節名詞讓人感覺更親切易懂，但如果文章中使用具體名詞和單音節名詞的頻率過高，也會使文章的風格過於做作，並使主題顯得過於簡單，甚至影響主題的表達，同時還會使讀者感到好像作者在採取一種居高臨下的姿態對他們講話。如果在名詞之外，其他詞類也大量使用具體的和單音節的詞，就會使寫出的文章像某些小報的新聞故事那樣，讀起來讓人覺得不舒服。

　　新聞語言當然應該是簡明、流暢、直接，但是如果某篇報刊上的文章使用了過多的具體名詞和單音節名詞，並且大量使用短句和較短小的段落，那麼這樣的文章連同這份報紙都會給人以單調乏味的感覺。下面的這篇文章就是一例：

Mountain cop saves seven ... and then slams 'Sir'!

A police sergeant led a mountain mercy dash to the white hell of Ben Aird in the Scottish Highlands yesterday.

He saved six stranded schoolboys. And then slammed their schoolmaster!

Sergeant Eric McCall (42), leader of Glen Aird Mountain Rescue Unit, led an eight-man team up the killer peak.

Five climbers have died on Ben Aird this year. And four died last year.

The mountain cop found the seven — six schoolboys and their teacher — huddled in a hollow 2,000 feet up.

The seven are from King Alfred School, Manchester. On their way down the killer peak, they got lost in a blizzard.

Darkness fell. They were stranded — in sub-zero temperatures!

Glen Aird Youth Hostel warden, 57-year-old Archie Bell, raised the alarm.

Sergeant McCall and his team risked death in an all-night search.

The seven were found at first light. The rescue team led them to safety.

And then the mountain cop slammed teacher Harold Barton (38).

'Only a half-wit wound take schoolboys up Ben Aird in these conditions,' said Eric. 'The man should be sacked!'

Two boys, Barry Appleton and Jason Wills, both 14, are suffering from exposure after their terrifying ordeal. The two are recovering in Newton Aird Hospital.

上面這段話是仿照了小報上新聞故事常用的標準英語的簡單形式寫成的。如果大報報導同樣的故事，也會使用簡化形式的標

準英語，但所用的詞彙要更加富於變化，句子和段落也比小報上的文章要長。看下面經過改寫後的情況：

School party saved on Ben Aird

Two Manchester schoolboys are recovering in Newton Aird hospital, Inverness, after a night on a Scottish mountain in sub-zero temperatures.

The two, Barry Appleton and Jason Wills, were with four other boys and a teacher, Mr Harold Barton, from King Alfred School, Manchester. Descending Ben Aird, they lost their way in a blizzard, and when darkness fell they dug in for the night.

After an all-night search, Glen Aird Mountain Rescue Unit found the school party at first light and led them to safety.

Police Sergeant Eric McCall, leader of the rescue unit, said: 'Only experienced climbers should risk Ben Aird in these conditions.'

Mr Barton said: 'We are grateful to the Glen Aird Mountain Rescue Unit, although we were fully prepared with emergency food, extra clothing and survival equipment.'

如果文章中抽象名詞的使用頻率過高，就可能會令人感到與具體熟悉的現實相脫離。除表達情感的詞彙之外，抽象名詞與具體名詞相比，更多以多音節構成。如果過多地使用多音節詞與抽象名詞，就會使文章顯得沈悶而且做作。看下面的例子：

A singular consequence of anticyclonic meteorological conditions is chromatic and acoustic aberration of television transmission. Since these atmospheric phenomena are beyond human control, no amelioration of sound or vision can be effected by manipulating the controls of the television receiving apparatus.

避免歧義

　　即使是寫作技巧嫻熟、經驗豐富的作者有時也會寫出帶有歧義的句子，如：

> Police were ordered to stop sleeping in shop doorways.
>
> Her Royal Highness broke a bottle of champagne over her bows and then slid stern-first into the river.
>
> In his farewell speech the retiring Member of Parliament for Newton Aird offered his best wishes to colleagues he had fought with for over thirty years.

作者在無意間寫出的這些意義含混的句子，不僅會讓讀者覺得可笑，還會損壞作者的權威性和可信性。經常性地出現這樣的謬誤還會影響作者及其所服務的機構的聲譽，如某報社及它的記者，地方政府機構及其官員，或者某教育中心及中心的學生等。

　　歧義和其他錯誤可以通過校對的方法來避免，但是校對所需要的高超的語言水平並不是每個人都具備的。作為學習者，我們只需要知道歧義是如何產生以及如何在寫作實踐中有效地避免就可以了。所以在這一部分中，我們主要考慮的是有關英語寫作的一般性技巧，目的是討論怎樣把意思表達清楚，不涉及文學創作中為了達到某種效果而特意使用的富有創意的歧義句。

　　在書面英語中產生歧義的原因主要有兩個。第一個原因在於作者在用書面標準英語寫作時，大腦中的感覺印象或原始材料還沒有形成某種必要的思想。詞彙的使用只佔我們思考過程的很小一部分，而且當我們思考問題時，往往是只在我們大腦內部發生資訊交流，並沒有表現為口頭或書面語言。當我們在這種情況下在大腦內部進行思考時，我們不必要去明確我們思

想的主題，因為我們知道、或者自認為知道我們自己具體在想什麼。構成我們這種內部交流內容的各種知識可能錯綜複雜，但在思考過程當中處於這一階段的知識只是以感覺印象的形式存在，並沒有形成有邏輯性的、明確的思想，或者結構完整的句子。

我們大腦內部交流的內容有時對於我們自己來說是顯而易見的，因此我們就會想當然地認為這些內容對於其他人來說也應該是明白無誤的。但是讀者只有通過我們的書面表達才能瞭解我們的想法，而用書面標準英語把這些想法表達出來則需要重新把它們組織成思想和語言。因此，寫作就需要某種程度上的思想分解能力，也就是使我們自己從完全發生在大腦內部的交流形式中脫離出來，然後才能把這種內心的思考過程有意識地形成思想和文字。

從這種意義上來說，我們好像是在給我們自己做翻譯。做翻譯時，最初的工作就是先要閱讀要翻譯的文章，這就使我們成為我們所寫文章的第一讀者，從而也使我們從自己的想法中超脫出來。而作為客觀公正的讀者，我們就有可能發現並消除寫作中出現的歧義或其他錯誤。這種客觀公正的態度是非常重要的。當然，我們不可能成為完全客觀的旁觀者，因為我們自身畢竟就是進行寫作的主體，但是如果想在這種「閱讀」過程中發現問題，就至少需要採取一種批評性的中立態度。孤芳自賞或者粗暴地反對批評意見，都會妨礙我們發現所寫的文章中和我們作為作者所存在的問題。因此，我們最好把自己假定為局外的旁觀者，帶著強烈的好奇心來看待我們所寫的文章，使我們自己的思想處於一種活躍開放的狀態。也只有這樣我們才能看到其他讀者在我們的文章中所看到的東西。

　　使書面英語產生歧義的的第二個原因在於英語語言本身。英語有超過50萬個的單詞及單詞的各種變體，有大量的詞具有兩個或兩個以上的意思，即像bat, light, stock和tail這樣的多義詞，還有變換無窮的句型，所有這些因素使英語擁有取之不盡的語言資源。但也正是這些因素還會使我們所說的話和所寫的文章混亂不堪，含混不清。在英語口語，尤其是在非正式場合的講話中，是容許歧義的存在的，因為講話者可以通過道歉、解釋、改正或重複的方法來彌補，直到聽者明白他的意思為止。而書面英語就不容許歧義的存在，因為作者不可能時刻在讀者身邊向他們解釋文章中有歧義的地方。

　　以上是造成歧義的兩個大的方面的原因，它們在現實的文章當中又各有不同的表現形式，而這些造成歧義的形式又是可以發現和避免的。下文中的一些例子出自學生和缺乏經驗的作者之手。目的當然不是讓他們出醜，而是透過他們的經驗，來幫助我們發現錯誤，並提供一些切實可行的消滅這些錯誤的方法。

◆ 半生不熟的思想

　　常見的歧義往往是由上述兩個經常交織在一起出現的原因造成的，即一是作者的想法尚未經過深思熟慮，形成思想，二是未成形的思想沒有用標準英語完全表達出來。

　　下面第一個例子中，作者討論的是一部小說：

> The actual time setting, which is some time around the turn of the nineteenth century, is relevant at times although not that important, because the book could be set in a different time.

作者在本句中四處使用了time這個詞，但他或者根本沒有意識到使用了這個詞的三種不同用法，或者知道這些不同但沒有把

它們表達清楚。短語The actual time setting是指小說的故事發生的歷史時期；some time around the turn of the 19th century的意思是十九世紀末；relevant at times的意思是在小說的某些情節發展階段或某些章節；a different time是指某一不同的歷史階段。有足夠耐心和愛心的讀者會從文中體會出這些短語的意思，但並非所有的讀者都具有這樣的耐心和愛心。所以這句話這樣寫會更好些：

> The historical period, which is the end of the nineteenth century, is relevant in some chapters but is not too important because the book could be set in a different period.

或者也可以這樣寫：

> The historical period is the end of the nineteenth century, and although this is relevant in some chapters it is not vital because the novel could be set in a different period.

好心的讀者也許能夠揣摩出下面這個例子的意思：

> A recruitment interview is a dialogue between two or more but it is not equal because one should control it while the other should do most of the talking.

作者對面試(interview)中不同角色的任務或責任有所瞭解，但這句話還是沒有表述清楚，因為這些任務沒有針對具體的人或者沒有把它們形成非常準確的思想和語言。下面這樣的說法就要比原來的句子清楚許多：

> A recruitment interview is a dialogue between the interviewer and the subject, or interviewee, but it is not an equal dialogue. The interviewer should control the dialogue but the interviewee should do most of the talking.

還有更明確的表達方法：

> Although a recruitment interview is a dialogue between the interviewer and the candidate, it is not a conversation between equals. The interviewer should control the dialogue in such a way that the candidate does most of the talking.

這類常見的歧義是可以避免的，方法就是不斷提醒自己，讀者只能通過我們所寫出來的東西才能瞭解我們的想法，並且要儘量把人物、地點、對象及事件等要素一一表達得明白無誤。

◆ 代詞指代不清

這種錯誤是上面講到的那種錯誤的另外一種表現形式，造成這種歧義的原因在於，在尚未明確所講的人或事物的情況下，作者卻想當然地認為讀者已經知道所討論的對象。

如果作者在一個句子中提到了兩位或更多位女士，然後在下一句話中用到代詞she，讀者就有可能不知道she到底指的是誰。依此類推，如果提到兩個以上的男士，隨後出現代詞he，提到兩群以上的人，隨後出現代詞they，提到兩個以上的事物，隨後出現代詞it，這些情況下都可能產生歧義。

下面例舉的這句話出自一位女學生之手，談到的是一位女作家所寫的以一位婦女為中心人物的小說。這位女學生大概知道她所使用的代詞it, her和she分別指的都是誰，但讀者只能猜測它們的意思：

> I think it helps the reader to identify with her character. Perhaps the reader has the same thoughts and feelings as she follows her throughout the book.

其中的第一個her (her character)，可能是小說作者所塑造的人

物或者是該人物所具有的性情及行為特徵；she (as she follows) 可能是小說的讀者 (即作者)，也可能是小說的作者，因為這兩個人都是女性；第二個 her (follows her) 則可能是小說的中心人物，也可能是小說的作者。

下面這個例子與上面一句話的情況類似：

> The Party has made a conscious decision to promote the policy in the city, and it is partly because of this that it is showing signs of growth.

It is showing signs of growth 中的 it 可能是指 the political party，也可能是指 the policy，還可能是指 the city。

在前一個例子中，讀者通過反復閱讀出現過相關代詞的段落，也許能夠推測出 it 是指什麼，以及 her 和 she 分別指誰，但他卻不一定有這樣的時間或心情，因為一個教師 (the examiner) 可能在一個晚上還要批閱其他三十篇學生寫的短文，某地方政府部門的主管也許在出席下午的會議之前要在早上讀完其他六份報告，招聘者說不定還要翻閱應聘一個職位的五十封求職信和個人履歷。所以，儘管我們不可能使我們所寫的東西絕對清楚明白，但出於我們自身利益的考慮，還是要儘量使我們所表達的意思能夠讓人正確地理解。

◆ 省 略

• 錯誤使用數位資訊

新聞報導中有時會給出一些形式簡略並略帶口語化的統計和數位資訊，雖然也能被廣泛接受和理解，但如果讀者僅從其字面意思來解釋的話，還是會出現一些因歧義而令人捧腹的情況，如：

A car left in a city car park is stolen twice a day.

For the third Saturday in a row a child was lost in the shopping centre.

Police report that five houses in the Cradle Bay district are broken into every weekend throughout the year.

這類歧義現象的產生是由於把有關事件發生頻率的統計數位過於簡化造成的。例如，按照上面第一句話的說法，其本意思應該是很多輛車被盜，結果卻變成了同一輛車在一天之內被盜兩次。類似這樣句子的意思應該更加完整地表達出來，有時還可以加上 on average 來幫助表明句意，如上面的第一、三兩句可以改寫為：

On average there are two incidents of car theft from city car parks every day.

Police report that on average there are five cases of house-breaking in the Cradle Bay district every week-end throughout the year.

上面例子中的第二句則需要較大的改動：

A child was lost in the city shopping centre on Saturday, the third such incident in successive weeks.

◆ 資訊欠連貫

　　有時歧義是由於作者丟失了重要資訊而造成的。這種丟失有可能在作者迫於較大壓力的情況下寫作時發生，但即使在這種情況下造成的歧義現象，仍然是作者想當然地認為讀者瞭解作者意圖的結果。下面這個例子中，作者這種想當然的想法就表現得十分明顯：

Three homeless men shared the bed and breakfast.

當然，多數讀者一看就能知道這句話中的 bed 和 breakfast 是口語化的用法，而且在句尾本該用 accommodation 這個詞 (Three homeless men shared the accommodation)，但還是有些讀者看過這句話之後會把它理解為三個人同擠一張床、同享一份早餐，這樣的解釋當然是讓人不可思議的。只有辨明情況之後，這樣的歧義才能消除。

再看下面這個例子：

> Churchill's wartime speeches in Parliament were widely read in Britain and overseas.

大多數讀者能夠意識到邱吉爾的演講先是發表在報紙上，然後才被廣泛傳閱。但仍然有人在讀過這句話之後會發現一個邏輯上的空缺，因此他在短時間內注意到的是句子的表述不清而不是其真正要表達的意思。只要把邏輯上的空缺補充完整，並把事情的前後順序表達清楚，就能避免這類歧義的產生。下面是這句話經過改寫之後的情況：

> Churchill's wartime speeches in Parliament were reported in the press and then widely read in Britain and overseas.

此外，本節的介紹中舉的兩個例子還表明，資訊的缺失有時會使句子意思顯得荒謬，甚至會對別人造成傷害。下面是把這兩個例子中的遺漏資訊補充完整後的句子，方括號中是補出的詞：

> Police were ordered to stop [people from] sleeping in shop doorways.

> Her Royal Highness broke a bottle of champagne over [the ship's] bows and then [the ship] slid stern-first into the river.

這兩個例子原來把一些相互矛盾的意象或思想放到了一起，我
們通過把丟失的資訊補充完整就消除了原句中的矛盾。

◆ 句 法

● 並 列

　　有時雖然句子的資訊完整，但由於句型 (句中單詞的排列順
序) 中使用了不合理的並列關係，同樣會產生意思荒唐的句子。
下面是從某些出版物中選取的例子：

> The two thieves escaped in a stolen car which was
> driven by a third member of the gang fitted with false
> number plates.

> Ian Botham was feeding the elephants with his chil-
> dren before he set off on the next stage of the long
> march for charity.

> MI5 will take over the responsibility of hunting down
> terrorists from Scotland Yard's Special Branch.

重新改變一下句子構成，這些句子意思表達上的不恰當之處就
可以避免：

> The two thieves escaped in a stolen car which was
> fitted with false number plates and driven by a third
> member of the gang.

> Ian Botham and his children were feeding the elephants
> before Mr Botham set off on the next stage of his long
> march for charity.

> MI5 will take over from Scotland Yard's Special Branch
> the responsibility for hunting down terrorists.

● 分詞短語

　　有時錯誤使用以分詞短語 (Participial Phrases) 開頭的句型也會造成歧義。當句子以分詞短語開頭時，後面必須馬上跟一個與之相關的名詞、代詞或名詞短語。如：

> Driving along Princes Street, he saw the Castle silhouetted against the skyline.

句中的 driving 是動詞 drive 的現在分詞形式，Driving along Princes Street 就構成了一個分詞短語，短語後緊跟的第一個詞是代詞 he，直接與動詞 driving 相關，即 he 是動作的發出者。下面這句話也是一樣：

> Beaten in the final of the 800 metres, Franky Dexter limped off the track.

Beaten 是動詞 beat 的過去分詞，Beaten in the final of the 800 metres 構成一個分詞短語，專有名詞 Franky Dexter 緊跟在該短語後，與動詞 beaten 直接相關，是該動詞的動作承受者。當名詞、代詞或名詞短語與分詞短語不相關時，就會造成歧義，甚至使句子意思變得荒唐。看下面的句子：

> Flying across the Scottish mountains, a herd of red deer scattered in panic.

> Rowing across the Highland loch, an osprey caught a trout.

由於這兩句話中的名詞短語 a herd of red deer 和 an osprey 與所在各句中的分詞短語毫不相關，於是句子中立即就產生了會飛的鹿和會划船的鳥這樣不合邏輯的錯誤。如果在分詞短語後都加上一個恰當的名詞、代詞或名詞短語，就會消除這兩句話中的歧義：

> Flying across the Scottish mountains, the <u>helicopter pilot</u> noticed a herd of red deer scatter in panic.
>
> Rowing across the Highland loch, <u>the old poacher</u> saw an osprey catch a trout.

同樣的規則也可適用於以過去分詞開頭的分詞短語。再看下面的句子：

> Educated in Canada, her books have been translated into seven language.
>
> Killed in a road accident the previous month, the President awarded the decoration posthumously to the infantryman.

這兩句話也產生了與前面的例子相似的句子意思上的荒謬：是書受過了教育而不是書的作者，已經去世的總統卻又死而復生。這兩句話可以做如下修改：

> Educated in Canada, <u>the author</u> has had her books translated into seven languages.
>
> Killed in a road accident the previous month, <u>the infantryman</u> was awarded the decoration posthumously by the President.

前面這兩個以過去分詞開頭的句子還可以做更徹底的修改：

> The author was educated in Canada, and her books have been translated into seven languages.
>
> The President awarded the decoration posthumously because the infantryman had been killed in a road accident the previous month.

• Only的使用

使用only這個詞時如果把位置放錯，也會造成歧義。例如

在下面這句話中，把only放在不同的位置就會產生不同的意思：

Sam borrowed a tape recorder from Derek.

先看把only放在句首的情況：

Only Sam borrowed a tape recorder from Derek.

這句話的意思是只有Sam而不是別人借了答錄機；如果把only放在Sam和borrowed兩個詞之間，句子的意思就變成了強調Sam是借了一台答錄機，而不是偷了或損壞了一台答錄機；當把only放在borrowed和a tape recorder之間，句子的意思就是Sam只借了答錄機，並沒有借別的東西；only放在句末Derek之後時，就表明Sam只向Derek借了答錄機，而沒有向其他人借。如果把only放在recorder和from之間就會產生歧義，意思可以是只借了答錄機而沒有借別的東西，也可以是只向Derek借了答錄機，而沒有向別人借。

◆ 一詞多義

許多簡單的、或者表面看起來簡單的英語詞都有兩個或更多的意思，這或許由於該詞是同音異義詞 (homonym)，或是多義詞 (polysemous)。

同音異義詞是指兩個或多個字雖然讀音相同和拼法一樣，但它們的意思和來源卻不相同。例如，last這個詞，在a shoe-maker's last中，它的意思是指人腳的模型，這個詞來自於古英語中表示「腳印」之義的last；帶有「最後的」這個意思的last則來自於古英語中的另一個詞laetest；表示「延續」或「繼續」之義的last源自古英語中的laestan。由此可見，三個不同的詞、三種不同的意思，卻使用了last這同一個簡單的形式。

　　所謂多義詞是指同一個單詞具有多種意思，而所有這些不同的意思卻都來源相同。例如snake這個詞，它來自於古英語的snaca，可以是指爬行動物蛇；可以指人身攻擊 (personal insult)，還可以作動詞，意思是蜿蜒、曲折前行，而且既可以是字面意也可以是比喻意；也可以用在snake-bird, snake-fish, snake-weed等複合詞中；還有像Snakes alive!這樣的感歎語；此外，它還在口語中用來指代技師所用的皮捲尺。

　　下面是一些多義詞的例子：

> air, bar, bat, bay, bit, cast, chap, die, dog, hack, vice, wake, ward, well, will, wind, yarn, yield.

上面例子中的一些詞，以及許多其他詞，它們的名詞和動詞具有相同的形式，如：

> bait, catch, engineer, guard, haunt, ring, trace, vault, veto, vote, water, zero, zigzag.

還有的詞的形容詞與名詞形式同形，如：

> academic, adult, delinquent, equal, evil, good, haemophiliac, introspective, neurotic, stoic, valuable.

像put up這樣看似簡單的表達方式，也有多種不同的用法，如果把除標準英語用法以外的慣用法及口語用法也考慮在內的話就更是如此，如：

> Mr Brown put up the *Vacancies* sign.
>
> He put up an American couple for the night.
>
> A child was put up to a prank by her brothers.
>
> Mr Brown would not put up with rowdy guests.
>
> Annoyed by one guest's behaviour, he shouted, 'Put up or shut up!'

Last year Mr Brown had to put up his prices.

This year he put up a plan to the local tourist association.

讓人感到意外的是，在學生的寫作中很少出現由於多義詞造成的歧義，而在新聞寫作中卻屢見不鮮。例如，在使用over這個詞所具有的與in connection with這個短語相同的意思時就導致了下面這樣歧義句的產生：

Police are holding two men over the fire in Edward Street.

An assistant finance officer has been suspended over the missing files.

與上述情況類似，記者們在報導不同的事件或在不同的情況下使用case這個詞時也造成了如下的歧義句：

Customs officials have been slammed in the smuggled arms case.

A company director is being held in a Moroccan drugs case.

Police are searching for an antiques dealer in a missing manuscript case.

本節開始時所舉的例子中的歧義也屬於同樣的情況，其中的fought with可以理解為fought against（與……進行鬥爭），也可以理解為fought alongside（並肩戰鬥）：

In his farewell speech the retiring MP offered his best wishes to colleagues whom he had <u>fought alongside</u> for over thirty years.

很多單詞的雙重語法功能（同時既是名詞又是動詞，或者既是形容詞又是名詞）使報紙上很多文章的標題產生歧義，其中有些看

起來近乎愚蠢的用法，有可能是編輯們為了達到某種效果而故意使用的雙關語，如：

> Health minister attacks dentists' body
>
> Doctors back nurses' body
>
> Labour left in pay bed fury
>
> Children hit as teachers strike
>
> Fish talks after skippers clash

因為這一部分中所出現的歧義都是由於詞義及詞彙的語法功能造成的，所以要想避免這種歧義的產生，或者有時出於調侃的目的而想故意造成歧義，唯一的辦法就是擴大詞彙量和提高對語法知識的掌握程度。為了達到這兩個目的，同時也為了提高拼寫能力，最簡單的方法就是使用字典。

◆ 公文用語

法律文書須用法律文體撰寫，這是無庸置疑的，但下面兩個例子本該是面對普通讀者的，卻使用了公文用語的語言形式。所節選的這兩個段落的語言風格，通俗地講是屬於官樣文章，可以很明顯地看出，它們都試圖讓所使用的語言顯得更正式，更貼近官方語言。這種語言風格冗長而費解，聽起來讓人感覺空洞乏味。

下面的第一個例子節選自一份政府報告：

> Both parties are agreed that the cause of the dispute is
> the rejection by the employees of the cleansing unit of
> a proposal by the District Council to pay them over-
> time money based on the amounts paid before the
> national strike action by the National and Local

Government Officers Association, which has disrupted
the District Council's normal pay process.

兩個政黨或團體可能是達成了某種協定，但讀者讀過這段話之
後卻很難明白具體達成什麼樣的協定。如果把它用更簡單的形
式寫出來，在不改變原義的情況下，文中所包含的複雜的資訊
是可以表達得讓人更容易理解。通過把這些資訊分隔成更小的
語言表達單位，也就是寫成更簡短的句子，並把它們按照時間
順序來排列，這樣就可以使上面這段話得到簡化。下面這個經
過修改後的段落保留了原文中的大部分用詞：

The national strike action by the National and Local
Government Officers Association (NALGO) disrupted
the District Council's normal pay process. The District
Council offered to pay employees of the cleansing unit
overtime money based on the amounts paid before the
national strike action by NALGO. The employees re-
jected this proposal. Both parties, the District Council
and NALGO, agree that the rejection of the pay proposal is the cause of the dispute.

第二個採用了費解的公文文章風格的例子節選自某公司的
員工手冊：

The minimum holiday entitlement, irrespective of the
employee's length of service, will be twenty days, not
including statutory bank holidays, except when an
employee terminates his employment before retiral age,
or is dismissed from employment following agreed dis-
ciplinary procedures. When employment is terminated
in either of these ways the employee's holiday entitlement for that year will be five days for each three
months or part thereof of employment.

像上一個例子一樣，我們修改這個例子，可以是改變其句子結構，同時還可以改變其用詞。由於公司中的每個人都有獲得最短假期的權利，所以 irrespective of the employee's length of service 這個短語就顯得沒有必要了；又由於法定銀行假期 (statutory bank holidays) 是最短假期之外附加的，所以用帶有否定意義的 not including 這個短語就會引起誤解。下面是把這段話經過修改之後的情況：

> The minimum holiday entitlement for all employees will be twenty days. In addition to the twenty days, all employees will receive the statutory bank holidays. Exceptions to this are, firstly, when an employee terminates his employment before retiral age, or, secondly, when an employee is dismissed from employment following agreed disciplinary procedures. When employment is terminated in either of these ways the employee's holiday entitlement for that year will be five days for each three months, or part of three months, of employment.

◆ 其他類型的意義含混

還有一些其他類型的意義含混現象難以歸類，但又是難以避免的，因為它們都隱藏在英語語言之中。這裏我們只能舉幾個例子。如下面這個例子，句子中的詞彙都是按照正確的語法和句型結構組織在一起，但讀起來仍然讓人感到像是舊時綜藝劇場對白的翻版，給人滑稽可笑的感覺：

> 'I didn't come here to be insulted.'

> 'No? Then where do you normally go to be insulted?'

下面也是一些無意間所造成的歧義句：

Andrew left his friend to pay the bill.

Andrew 和他的朋友，到底是誰付的賬呢？

Jeremy heard his sister from inside the house. 或是
From inside the house Jeremy heard his sister.

是誰在房子裏呢，是 Jeremy，還是他的妹妹，或者是兩個人都在房子裏？

Mr Pendleton was not invited to the party because he was the *Clarion* editor.

這句話的意思到底是因為 Mr Pendleton 是編輯才沒有被邀請參加晚會呢，還是他被邀請參加晚會的原因並非是因為他是編輯呢？

當我們在受到壓力的情況下進行寫作時，像以上這樣歧義性的錯誤在所難免。我們只有對所使用的語言加倍小心謹慎，才能使我們自己成為合格的作者和讀者，也才能更容易地發現那些歧義現象。如果在有些情況下我們自己也很難確定怎樣寫才算正確，那麼我們就要把句子寫得儘量明白無誤。

第六章 | 造 句

簡單句

英語中最容易辨別的語言單位是單詞，前文我們已經討論過如何準確地辨別詞以及怎樣有效地使用詞。但當我們在撰寫論文、報告、小說或者是新聞故事等這樣連貫的語篇時，句子和段落就成了我們所要考慮的重要的語言單位。

一個標準的英語句子是能夠進行語法分析的最大語言單位，也是可以進行文體風格分析的最小語言單位，而語法和文體這兩個概念所各自包含的要素是相互獨立的，而且一種好的文體風格要求以正確的語法為基礎。因此，我們在本章討論句子結構的過程中，同時還要考慮語法和文體方面的因素。在正式討論句子結構之前，我們先來簡單地瞭解一下書寫句子時大腦的思維活動過程，這對我們理解句子結構是有益的。

所有語言的運用，不管是口語還是書面語，都相當於一個編碼過程。大腦左半球的電化學能被轉變成感覺印象，這些印象又經過提煉加工成為思想，也就是大腦中所產生的想法、形象及感情。隨後，所形成的思想又被重新編碼，或被「翻譯」成語言，最後才形成書面標準英語。

如果你在這裏是第一次讀到關於我們對大腦活動的描述，可能會感到這些活動過程有些複雜，但是既然你能夠讀懂我們上面所寫的這段文字，這就説明你的大腦裏同樣在進行著正如

我們所描述的活動過程。過程中的最後一個階段，即把思想轉化成書面標準英語的階段，與其他階段有所不同。此前的階段都屬於大腦先天的、自然的活動，書面標準英語就是大腦內部這些活動的外在表現形式，它的媒介是字母，而字母不是大腦本身所固有的，而是一種人造的因素。

　　與口語或尚未用口語表達出來的人的內心思想相比，書面標準英語要受到更多規則的限制。這些規則包括拼寫、語義、語法、標點及句法，也就是構成句子和段落結構的所有要素。句法這個詞的名詞形式syntax以及形容詞形式syntactic都來自於希臘語，意思是安排、排列。所有上述規則構成了一套或一系列的規範，我們要想使自己大腦中的語言在表達出來之後能夠被讀者所理解，就要首先使「大腦內語言」(inner language) 符合這些規範。任何具有初級思維活動能力，並且能夠形成大腦內語言的人，或者任何能夠讀懂我們這裏所寫的文字的人，應該說都具備學習和使用這些規範的能力。

　　這些規範一經掌握，我們就能正確使用英語這一靈活而又變化無窮的語言，也能讓瞭解這些規範的讀者理解我們所寫的文章，並且與之進行思想上的溝通。擁有五十多萬個詞彙及其各種變換形式的英語語言資源，能夠衍化出無窮的句型結構，而且讓我們把單詞進行具有創意的組合，寫出新穎獨特的句子。

◆ 句子的定義

　　句子是由一組單詞構成，其中一般必須包括一個限定動詞，並且必須是一個完整的表達交流資訊的單位。當然這個定義所講的只是一般情況，在個別情況下，句子中有可能沒有限

定動詞，或表達的資訊並不完整。幾乎在所有長度超過兩段或三段以上的文章中，都能找到三種句型：**簡單句**（simple sentence）、**複合句**（compound sentence）和**複雜句**（complex sentence）。* 此外還有可能出現第四種句型，即複合句與複雜句混合在一起的句子。所有這四種句型我們都將在本章中詳細講述，本節我們主要先討論一下簡單句的情況。

一個標準的英語句子中通常都要有一個限定動詞，也就是帶主語的動詞。動詞的主語，即該動詞所在的句子的主語，是動詞所表示的動作的執行者。看下面的例子：

主語	動詞	賓語
A thunderstorm	ruined	the barbecue.
Andrew and Hannah	entered	the yellow marquee.
We	followed	them.

從這些例子可以看出，動詞的主語一般是名詞thunderstorm、名詞短語Andrew and Hannah或者代詞we。

用於祈使語氣的表示命令的動詞則打破了這一常規，它們前面不帶主語，其暗含的主語是you，如：

[You] Stop! [You] Listen! [You] Calm down.

組合在一起的一組單詞中，如果沒有限定動詞，一般就不能成為標準的英語句子，除情態助動詞之外的所有動詞都有非限定形式。我們在談到動詞的一節中已經瞭解到，動詞的非限定形式有以下幾種：

---

* 一般英語語法書把compound sentence譯做並列句，而complex sentence譯做複合句。

不定式：to ruin, to enter, to follow

以 -ing 結尾的現在分詞：ruining, entering, following

以及過去分詞 (跟在助動詞 have 或 had 之後的動詞形式)：ruined, entered, followed.

不包含限定動詞或非限定動詞的一組詞當然也能向讀者傳達資訊，但這一組詞不僅在語法上不完整，缺少了動詞所表明的動作或狀態，也使得文體形式有所欠缺。正因如此，下面這幾個例子都不是標準的英語句子：

A new warning by the police to city motorists.

A second fatal accident this month on the city by-pass.

A one-year driving ban and a £1,000 fine for the careless driver.

如果在上面的每個句子中都加上一個限定動詞，並且避免使用 There is, There was 或 There will be 這樣單調的形式開頭，所得到的句子就可以既符合語法上的要求，又符合文體上的要求：

Police *have issued* a new warning to city motorists.

For the second time this month a fatal accident *has occurred* on the city by-pass.

A one-year driving ban and a £1,000 fine *have been imposed* on the careless driver.

下面這些例子中雖然有動詞，但這些動詞都是非限定形式，因而也不符合標準英語的要求：

Mr Leonard Vedley *to seek* planning permission for a Cradle Bay marina development.

A marina development *proposed* for Cradle Bay.

Mr Vedley *promising* 150 new jobs at the proposed Cradle Bay Marina.

第一個例子中的動詞to seek是不定式，第二例中的proposed是過去分詞，第三例中的promising是現在分詞。給它們加上助動詞之後，就可以把原來的非限定形式動詞變成限定動詞：

> Mr Leonard Vedley *is to seek* planning permission for a Cradle Bay marina development.

> A marina development *has been proposed* for Cradle Bay.

> Mr Vedley *is promising* 150 new jobs at the proposed Cradle Bay Marina.

添加限定動詞之後，這些例子就符合了語法和文體的要求，變成了標準的英語句子。

◆ 句子的賓語

前面列舉的三個例子說明了句子中主語和動詞之間的關係，同樣也說明了及物動詞與賓語之間的關係。我們再看這三個例子：

主語	動詞	賓語
A thunderstorm	ruined	the barbecue.
Andrew and Hannah	entered	the yellow marquee.
We	followed	them.

及物動詞的賓語用來表明該動詞所表示動作的對象或結果。如同主語一樣，用來作賓語的可以是名詞barbecue、名詞短語the yellow marquee和代詞them。

Barbecue, the yellow marquee, them這幾個賓語都是直接跟在動詞後，稱為**直接賓語**。賓語還可以進一步擴展，為句子

添加更多的資訊，擴展出來的部分稱為**間接賓語**，因為這一部分常常不直接跟在動詞之後。下面這幾個句子都包括主語、動詞、直接賓語和間接賓語幾個成分：

主語	動詞	直接賓語	間接賓語
The police	have issued	a new warning	to city motorists.
A local businessman	will seek	planning permission	for a Cradle Bay development.
Mr Leonard Vedley	is promising	150 new jobs	at the Cradle Bay Marina development.

當句子中的動詞是及物動詞時，其後必須跟直接賓語，這樣才能符合語法和文體上的要求。下面是幾個錯誤句子的例子：

City councillors took

The Chamber of Commerce will donate

Students at Central University need

給上面的每個例子都加上一個賓語，就變成了一個完整的表達資訊的單位：

City councillors took a difficult decision.

The Chamber of Commerce will donate £2,500 to local charities.

Students at Central University need a bigger library.

把動詞、直接賓語和間接賓語放在一起，我們有時把句子的這一部分叫作謂語，指由句子的主語所表達的陳述。因此，一個句子的結構又可簡單地劃分為主語和謂語，如：

主 語	謂 語
The police	have issued a new warning to city motorists.
A local businessman	will seek planning permission for a Cradle Bay development.

到目前為止我們所討論的句子中都只有一個限定動詞，這樣的句子在語法上稱為簡單句。簡單句可以用下面的形式表示：

　　主語 + 動詞 + 賓語 + 間接賓語

或是

　　主語 + 謂語

把句型表示成公式的形式，這樣在結構上和語法上看起來都比較簡單明瞭，但是為了避免單調乏味，多數文章中的段落都要不斷變換句型，有時用簡單句，有時用複合句，有時用複雜句，有時又複合句與複雜句混用。僅就簡單句一種句型來説，通過使用不同的連接方式和不同的擴展形式，也可以變換出多種多樣的句子。

● 連接與擴展

　　使用連詞and、副詞also以及連接短語as well as, along with, in addition to和on top of等，是擴展簡單句的一種方法，它們可以使句子表達更多的資訊，也可以使句子形式富於變化，如：

Vitesse Bordeaux *and* Cracow Solidarnoz met in the cup final.

Charles Auriol, Chairman of Vitesse Bordeaux, is *also* chairman of three other companies in the Bordeaux area.

Women *as well as* men sang in the streets of Bordeaux after Vitesse's cup win.

The victory champagne, *in addition to* the brandy at half-time, affected the Vitesse Bordeaux Chairman.

Their cup-winning bonus, *on top of* other cash awards *and along with* their annual salaries, made Vitesse Bordeaux the highest paid team in France.

此外還有一些其他用於擴展和連接句子的詞和短語，如 besides, and besides 和 over and above。

● 名詞短語

　　另一種擴展句子的簡潔的方法是，把單個的單詞擴展為短語，如把名詞、形容詞、介詞和副詞擴展為短語。所謂短語就是兩個或兩個以上放在一起的一組單詞，而且其中沒有限定動詞。名詞短語就是以名詞為中心詞的短語。

　　上面幾個例子中出現了以下一些名詞短語：

Chairman of Vitesse Bordeaux, chairman of three other companies, the victory champagne, the Vitesse Bordeaux chairman, Their cup-winning bonus, the highest paid team in France.

每個短語的中心詞都是名詞，有三個短語的中心詞是 chairman，其他幾個的中心詞分別是 champagne, bonus 和 team。把名詞擴展成名詞短語之後，句子的意思也更加豐富，句型也富於變化。

● 形容詞短語

　　上面有些名詞短語中包含有形容詞，如：

other companies, *victory* champagne, *cup-winning* bonus

但每一個短語的中心詞都是名詞，其中的形容詞只是用來修飾名詞。在其他有些短語中，短語的中心詞為形容詞，這樣的短語叫做形容詞短語，如：

Matthew Ray, the new Member of Parliament, is *much too ambitious.*

The editor of the *Daily Clarion* is *hard-working, fair-minded and more objective than the former editor.*

Kiln Acres, the site of the old brickworks, is *completely derelict.* The area is *the bleakest in the region.* The cost of reclamation, however, would be *far too high.*

● 介詞短語

　前面談到介詞時 (見第82–86頁)，我們已經瞭解到這一類功能詞的重要作用，還從中知道了介詞是介詞短語中的中心詞，如：

The Australian XV showed effort and artistry *in a high-scoring match.*

Experienced archaeologists will excavate an Iron Age site *near the city centre.*

下面這個句子中則出現了兩個介詞短語 for new orders 和 at home and abroad：

Electronic engineering factories are competing *for new orders at home and abroad.*

我們可以把介詞短語放在句子開頭，從而使簡單句的句型結構有更多的形式，如：

> *On the third Saturday in December* city shoppers went on a Christmas spending spree.

> *After a heated debate* the council accepted the planning proposal for the marina development.

● 副詞短語

　　副詞短語可以使我們能夠對簡單句中動詞的意義進行擴展，如：

> The editor publishes *without fear or favour*.

> *Slowly and painstakingly* the archaeologists excavated the Iron Age site. *Only once before* had they dug near the city centre. Now they worked *with great enthusiasm*.

> *As a matter of urgency*, electronic engineering factories are competing for new orders.

這些例子告訴我們怎樣通過添加短語來擴展簡單句的意思和改變其結構。通過改變短語在句子中的位置，我們不僅能夠改變句型結構，還可以改變文章的節奏和不同的強調重點，這樣就可以把讀者的注意力集中在你所要強調的地方。

● 連接、擴展及文體風格

　　在句子的連接方面，最好使用簡單的連接手段，並儘量避免使用指代性的表達方式，這是一個一般性的指導原則。如果刻意使用那些精心選定的連接方法，就會使文章的風格顯得矯揉造作，同時也就陷入了一個經常被人嘲笑的文風「過於優雅」的誤區，也就是在文章中試圖盡力避免重複同一個關鍵字或短語，而結果卻往往適得其反，因為這種故意變換連接方式的作法有時比重複同一個表達方式來銜接句子的方法更顯做作。

例如，某報記者在撰寫一篇關於他的一個攝影記者同事獲獎的報導中，第一次提到該同事時用的是a prize-winning photographer，這在標準英語中也算得上是一個事實性的陳述；第二次提到時，就改用了the ace lensman這一新聞報導中經常使用卻毫無新意的表達方式；隨後又用了the super snapper，雖然新穎別致讓人感到親切，卻又不符合標準英語的規範；最後則使用了the prince of the pics，選擇這個短語的目的則完全是為了不與前面的指代方式重複，表達了與前幾個指代方法毫無兩樣的意義。如果在指代人物時沒有變換這麼多的花樣，而只是簡單地重複使用photographer，再加上該攝影記者的姓名，以及人稱代詞he，這樣寫出的這則新聞報導會讓人覺得讀起來更加順暢。從這個例子我們就可以看出，所謂「過於優雅」的文風確實具有諷刺意味，因為刻意變換指代方式的作法其實更顯笨拙和生硬。

使用描述性的連接和句子擴展給文體風格方面帶來的問題更多。比如，如果完全依賴擴展短語來擴展簡單句，就會使句子中唯一的一個動詞難以負荷太多的資訊，即使這樣的句子可能從語法方面來講是正確的，但卻不符合文體的要求，因為它會轉移讀者的注意力，使讀者更多地考慮的是文章的寫法而不是文章所要表達的意思。看下面的例子：

The fair-minded, hard-working city councillors, the elected representatives of the people, finally took a difficult decision on the marina development after a long and sometimes heated debate.

可以看出，句中唯一的一個動詞took所承載的大量資訊已經使它幾近難以承受了。如果文章中使用過多的類似上例的描述性

語言，就會使文章顯得詞藻過於華麗，語言過於放縱，即使不
諳寫作技巧的讀者也會感到其文風矯飾而做作，並因此而懷疑
作者只是在玩弄詞藻。

　　但是，如果文章中不用或少用帶有描述性擴展成分的簡單
句，就會產生另外一種矛盾。試想，如果文章中連續兩三個段
落完全使用簡單句的話，肯定會使讀者感到厭煩。一成不變地
使用主語＋動詞＋賓語這樣單調的句型，不僅造成句子結構
的重複，還會使文章的節奏顯得重複拖遝，斷斷續續。要解決
這一矛盾，可以採取短句和長句配合使用的方法，即除了使用
簡單句外，還要使用一些有兩個或更多限定動詞的句子，也就
是包括多個從句的句子。

複合句

　　在講到連詞時（見第82–87頁），我們已經知道連詞可以用來
引導分句。所謂分句就是一個比短語大而比句子小的語言單
位，並且其中包含一個限定動詞。下面這個例子中使用了連詞
either ... or和兩個限定動詞stay和drive：

> *Either* you stay overnight at Parsemer/ *or* you drive on
> to the city of Grantown.

第二個例子中使用的連詞是but，兩個從句中使用的限定動詞都
是is：

> Aldridge Tower at Upper Sallow is derelict/ *but*
> Thornham Hall in Lower Sallow is still inhabited.

同樣，最常用的連詞and可以在一個句子中用來連接兩個分
句，如：

Rock bands attract one kind of audience/*and* folk groups attract another.

兩個以上的連詞可以用來連接三個以上的分句，但當句子中使用兩個以上連詞時就會使句子結構顯得重複、囉嗦，如：

Some members of the council opposed the marina scheme/*but* a majority supported it/*and* the planning application was approved.

由連詞連接在一起的兩個或多個分句構成的句子叫做複合句，所謂複合 (compound) 在這裏其實就是把兩個或多個要素放在一起的意思。複合句中的每個分句都具有相同的語法功能，稱為一個主句。如果把句中的連詞去掉，每個主句都可以從原來的複合句中分離出來而單獨成句。把這一規則套用到上面這個句子中，我們會發現，句子中幾乎所有的主句都可成為一個完整的句子，只有其中的 a majority supported it 有些例外，但如果把代詞 it 替換為名詞短語 the marina scheme，也可變為標準的英語句子：

A majority supported the marina scheme.

由於連詞的作用就在於連接兩個語言單位 (這裏是連接兩個主句)，如果打斷這種連接，使兩個主句變成兩個句子，並且仍然保留連詞的話，有時就會給讀者造成困惑。雖然語法上也容許句子以連詞開頭，但如果重複使用這種句子結構，就會使文章的語言風格顯得極不自然，並造成一種斷斷續續的語言節奏。看下面的例子：

A team from the Young Farmers Club entered the annual raft race. And came second. The young farmers could have won. But their combined weight almost sank their raft. They raised over £ 1,000 for charity.

> And met their target. But they hope to do better next
> year.

上面這段話中的所有句子都使用了簡單的語法結構，但文章的風格卻顯得矯揉造作。記者們有時使用這種節奏緊迫的語言風格是為了讓人對他們所講述的主題更感興趣，但是假如讀者所注意到的只是他們的語言風格而不是所講述的內容本身，效果就會適得其反。如果我們把上面這段話中語法結構簡單的句子變成複合句，就會取得更加明顯的效果：

> A team from the Young Farmers Club entered the
> annual raft race and came second. The young farmers
> could have won but their combined weight almost sank
> their raft. They raised over £ 1,000 for charity and
> met their target, but they hope to do better next year.

　　經過修改後的這段話中包括三個複合句，比修改前包含七個簡單句時讀起來要流暢得多。即使如此，經修改後的這段話還是重複使用了同樣的句子結構，仍顯得有些單調。可見，僅靠簡單句和複合句還不足以使讀者在閱讀較長的文章時始終保持興味盎然，只有再學會運用第三種句型，即複雜句，我們才能在更多的句型選擇中使所寫的文章避免單調乏味。

複雜句

　　一個複雜句 (Complex Sentence) 中一般包括一個主句和一個或多個從句。Complex這個形容詞在這裏的意思是「由兩個或多個相關部分構成的」。正如我們前文所講到的那樣，主句可以從整個句子中分離出來，能夠形成一個完整的資訊單位，並且可以獨立存在，而從句一般不能形成完整的資訊單位或完整的

句子，它的部分意思的表達需要依賴於主句。從這種意義上說，從句是從屬於主句的。如：

> Positron's drummer is Trick Fraser, who begin his career in the National Youth Orchestra.

其中的主句是Positron's drummer is Trick Fraser。我們用上面講到過的主句的驗證方法來對它檢驗一下：Positron's drummer is Trick Fraser這一部分在語法和語義上都是完整的，並且能夠獨立成句，所以我們說它是一個主句是正確的。再看句子的剩餘部分：

> who began his career in the National Youth Orchestra

這一部分當中，有限定動詞began，其主語為代詞who，在語法上完全符合一個完整句子的要求，但我們也可以明顯地看出，句子的這一部分表達的意思不完全，不能滿足文體要求，也不能構成一個完整的資訊單位，而且它的意思需要依賴於主句才能表達清楚，因此是複雜句的一個從句。

◆ 修飾性從句和與人有關的名詞

上面例子中的who began his career in the National Youth Orchestra這部分是一個用來修飾主句中專有名詞的典型從句，在這句話中的專有名詞是Trick Fraser。當從句用來修飾主句中的一個指人名詞時，該從句通常以關係代詞who, whom或whose開頭，它所修飾的並且與之相關的名詞稱為**先行詞**，也就是指在關係代詞之前的詞。

我們要記住這樣幾條規則：who要與he, she, they相配合，whom要與him, her, them相配合，whose則要與his, hers, theirs

相配合。下面這樣一些簡單的公式可以幫助我們牢固地記住這些規則：

who = he, she, they

whom = him, her, them

whose = his, hers, theirs

在語法上，為了使定語從句得到簡化，標準英語中常把關係代詞whom省略掉。如：

Trick Fraser is a musician *whom I admire.*

這句話中的從句whom I admire相當於I admire him，指的是主句中的先行詞musician。在類似的句子中，whom可以省略掉，那麼上面這句話就可以寫成：

Trick Fraser is a musician *I admire.*

上述句子中的I admire仍然是一個定語從句，用來修飾先行詞musician。

另外，標準英語中有時還要求在關係代詞前加上一個介詞，即如to whom, for whom, from whom, with whom, about whom等。如：

The musician *from whom I learned most* is Positron's keyboards player, Ward Nettles.

Positron's drummer, *about whom the critics are divided*, began his career in the National Youth Orchestra.

從句from whom I learned most差不多與I learned most from him相當，修飾的是主句中的先行詞musician；從句about whom the critics are divided則與the critics are divided about him大致相當，修飾的是主句中的名詞drummer。

下面是一個以關係代詞whose開頭的定語從句的例子：

> Trick Fraser, *whose parents are amateur musicians*, is leaving the group next month.

這句話中的從句whose parents are amateur musicians就相當於 his parents are amateur musicians，它修飾的是作先行詞的專有 名詞Trick Fraser。

用來修飾指人名詞的定語從句一定要以關係代詞who, whom或whose來引導，而關係代詞that和which一般用來引導 修飾主句中代指事物名詞的從句。例如，標準英語中不容許出 現下述這樣的句子：

> Several musicians that were once members of the National Youth Orchestra are now playing professionally.

◆ 包含性定語從句和非包含性定語從句

定語從句的意義往往由如何對該從句進行標點來決定。 如：

> The fast bowler *who took six wickets* was named the man of the match.

這句話的意思是指，主句中的單數名詞bowler (板球手) 是許多 板球手之一。用下面的方式表達出來就更明確：

> The fast bowler *who took six wickets* [as distinct from the other fast bowlers] was named the man of the match.

如果我們把這句話中的定語從句用逗號隔開，即：

> The fast bowler, *who took six wickets*, was named the man of the match.

表示這句話中所涉及的只有一個板球手。正是所使用的逗號把

板球手限定為只有一個，這就使得這個詞既在語法上具有單數形式，又在意義上排除了其他可能性，從而也就進一步強調了該名詞的獨有特性。

下面是一個相似的例子：

The busker *who played the clarinet* entertained the Saturday shoppers.

這句話中沒有逗號，就表明除了演奏黑管的街頭藝人之外，可能還有一些其他沒有演奏黑管的或沒有給星期六的購物者帶來娛樂的街頭藝人。現在我們用逗號把上面這句話中的定語從句隔開：

The busker, *who played the clarinet*, entertained the Saturday shoppers.

顯然，這句話裏提到的就只有一個街頭藝人，還是隔開定語從句的逗號把所修飾的名詞限定為一人，即只有獨一無二的一個街頭藝人演奏。

當主句中的被修飾名詞為單數時，應遵循以下規則：

如果who所引導的從句由逗號隔開，則句子所涉及的只有該名詞所指代的一個人，不包括其他人；

如果who所引導的從句沒有被逗號隔開，則從句對該名詞沒有限定作用，它所指代的人並不把其他人排除在外，而是指其他多個人中之一。

如果主句中的被修飾名詞是複數，情況就大不一樣了。在下面的例子中，從句仍然以紅色斜體字來表示：

Daily Clarion journalists *who work unsocial hours* get overtime payments.

現在我們把這句話變成下面的結構：

> Overtime payments are given to *Daily Clarion* journalists *who work unsocial hours.*

顯然，這裏的定語從句who work unsocial hours指的是複數名詞journalists，但我們還是不清楚它到底是指*Clarion*這家報紙的所有記者還是指它的部分記者。如果把這句話改寫成下面的形式，就可避免句子意義含糊：

> *Daily Clarion* journalists, *who work unsocial hours,* get overtime payments. 或者：

> Overtime payments are given to *Daily Clarion* journalists, *who work unsocial hours.*

從句與主句用逗號隔開，就表示從句所指的是*Clarion*這家報紙的所有記者。被逗號隔開的從句不僅修飾先行詞journalists，而且還起到其同位語的作用，即指所有記者。逗號的使用使得先行詞所代表的所有人都被包括在內。如果不使用逗號，who所引導的定語從句所指代的就只有部分記者，如：

> *Daily Clarion* journalists *who work unsocial hours* get overtime payments.

這句話的意思就是那些沒有在規定工作時間以外工作的記者就得不到加班費，用下面的方式可以更明白地表明這樣的意思：

> *Daily Clarion* journalists *who work unsocial hours* [as distinct from other journalists who do not] get overtime payments.

當主句中被修飾的名詞為複數時，應遵循的規則是：

> 如果由who所引導的定語從句被逗號分隔開，被修飾的名詞就包括所有該名詞所指代的每一個人；

如果由who所引導的定語從句沒有被逗號分隔開，就不一定包括被修飾名詞所指代的每一個人，該定語從句也就只用來指代其中的一部分人。

對於這種結構相同，但標點的不同會引起意義不同的從句，過去的語法術語把它們稱為限制性定語從句和非限制性定語從句，但是我們認為這兩個術語會引起意義上的模糊，所以這裏就用包含性定語從句和非包含性定語從句來區分。

◆ 修飾性(定語)從句與指物名詞

當定語從句所修飾的不是指人的名詞，而是指動物或其他事物的名詞時，一般以關係代詞that或which來引導。對that和which的用法加以區分非常重要，尤其在需要對包含性定語從句和非包含性定語從句加以區別時，區分這兩個詞的作用就尤為關鍵。例如：

> The drugs hot line *that was set up in the Cradle Bay district last year* is appealing for funds.

句中的從句that was set up in the Cradle Bay district last year表明，在其他地方可能還有其他的drugs hot lines (禁毒熱線)。如果在這句話中使用關係代詞which，並且用逗號把從句與主句分隔開，意思就不太一樣了：

> The drugs hot line, *which was set up in the Cradle Bay district last year*, is appealing for funds.

這句話中所涉及的drugs hot line就只有一個了。

當主句中被修飾的名詞為複數時，用that和which引導定語從句的情況與被修飾名詞為單數時所表示的意思相同。如：

Cradle Bay hotels *that depend on the tourist trade* are doing little business this year.

這句話的含義是在Cradle Bay這個地方還有不依賴旅遊業維持生計的旅館。如果我們把that替換為which，再用逗號把從句與主句隔開，句子的意思就會有所改變：

Cradle Bay hotels, *which depend on the tourist trade*, are doing little business this year.

這樣就表明所有的旅館都以旅遊業維生。下面的例子也與此類似：

Clubs and societies *that meet in Wellington Hall* will pay an increased hire charge next year.

這句話的含義是有些俱樂部和社團不在Wellington Hall集會，而如果把句子變成這樣：

Clubs and societies, *which meet in Wellington Hall*, will pay an increased hire charge next year.

意思就是所有的俱樂部和社團都在Wellington Hall集會，並將提高租借費用。

如果定語從句所修飾的是主句中表示地點的名詞，則從句一般以where, in which或at which來引導。如：

There is the old boat yard *where/in which* the first Cradle Bay lifeboat was built.

如果定語從句所修飾的是主句中表示日期或時間的名詞，則從句一般以when或at which來引導。如：

Sunday morning is the time *when/at which* the city centre is quietest.

最後，如果定語從句所修飾的是主句中表示事件或某種情況的

名詞，從句的引導詞一般為 where, when, at which 或 in which。
如：

> Dr Somerford went to the graduation ceremony *where/ at which/in which her niece was awarded a BA degree.*

在複雜句中使用定語從句，可以為我們提供多種句型選擇。
如：

> Geoff Rimmer won the junior motor cycle scramble last year. He is competing again this year.

這是一個簡單句，可以變成複合句：

> Geoff Rimmer won the junior motor cycle scramble last year and he is competing again this year.

還可以變成複雜句：

> Geoff Rimmer, who won the junior motor cycle scramble last year, is competing again this year.

以下是簡單句：

> Geoff's machine was built by his father. Geoff is only seventeen years old.

這兩個簡單句的順序可以顛倒，並用連詞連接成一個複合句：

> Geoff is only seventeen years old, and his machine was built by his father.

還可以把這兩個簡單句變成一個更加簡潔、緊湊而流暢的複雜句：

> Geoff, whose machine was built by his father, is only seventeen years old.

再看一個簡單句例子：

Cradle Bay was once a busy fishing port. Cradle Bay is now the site of the new marina.

同樣，這兩個簡單句可以變成一個複合句：

Cradle Bay was once a busy fishing port but is now the site of the new marina.

也可以變成兩種不同的複雜句，第一種是這樣的：

Cradle Bay, which was once a busy fishing port, is now the site of the new marina.

這句話中的主句是 Cradle Bay is now the site of the new marina，從句是 which was once a busy fishing port。第二種變法：

Cradle Bay, which is now the site of the new marina, was once a busy fishing port.

這樣，句子中的主句就變成了 Cradle Bay was once a busy fishing port，從句是 which is now the site of the new marina。

應該注意，有些簡單句並不能連接成意思順暢的複合句。例如下面兩個簡單句：

Geoff Rimmer's father, Jack, owns a lobster boat. The boat was built twenty years ago.

如果把它們連接成複合句，從結構上和文體就都顯得牽強：

Geoff Rimmer's father, Jack, owns a lobster boat, and it was built twenty years ago.

但如果把這兩個簡單句變成一個複雜句就好得多：

Geoff Rimmer's father, Jack, owns a lobster boat *that was built twenty years ago.*

這句話裏的主句是 Geoff Rimmer's father, Jack, owns a lobster boat，從句是 that was built twenty years ago。還可以變成下面

這樣的複雜句，雖然不如上面這句話讀起來順暢，但也是符合
規則要求的：

> The lobster boat *that Geoff Rimmer's father, Jack, owns*
> was built twenty years ago.

最後再看一個例子，通過它我們可以瞭解到怎樣把兩個簡
單句以不同的方式結合到一起，以使句子結構和節奏都富於變
化。這兩個簡單句是：

> Jack Rimmer has lived in Cradle Bay for sixty years.
> Cradle Bay was once a busy fishing port.

我們可以把這兩個句子變成幾種複雜句，每一種的基本意思不
變，但所產生的句子節奏和所強調的重點有所不同。變成複雜
句後的從句以紅色斜體字來表示：

> Jack Rimmer has lived for sixty years in Cradle Bay,
> *which was once a busy fishing port*.

> Jack Rimmer has lived in Cradle Bay, *which was once
> a busy fishing port*, for sixty years.

> For sixty years Jack Rimmer has lived in Cradle Bay,
> *which was once a busy fishing port*.

> Cradle Bay, *where Jack Rimmer has lived for sixty
> years*, was once a busy fishing port.

另外，還可以表達成一個主句帶兩個從句的句子：

> Cradle Bay, *which was once a busy fishing port*, is
> *where Jack Rimmer has lived for sixty years*.

我們看到，同樣的意思用五種句子的變換形式表達了出來，再
加上前面舉過的例子，我們已經知道怎樣運用定語從句和複雜
句來改變句子的長度、結構、強調重點以及文章的節奏。這些

例子還説明，使用複雜句可以讓我們更緊湊、更流暢和更簡潔地組織和表達資訊，從而更有效地使我們所要表達的思想深入到讀者心中。

在這一部分所舉的例子中，所有的從句都是以關係代詞 who, whom, whose, which 和 that 來引導，修飾主句當中的名詞，因此我們可以把這類從句叫作形容詞性從句。

◆ 嵌入式從句

在上面一部分所舉的一些例子中，由 **who** 所引導的從句是插入或嵌入主句中的。如：

> *Daily Clarion* journalists *who work unsocial hours* get overtime payments.

這句話的主句是 *Daily Clarion* journalists get overtime payments，從句就插入在主句裏。

這種把從句插入主句的方法有兩個用途，一是可以使句子以非常簡潔的方式容納更多的資訊，二是便於我們改換句型。但是，採用多重嵌入的句式就會產生不良後果。如果主句中包含一個嵌入的從句，從句中再包含另外一個嵌入的從句，這樣的嵌入就會產生反效果。如：

> Positron's drummer, about whom the critics — most of whom are not professional musicians and whose knowledge of music is sometimes limited — are divided, began his career in the National Youth Orchestra.

主句 Positron's drummer began his career in the National Youth Orchestra 中插入了嵌入的從句 about whom the critics are divided，在這個從句中再次插入了從句 most of whom are not

professional musicians和whose knowledge of music is sometimes
limited。

　　這樣一個句子中包含了過多的資訊，而且顯得零亂繁雜，
主句中的主語Positron's drummer與它的謂語began his career in
the National Youth Orchestra分隔得太遠，使得主句的意思讓
人難以理解。這樣，就使文章的風格忸怩晦澀，意義表達不明
確，而且還會使讀者感到厭煩。

◆ 從句作動詞的賓語

　　在句子結構與風格一部分中，我們已經知道簡單句裏的動
詞後往往要跟一個名詞或代詞作動詞的賓語，這樣的簡單句句
型為主語 + 動詞 + 賓語。如果把這一句型中的賓語用一個從
句來代替作主句動詞的賓語，簡單句就擴展為一個複合句。因
為這類從句的作用相當於一個名詞，我們就把這種從句叫作名
詞性從句。

　　這類從句往往用關係代詞**that**或**what**來引導，如：

> Jean-Paul Chambery, manager of Vitesse Bordeaux,
> thought *that his goalkeeper was excellent.*

這句話中，從句that his goalkeeper was excellent是主句中動詞
thought的賓語，說明所想的內容。再如：

> In the second half, Chambery saw *that Cracow*
> *Solidarnoz had lost their rhythm.*

同樣，從句that Cracow Solidarnoz had lost their rhythm是主句
中動詞saw的賓語。

　　這兩個句子中的從句都是以that開頭。同樣的句子結構中
的從句還可以用what來開頭，如：

The Bordeaux team knew *what they had to do to win.*

從句what they had to do to win是主句中動詞knew的賓語，説明該運動隊所「知道」的事情。再如：

Solidarnoz's manager did not understand *what had gone wrong with his plan.*

從以下部分的內容中，我們可以瞭解到第三種從句，它給我們提供了更多的句型選擇。

◆ 狀語從句

這裏所講的更多的句型選擇來自於一種可以修飾主句中動詞或可以改變該動詞意義的從句。正由於這種從句可以像副詞一樣修飾動詞，我們就把這類從句叫做**狀語從句**（Adverbial Clauses）。在這一部分中，我們來討論一下幾種主要狀語從句的結構和功能。

• 表示轉折意義的狀語從句

我們可以用很多種句子結構方式使從句的意思與主句中動詞所表明的動用作相反或相對。這種表示轉折意義的從句常以下列表達方式開頭：

although, despite, in spite of; if, even if; provided that, so long as, as long as; in case, lest, unless; however, no matter, whether, whatever.

這些表達方式不僅為我們提供了多種構成轉折從句的方法，還可以使我們準確地表達出每句話所説明的不同程度的相反或相對意義，滿足不同情況、不同讓步條件的要求。但很多作者往往忽視這些表達方式的用法，一味地使用however來表示意思的轉折，而且有時還會造成錯誤。

我們前面已經講到過（見第260–62頁），表示相反或相對的最簡單的方法是用連詞but連接兩個主句。但有些教師和新聞記者反對過多使用以but引導的分句，甚至毫無理由地反對使用以but開頭的句子，代之以however引導的分句或結構，因此時常造成用法的混亂。

下面是一個可以使用however從句的例子：

> The reporters could not satisfy the *Clarion* editor *however hard they worked.*

從句however hard they worked中的however大致相當於no matter how, in whatever manner或by whatever means，意思是「無論如何、不管怎樣」。如果把主句和從句的順序顛倒一下，所得到的句子同樣成立，並且句子的意思不變，however的用法也不變：

> *However hard they worked,* the reporters could not satisfy the *Clarion* editor.

再看下面這兩個主句與從句順序顛倒的例子：

> Beppi's Bistro could not attract new customers *however hard the manager tried.*

> *However hard the manager tried,* Beppi's Bistro could not attract new customers.

在這兩個句子中，引導從句的however的意思都相當於no matter how。

下面是一些however這個詞被混亂使用的典型例子：

> *However,* the editor was a fine journalist.

> *However,* the *Clarion* editor sometimes muttered a compliment.

However, Beppi's bistro still made a small profit.

However, Beppi still had his regular customers.

　　這幾句話中however的用法與前面例子中的用法不同，它在這裏的意思就相當於nevertheless, even so, despite this或者but。其實它們都可以用but來代替。這幾個句子中都只有一個動詞和一個分句，however只是一個單獨的副詞，而不是一個分句。However有時並不用來表示意思的轉折，而是像Basically, Hopefully或Frankly這樣的詞一樣，放在句首來加強語氣，沒有太多的實際意義。如果在however之後插入一個逗號，這種只有一個分句的句子結構還是清楚的，但逗號往往被錯誤地省略掉，應引起我們的注意。

　　「這樣做有必要嗎？」學生們時常會就標準英語的方方面面的規則提出這種疑問。應該指出，這裏我們強調逗號的用法是有必要的，原因有二：其一，當逗號被錯誤地省略掉時，前文所講到的however的兩種用法就會混淆。我們來比較一下下面這兩個句子：

However you feel, sentence structure can clarify the meaning of what you write.

However, you feel sentence structure can clarify the meaning of what you write.

雖然這兩句話中詞彙的排列順序相同，但however的用法和意義是不一樣的。第一句中的從句However you feel的意思是「不管你怎麼想」或「無論你感覺如何」；第二句中的however是一個副詞，意思是「然而」、「不過」或「即使如此」。但是在第二句中，如果對however的用法要求不十分嚴格，並且這個句子前面

再有一個主句，就可以把它看成是與前面這個分句之間的一個
狀語連詞，作用相當於but。

　　當像however這樣的詞用來引導從句和只作為一個單詞的
這兩種用法被混同起來時，其中一種用法用會逐漸代替另外一
種用法，而另外一種用法也就會因此而慢慢從語言中消失。這
種情況對於作者來說還有另一個不利之處，就是了解這兩種用
法區別的讀者不得不打斷閱讀的連貫性，去猜測作者所要表達
的意思；即使短暫的停頓，都會把讀者的注意力從理解文章的
意思上，分散到考慮作者的寫作手法上。如果在however用作單
獨的詞時後面不加逗號，讀者的停頓時間就會更長，甚至會引
起對閱讀的反感。

　　要注意同一表達方式的不同用法區別的第二個原因在於，
如果混淆了這種區別，就會失去語言用法上的多樣性，以及隨
之而來的文章節奏和結構上的多樣性，以這裏提到的however的
用法為例，我們所不斷接觸到的就只有它作為從句引導詞的用
法，而失去了它的另一個用法。如果作者不注意這種區別，即
使不熟悉寫作技巧的讀者也會感到作者的寫作能力有限。通過
使用不同的表達方式作為句子的開頭，就可以避免這種同一用
法的重複，也可以使只有一個分句的句子結構變得更有活力。
如：

> The reporters, however, respected the editor.
>
> The *Clarion* editor, however, sometimes muttered a
> compliment.

　　這裏所要強調的是，我們所能夠形成的精微而複雜的思想
以及向讀者表達這些思想的能力，不能因語言的使用不當而受
到阻礙。

• 其他表示轉折意義的狀語從句

通過上文，我們很明顯地看出，以however開頭的從句表達的是轉折的意義。此外，還有一些表達方式可以表達同樣的意義，如：

> even if, no matter, whether, whatever, despite, in spite of

看下面的例子：

> *Even if local residents object*, the marina development will go ahead.

如果把even if引導的從句放到主句之後，句子的意思保持不變：

> The marina development will go ahead *even if local resident object*.

用下面這些表達方式引導的從句，不管是放在主句之前還是主句之後，句子的意思同樣保持不變：

> no matter, whether, whatever, despite, in spite of

如：

> No matter what local residents say, ...
>
> Whether local residents object or not, ...
>
> Whatever local residents say, ...

Despite和in spite of兩個表達方式用在副詞短語中（不帶限定動詞）比用在狀語從句中更能使句子顯得簡潔明快，如：

> *Despite local objections*（副詞短語）, the marina development will go ahead.
>
> *In spite of local objections*（副詞短語）, ...

看下面一些副詞或副詞短語：

> provided, provided that, so long as, as long as, in case, lest, unless

這些表達方式的意思是，必須首先滿足某些條件或做出某些讓步，主句中動詞所表明的動作才能發生。如：

> *Provided enough good climbers volunteer*, a fells rescue unit will be formed.

> A fells rescue unit will be formed *as long as enough good climbers volunteer*.

以及：

> Miriam Levy will not feel confident in the piano solo *unless she gets more rehearsal time*.

> The National Youth Orchestra rehearsed Elgar's overture 'In the South' *in case they needed an encore*.

Provided that 和 lest 這兩種用法在標準英語中已經顯得有些古舊，我們現在常常代之以 provided 和 in case。

此外我們還可以選擇 although 和 if 作為這類從句的開頭，如：

> Miriam Levy felt nervous *although she had rehearsed the solo thoroughly*.

> *If Miriam felt nervous* it was not apparent in her polished performance.

我們往往過多地使用 if 來引導這類從句，為避免這種情況，我們可以適當地多選用上面列出的一些其他表達方式。

最後，如果把兩個或更多的人或事物進行直接比較，可以使用以 as, as if 或 than 引導的從句。如：

The atmosphere in Beppi's is *as lively as it was.*

Beppi Serafini spoke about his Bistro *as if it were a gourmet restaurant.*

Beppi's prices are much higher *than they were last year.*

As 和 than 的用法可以靈活變換，如 as much as, more than, less than。

我們如果用上面的某些表達方式來連接兩個簡單句，就可以得到多種不同結構的句子，而且可以使它們的基本意思保持不變。看下面兩個簡單句：

Franky Dexter has been selected for the 800 metres.
He missed most of last season because of injury.

下面是這兩個簡單句的不同連接方式，其中的第二句和第四句分別與第一句和第三句的主句和從句的順序顛倒：

Franky Dexter has been selected for the 800 metres *despite/in spite of missing most of last season because of injury.*

Despite/in spite of missing most of last season because of injury, Franky Dexter has been selected for the 800 metres.

Franky Dexter has been selected for the 800 metres *although he missed most of last season because of injury.*

Although he missed most of last season because of injury, Franky Dexter has been selected for the 800 metres.

再看下面兩個簡單句：

Franky could win the race. He will have to train hard.

我們可以把這兩句話合併為一個複合句：

Franky could win the race but he will have to train hard.

如果變成複雜句，就可以得到多種句式，當然也包括主句與從句順序互換的情況：

Franky could win the race *if he trains hard.*

If he train hard, Franky could win the race.

Franky could win the race *provided he trains hard.*

Provided he trains hard, Franky could win the race.

如果把從句嵌入主句中，我們還可以得到另外兩種句式：

Franky, *provided he trains hard,* could win the race.

Franky could, *if he trains hard,* win the race.

再看一個複合句子：

The training might prove rigorous but Franky is determined to win.

這個複合句可以變成下面幾種複雜句的形式：

Even if the training proves rigorous, Franky is determined to win.

Franky is determined to win *even if the training proves rigorous.*

No matter how rigorous the training proves, Franky is determined to win.

Franky is determined to win *no matter how rigorous the training proves.*

However rigorous the training proves, Franky is determined to win.

Franky is determined to win *however rigorous the training proves.*

• 強勢轉折結構

有些具有轉折意義的表達方式，如表示直接必然結果的 therefore，還有 even so 和 otherwise，稍顯古舊的 neverthe-less，以及 however 等，都有強調的意味，因此在標點和結構上比其他表示轉折關係的從句要求更嚴格。與這些加強轉折意義詞彙相似的還有一些表示遞進或確認意思的強調表達方式，如 indeed 和略顯過時的 furthermore。

標準英語中不容許出現下面這樣結構的句子：

The drugs hot line ran out of funds, *the service there-fore had to be abandoned.*

Only five experienced climbers volunteered, *even so a fells rescue unit was formed.*

也不能用下面結構的句子來表示意思的遞進：

Mike Carter is the youngest player in the Australian XV; *indeed, he is the youngest first-class player in Australia.*

以上三個句子都缺乏句子結構上所要求的傳達資訊所必須具備的完整性和統一性。每個句子中實際上都包括兩層意思，我們可以有兩種方法來組織這些句子。第一種方法是用分號把這些句子分隔為兩部分陳述：

The drugs hot line ran out of funds; *the service, therefore, had to be abandoned.*

Only five experienced climbers volunteered; *even so, a fells rescue unit was formed.*

Mike Carter is the youngest player in the Australian XV; *indeed, he is the youngest first-class player in Australia.*

在這三個句子中，分號使原來的句子變成了包含兩個主句的複合句。在therefore, even so和indeed幾個詞之前和之後出現的逗號給句子造成了一個停頓，因而對其所在的分句起到了強調作用。

第二種方法就是把原來不當的句子明明白白地寫成兩句話：

> The drugs hot line ran out of funds. The service, therefore, had to be abandoned.

> Only five experienced climbers volunteered. Even so, a fells rescue unit was formed.

> Mike Carter is the youngest player in the Australian XV. Indeed, he is the youngest first-class player in Australia.

同樣，這裏放在therefore, even so和indeed之前和之後的逗號也是對其所在分句起到強調作用。

此外還有第三種方法，就是把句子中的therefore和even so省略掉，變成一個複雜句，其中包括一個主句和一個原因狀語從句(見下文)或讓步狀語從句。不過這樣變化的結果與原來句子的意思不太相同，因為這樣就缺少了由therefore和even so所產生的強調作用。下面是用這種方法變化後的句子：

> *Because the drugs hot line ran out of funds*, the service had to be abandoned.

> A fells rescue unit was formed *although only five experienced climbers volunteered.*

• 表示對比、方式和方法的從句

如果兩個事物的對照只是出於比較而不是出於對立，或者

我們想要表達出做某事的方式或方法，有多種句式可供選擇。

一種就是利用現成的形容詞或副詞的比較級形式。例如 (下面句子中用 / 表示不同分句的分隔) ：

> Hill farmers in the Northwest claim / that costs are *much higher* / *than they were last year* / but that incomes are *lower* / *than they have been for many years.*

這句話中，形容詞比較級 higher 修飾的是名詞 costs，比較從句 than they were last year 修飾的是動詞 are。同樣，形容詞比較級 lower 修飾的是名詞 incomes，而比較從句 than they have been for many years 則修飾的是第二個 are。

可以用來構成比較句式的還有副詞短語 as ... as, more ... than 和 less ... than，如在下面的句子中，as hard as 和 less hopefully than 就是副詞短語：

> Most farmers are working as *hard* / as they can / but they face the future *less hopefully* / than they have ever done.

副詞 hard 修飾動詞 are working，比較狀語從句裏 as they can；副詞的比較級 less hopefully 修飾動詞 face，比較狀語從句是 than they have ever done。

同樣是 as ... as 這個短語，還可以用來引導方式狀語從句，修飾主句中的動詞，表明某事是怎樣做的，如：

> Dr Craig broke the news about the drugs hot line *as gently as he could.*

下面是由 as ... as 引導的方式狀語從句的兩種變換形式的例子：

Just as he had feared, the venture collapsed through lack of funds.

Dr Craig felt *as if he were personally responsible for the failure*.

當然，表示方式方法時還可以用短語，如：

Dr Craig broke the news *as gently as possible*.

He felt *personally responsible* for the failure.

• 表示原因和目的的狀語從句

要想解釋主句中所表達動作的原因或目的，一般的方法是使用以 because, since 或 as 開頭的狀語從句，這三個詞通常是可以互相替換的。這樣構成的複雜句，就像多數複雜句一樣，主句和從句的順序可以互相顛倒，如：

Central University Students' Association's Green Week was poorly attended *because / since / as the event was not publicized*.

Because/since/as the event was not publicized, Central University Students' Association's Green Week was poorly attended.

Because Central University Students' Association's Green Week was not publicized, the event was poorly attended.

現在人們越來越少地使用以 for 開頭的原因狀語從句，這大概是由於人們多傾向於使用上面提到的三個表達方式來表示原因，或者是由於 for 的這種用法正慢慢被它的介詞用法所取代。但是像下面這樣的用法也是符合規範的：

At the end of the debate on capital punishment MPs

did not vote along party lines, *for they saw the issue as one of personal conscience, not party dogma.*

　　另外一個更加直接的表示原因的方法就是用 reason 這個詞，如：

The reason Matthew Ray voted against capital punishment was his fear of making a fatal error.

這句話的主句是 The reason was his fear of making a fatal error，從句 Matthew Ray voted against capital punishment 可以看作是一個形容詞性的從句，用來修飾名詞 reason。當然，把它看成是什麼樣的從句並不重要，重要的是作者能夠正確有效地使用。短語 the reason why 雖然聽起來有些語義上的重複，但也屬於一個正確的習慣用法。

　　現在我們要從原因狀語從句轉向目的狀語從句的描述，此時我們再次發現英語語言的發展有著前後不統一的情況。以 that, so that 和 in order that 引導的目的狀語從句仍然可以使用，但在現代標準英語中就顯得有些古舊。例如：

Train hard *that you may win.*

Train hard *so that you may win.*

Train hard *in order that you may win.*

這樣的句子在今天的英語中已經很少出現，前兩種情況一般被簡化為用動詞不定式 to win 來表示，即：

Train hard *to win.*

上面第三句中的從句 in order that you may win 往往被簡化為 in order to win。像 to win 和 in order to win 這樣簡化的結構仍可被稱為從句。

• 因果狀語從句

因果狀語從句可以由so ... that和such ... that兩個表達方式來引導，如：

> The Green Week was *so badly attended that* the stall-holders out-numbered the visitors.

> The event was *such an embarrassment that* the Vice-President of the Students' Association resigned.

從語法規則上來說，so和such應該隸屬於主句，而that則隸屬於從句，但我們很容易認為so badly attended that和such an embarrassment that分別是一個完整的、不可分割的短語。

• 時間和地點狀語從句

在表達時間的句子中，主句與從句所表達時間概念的不同或相同決定了句子結構的選用。表示動作的同時性的從句一般以下面的副詞或副詞短語引導：

> when, whenever, while, as, as soon as, just as, even as

如下面的句子：

> *When she is sick of the city* Barbara returns to the Isle of Skye.

> *Whenever she sets foot on the island* Barbara feels free.

> She walked down to the shore *while the village was still asleep.*

> Rain began to fall *as Barbara walked along the shingle.*

短語as soon as, just as和even as一般表示更強的同時性或突然性，如：

As soon as/Just as/Even as she reached the bay the oystercatchers flew off.

如果主句和從句所表達的時間概念不同，從句所使用的引導詞一般為before, after, till, until和since等，如：

Upstart Genes played for an hour *before Positron came on stage.*

Positron's road crew went to work *after the audience left.*

The crew kept going *till/until every item was in the van.*

Fran Prasana has been singing with Upstart Genes *since she left art college six years ago.*

最後，用來引導地點狀語從句的詞一般為where, wherever, anywhere和everywhere，其中，where用於指代地點的簡單表達方式，如：

Upstart Genes' tour ended *where it had begun,* in Hamburg.

而wherever的意思則是「在任何地方」或「到任何地方」，或者「無論何地」，與anywhere的意思基本相同，表示「任何地方」，如：

In their first year as a band Upstart Genes played *wherever/anywhere they could.*

下面是以everywhere開頭的地點狀語從句的例子：

Now Upstart Genes attract big audiences *everywhere they play.*

Nowhere這個詞用在短語中比用在從句中更好些，如：

The harsh grandeur of the Isla of Skye is like *nowhere else in the world.*

> On some parts of the island signs of human habitation
> are *nowhere to be seen*.

下面的例子進一步證明了我們前面所講到的一種情況，即把多個簡單句變成包含狀語從句的複雜句後，就會更顯得富於變化，更加流暢、簡潔而且有説服力。例如下面這兩個簡單句：

> At the age of sixteen Felicity Ward wrote news items
> for her local newspaper. She was still at school at that
> time.

這兩個簡單句可以變成如下幾種複雜句的形式：

> At the age of sixteen Felicity Ward wrote news items
> for her local newspaper while she was still at school.

> At the age of sixteen while she was still at school, Felic-
> ity Ward wrote news items for her local newspaper.

> Felicity Ward wrote items for her local newspaper when
> she was sixteen and still at school.

> Felicity Ward wrote news items for her local newspa-
> per when she was a sixteen-year-old schoolgirl.

> When she was aged sixteen and still at school, Felicity
> Ward wrote news items for her local newspaper.

> Felicity Ward, when she was sixteen and still at school,
> wrote items for her local newspaper.

再看下面兩個簡單句：

> At the age of nineteen, Felicity went to Central
> University. There she began to edit the University
> magazine *Zymogen*.

這兩個句子可以合併為一個複合句：

> At the age of nineteen, Felicity went to Central

University, and there she began to edit the University magazine *Zymogen*.

或者也可以變成帶一個時間狀語從句和一個地點狀語從句的複雜句：

When she was nineteen, Felicity went to Central University, where she edited the University magazine *Zymogen*.

把兩個簡單句變成一個包括一個主句和兩個從句的複雜句，就使資訊的表達顯得緊湊而順暢。

再看下面三個簡單句：

Felicity edited *Zymogen* for three years. She then graduated. She joined the *Daily Clarion* as a reporter.

這三個句子可以合併為下面幾種複雜句：

Felicity edited *Zymogen* for three years until she graduated, after which she joined the *Daily Clarion* as a reporter.

For three years Felicity edited *Zymogen* until, after graduating, she joined the *Daily Clarion* as a reporter.

When Felicity graduated after editing *Zymogen* for three years, she joined the *Daily Clarion* as a reporter.

複合－複雜句

先看三個簡單句：

Felicity Ward edited *Zymogen* for three years. She then graduated. She joined the *Daily Clarion* as a reporter.

這三個簡單句可以用複合句和複雜句合併成一句，得到一個包括兩個主句和一個從句的複合–複雜句，如：

(a) Felicity Ward edited *Zymogen* for three years until she graduated, and then she joined the *Daily Clarion* as a reporter.

(b) After Felicity Ward had edited *Zymogen* for three years, she graduated and joined the *Daily Clarion* as a reporter.

(c) When Felicity Ward has edited *Zymogen* for three years, she graduated and joined the *Daily Clarion* as a reporter.

(d) Felicity Ward graduated after she had edited *Zymogen* for three years, and then she joined the *Daily Clarion* as a reporter.

上述 (a) 句中的副詞性連詞 until 引導一個時間狀語 until she graduated；連詞 and 連接的主句 and then she joined the *Daily Clarion* as a reporter 與句子開頭的主句 Felicity Ward edited *Zymogen* for almost three years 具有相同的語法地位。 (b) 句中的狀語連詞 after 引導時間狀語 After Felicity Ward had edited *Zymogen* for three years，連詞 and 引導的分句 and joined ... as a reporter 與另一分句 she graduated 構成了整個複合–複雜句中複合句的部分。 (c) 句以一個時間狀語開頭，隨後是一個分句 she graduated，最後與此分句相並列的複合句的第二個分句 and joined ... as a reporter。 (d) 句以分句 Felicity Ward graduated 開頭，後面跟一個時間狀語從句 after she had edited *Zymogen* for three years，然後是第二個分句 and then she joined the *Daily Clarion* as a reporter。

　　複合–複雜句中可以有兩個以上的分句和一個以上的從句，如：

When Fran Prasana, who was studying art at Central College, told her family that she was joining Upstart Genes as the lead singer, her father was alarmed and her mother was bewildered but her young sister was delighted.

上面這句話中有三個分句：

her father was alarmed

and her mother was bewildered

but her young sister was delighted

還有三個從句，一個是時間狀語從句，修飾幾次出現的動詞 was：

When Fran Prasana told her family

另一個是定語從句，修飾專有名詞 Fran Prasana：

who was studying art at Central College

還有一個是名詞性從句，作動詞 told 的賓語：

that she was joining Upstart Genes as the lead singer

再看一個例子：

Upstart Genes rehearsed whenever they had time, played gigs anywhere they could and travelled hundreds of miles a week, but they did not achieve the success they longed for until Fran Prasana, whose voice is ideal for the band, joined them.

這句話中有四個分句：

Upstart Genes rehearsed

[Upstart Genes] played gigs

and [Upstart Genes] travelled hundreds of miles a week

　　　　but they did not achieve the success

此外還有五個從句：

　　　　whenever they had time

這是一個時間狀語從句，修飾動詞rehearsed；

　　　　anywhere they could

這是一個地點狀語從句，修飾動詞played；

　　　　[that] they longed for

這是一個定語從句，修飾名詞success；

　　　　until Fran Prasana joined them

這是一個時間狀語從句，修飾動詞短語did not achieve；

　　　　whose voice is ideal for the band

這是一個定語從句，修飾專有名詞Fran Prasana。

　　複雜句和複合–複雜句給我們提供了無數種句式選擇，可以使我們寫出流暢、簡潔而又富於變化的句子，又由於我們可以在句子中對詞彙進行富有創意的組合，這樣又可以使我們寫出的句子新穎獨特。在隨後的幾章中，我們會看到，句子和詞彙的使用及其不同的使用方法所產生的不同效果，對於段落及篇章的寫作都有著重要的影響。

第七章 | 段落結構

前面我們曾把句子定義為「完整的交流資訊的單位」，而段落就可以說是由一系列句子組成的對所要交流資訊的完整敘述。

在標準英語中，對段落的長度和結構都沒有嚴格的界定，可以像新聞類文章中那樣，每段話可能只有一個句子，也可以像教科書上或非小說類作品中的段落那樣，包括很多句子和成百上千的單詞。一個段落可以是對某些具有相同特徵事物的簡單而客觀的描述，如可以對你自己房間裏的明星海報、風景畫以及照片等進行一番描繪；還可以是思維過程中一連串精妙想法的展現，或者是對一個人性格的各個方面的分析，也可以是一場正規的辯論或學術爭論中邏輯過程的推理。

用這樣的方式把一系列相關的內容放在一起，就有了主題上和句子之間的連貫性。也就是說，通過把句子組織成一個段落的過程，實際上也是把我們的思想巧妙地組織成一個整體的過程。即使是構思很簡單的一個段落，也可以幫助我們澄清思想，並使思想有條理，進而把我們的思想清楚明白地向讀者表達。

在對話中如果有兩個或多個說話者時，分段還可以用來幫助分清對話的層次，這一點我們已經在第125–26頁介紹過了。

就像書面標準英語的很多其他方面一樣，段落首先是由印

刷商使用。起初，在兩個不同的話題之間或在兩個不同的説話者所説的話之間，印刷商是在文本中用一個類似於字母P或倒轉的P的符號來進行分隔，後來，為了使這種話題的轉換顯得更明顯，印刷商就開始讓每個新的話題都另起一行，並在靠左邊距的一邊縮進。這一習慣性的作法漸漸成為了人們通用的慣例，從而也就為書面英語又增加了一條規則。

　　由於一個段落中往往包括一系列相關的內容，而不僅僅是某一個內容，所以也往往包括多個句子。當然，只包含一個句子的段落在標準英語中是容許的，而且這樣的段落可以非常有效地表達簡短、確定而有力的陳述。

描寫事實的段落

　　下面這個簡短的段落按照一定的次序陳述了一系列的事實：

> The front page of modern broadsheet, or 'quality', news-papers normally carries five or six news stories. A prominent headline above the leading story is designed to catch the reader's eye, and this appeal is strengthened by the use of news photographs, sometimes in full colour. Colour is also used in front-page advertisements, including house advertisements in which the newspaper promotes selected articles in that day's issue.

這一段中的三句話圍繞著同一個話題，即關於現代大報的話題，進行了一系列的陳述。其中的第一句是簡單句，第二句是複合句，第三句是複雜句。第一句話在引出所討論話題的同時，也是作為這段話所陳述的事實之一，隨後的兩句是就同一話題又增加的一些新的陳述。這樣安排雖然也確實構成一個段

落，但讀起來讓人感覺就像一個目錄中的各個條目一樣鬆散地排列在一起。如果我們能夠把這段話的主題更加明顯地突出出來，讀者就會更準確地抓住段落的大意，文章也就更能吸引讀者的注意力。

要做到這一點，我們可以在段落中使用主題句。所謂主題句就是能夠明確表明段落的話題或主題的句子。主題句有時也叫關鍵句，因為它往往是我們抓住段落主旨的關鍵。最簡單的方法是把主題句放在段落的開頭，如，可以把下面這句話放在上面所例舉的那段話的開頭：

Newspaper design is constantly changing.

如果這段話有了一個像這樣直接明瞭的主題句，相信讀者都能夠理解段落的大意。下面這個主題句對我們更有啟發：

A newspaper achieves its effects through page design as well as editorial content.

段落起首的主題句可以使段落的意思更加明確而集中，這種意思的明確和集中還可以由特意放置在段落末尾的結尾句得到進一步加強。使用這樣的結尾句可以使段落在作者的有意控制下收尾，而不至於讓人感覺唐突或拖泥帶水。一個段落的結尾，甚至更大一些的篇章如散文、報告或學術論文等的結尾，不僅僅代表該段篇章的結束，它還應該是我們在篇章的結尾處所形成的觀點或看法的一種合理的説明。如果給前面所例舉的那段話加上一個有力的結尾句的話，這句話就應該既能概括前面幾句話的內容，又能使整段的意思集中起來。下面是給這段話加的一個結尾句的例子：

The effect of these devices is to make the modern broadsheet newspaper a visual as well as written medium of communication.

加上了一個開頭的主題句和結尾的收尾句之後，這段話就基本符合一個規範的段落的要求了，包括了開頭、發展和結尾三個部分，結構嚴謹，自成一體。下面是這段話變化之後的情況：

> A newspaper achieves its effects through page design as well as editorial content. The front page of modern broadsheet, or 'quality', newspapers normally carries five or six news stories. A prominent headline above the leading story is designed to catch the reader's eye, and this appeal is strengthened by the use of news photographs, sometimes in full colour. Colour is also used in front-page advertisements, including house advertisements in which the newspaper promotes selected articles in that day's issue. The effect of these devices is to make the modern broadsheet newspaper a visual as well as a written medium of communication.

但是如果我們想要進一步討論關於報紙版面設計的問題，而不是到此為止，又該怎麼樣寫呢？例如，如果在這段關於大報的版面設計的段落之後跟的是一段關於小報版面設計的內容，那麼這一段的結尾句 The effect of ... medium of communication 就顯得不太合適了。這樣的話，我們就需要一個既能引出新話題，又可以把兩個段落的內容銜接起來的句子。

我們可以在下一段的開頭直接用一個能起到連接作用的主題句，如：

> Tabloid, or 'popular', newspapers are even more dependent on page design.

這句話中的 Tabloid 一詞就引入了一個新的話題，page design 又表明了與前文的聯繫，而 even more dependent 則表示這一段的內容與前一段形成對比，從而使話題進一步擴展。

　　另外，還可以用一個長度較長、內容更豐富的句子，既作為新話題的引入和與前文的連接，又可以把兩段的話題統一起來，如：

> Page design is even bolder in tabloid newspapers, where there are bigger headlines, more photographs and a greater use of colour.

這句話不僅實現了上下文的連接，還能很容易地引導讀者從一段過渡到下一段。隨後的內容就可以像前一段中一樣，進行順理成章的陳述，如，下面這部分可以作為上面這個主題句之後的內容：

> Some editors attach so much importance to visual effects that they allow the designer rather than the chief sub-editor to plan the front page. The focal point is always a photograph, and wherever possible the photograph is a close-up in full colour.

　　第一段中的結尾句只提到了大報，我們可以再給它加上小報這一陳述對象，並把medium變成複數media，整個句子就變成了這樣：

> The effect of these devices is to make modern newspapers, both broadsheet and tabloid, visual as well as written media of communication.

我們來小結一下上面例舉的兩個段落中所使用的寫作技巧。首先，第一段中的整個段落由一個主題句引導：

> A newspaper achieves its effects through page design as well as editorial content.

隨後的部分則詳細描述大報頭版的設計，來對主題句加以證明和陳述。

　　從第一段向第二段的過渡由第二段開頭的一個過渡句來實現，這句話還同時作為第二段的主題句：

> Page design is even bolder in tabloid newspapers, where there are bigger headlines, more photographs and a greater use of colour.

第二段敘述的是小報頭版的版面設計這一由主題句所引導的主題，並與第一段的內容形成了對比。

　　在第二段的末尾，使用了一個結尾句來總結前文，並使兩段內容得到統一：

> The effect of these devices is to make modern newspapers, both broadcast and tabloid, visual as well as written media of communication.

下面是整個這兩段話的情況：

> A newspaper achieves its effects through page design as well as editorial content. The front page of modern broadsheet, or 'quality', newspapers normally carries five or six news stories. A prominent headline above the leading story is designed to catch the reader's eye, and this appeal is strengthened by the use of news photographs, sometimes in full colour. Colour is also used in front-page advertisements, including house advertisements in which the newspaper promotes selected articles in that day's issue.
>
> 　　Page design is even bolder in tabloid newspapers, where there are bigger headlines, more photographs and a greater use of colour. Some editors attach so much importance to visual effects that they allow the designer rather than the chief sub-editor to plan the front page. The focal point is always a photograph, and wherever possible the photograph is a close-up in

full colour. The effect of these devices is to make modern newspapers, both broadsheet and tabloid, visual as well as written media of communication.

在這兩段話中，除了結尾句的總結和解釋之外，還包括一些客觀的敘述。如果所討論的是一個更加引人深思的主題，或者我們要對主題進行嚴密的推理論述，這時就要用不同的方法來組織段落結構。

描寫思想的段落

當我們從不同的角度對同一主題的內容進行陳述時，就要用不同的段落結構方法，例如，還是上面舉過的那段話，如果談論的話題變成了對各種報紙的評價，或是討論新聞與讀者的關係，而不是僅對報紙頭版的內容和形式做事實性的描述，那麼段落的寫法也就不一樣了。在下面一個作為示範的段落中，所有資訊先是以時間為序排列，並寫成一些比較零碎的筆記形式，作為段落的草稿。這也是許多文章或段落剛開始寫作時的做法。如：

Daily Mail launched 1896; by 1900 mass circulation of 1 million copies a day at half-penny a copy. Cost low because long print run gave low unit cost, and income from advertising; cost made it affordable; daily publication — new issue every morning — made it disposable; newspapers as commodities to be used and discarded. Since newspaper was disposable, so news too was disposable. Then news as a commodity, read and then discarded; news agencies selling news — e.g., Press Association and Reuters. Now newspaper advertising managers sell space to advertisers by promising

thousands or millions readers. If readership bought and
sold, then readers too are a commodity.

　　這段草稿以關於 *Daily Mail* 這份報紙的一個事實性的陳述開頭，結尾卻出人意料地說報紙的讀者本身也是一種商品。如果用這段草稿來為報紙寫一則新聞故事，記者就會按照新聞寫作的常規，改變時間順序，把故事的最終結果放在開頭句中（開頭一句也叫導語），以引出新聞的話題並體現新聞故事的即時性。但是，就作為範例的這一段而言，我們最好還是保留草稿中原有的順序，因為這個順序可以看作是一個符合邏輯的思維過程，一環緊扣一環，最後得出一個有力的結論。

　　應該注意到，草稿的開頭一句話雖然提到 *Daily Mail* 這家報紙，但它並不能用來作段落的主題句，因為這段話的真正話題並非是 *Mail* 這份報紙，而是有關大批量發行報紙與其讀者的問題。構思這段話的時候我們應考慮到這一點。下面就是寫好之後的段落：

Britain's first mass-circulation newspaper was the *Daily
Mail*, which was launched in 1896. Only four years
later, in 1900, the *Daily Mail* had a circulation of one
million copies a day. Part of the *Daily Mail*'s popular
appeal was its cheapness, one half-penny, at a time
when other newspapers cost up to ten pence. The low
cover price was possible because the long print-run led
to low unit costs; that is, the expense of news-gathering,
writing, editing, typesetting and printing was spread
over one million copies compared to the 50,000 or
100,000 copies of other newspapers. Another factor
influencing the cover price was that some of the *Daily
Mail*'s income came from advertising revenue, which
meant that part of the production cost was borne by

advertisers. Mass-circulation newspapers became easily affordable and, since a new edition appeared every morning, they came to be seen as disposable, things to be used and then discarded. As newspapers came to be treated as commodities, so too did their contents. Organizations that existed to buy and sell news — the Press Association, the national news agency established in 1868, and Reuters, the international news agency established in 1851 — increased their activities to meet the growing demands of newspaper and their readers. Newspaper proprietors, unlike most of their editors, saw their publications as commercial operations rather than as information services, and sold space in the pages of their newspapers to advertisers. Advertising agencies were formed to buy and sell space just as the news agencies bought and sold news, and so the spaces, along with the advertisements that filled them, came to be seen as commodities. Today, most newspapers have advertisement managers, who sell space to advertisers and advertising agencies by promising so many thousands or millions of readers. The promise is made in letters, or 'mailshots', to advertising agents and in newspapers' self-promoting house advertisements, the assumption being that whoever reads the newspapers also reads the advertisements. Now that readerships are being bought and sold in this way, readers too have become commodities in the world of mass-circulation newspapers.

　　這段話的開頭一句提示出了該段後面部分的內容和寫作者的思路，因此可以把它看作是該段的主題句，但它並不是唯一的主題句。這段話的內容逐步深入，意思層層推進，並在最後的結尾句中得到了結論。這段話的最後幾個字the world of mass-circulation newspapers既總結了前文的論述，又與段首的第一句話相呼應，並且還不止於此，它還是整個這段話的落腳點，因此最後這句話才是這段話的真正主題句。

如果結尾句具有上述的雙重功能，段落的結構安排就更要體現出一個循序漸進的層次，從而自然而然地達到段落最後的結論。上面這個示範段落就做到了這一點，它用句與句之間相互關聯、有時又用相互呼應的意思，以及通過不斷強調像read, reader, readership這樣的詞，使整個段落形成了一條連貫的思路。

我們在本章的開頭已經提到過，標準英語在段落的長度和結構方面容許有較大的靈活性，例如，上面用來做示範的這個段落就可以拆分為兩個甚至三個段落，這就是這種靈活性的一個證明。如果拆分成三段，第二段就可以從As newspapers came to be treated as commodities開始，第三段從Today, most newspapers have advertisement managers開始。在這種情況下，如果所寫的主題對於段落的長度沒有嚴格要求的話，我們就可以採取其他的標準來劃分段落的長度，其中最為穩妥的辦法就是按照讀者的要求和能力來劃分，簡言之，就是看讀者能夠接受一段話中有多少詞彙和表達多少思想。

描寫人物的段落

我們時常要寫一些關於人的生活、性格或事業等方面的文章，所寫的人物可能是歷史人物，也可能是小說或戲劇中的人物：可能是你在小說中塑造的人物，這個人物還可能就是你自己，或者可能是你在履歷中所描述的自己。為了說明描寫人物的段落的寫法，我們下面所用的示範段落就選用了人物傳記方面的題材。

　　這段話所使用的是標準英語句子，但故意寫得重複囉嗦，並且句子順序也隨意排列。段落的長度大約有220個詞，只用一個段落來寫有些不妥，另外還需要增加或刪減一些細節方面的內容。先看這段話的原文：

> His second book, *In at the Kill: Blood Sports in Britain*, once again caught the public imagination. His powerful descriptions and starkly revealing photographs of blood sports persuaded many landowners to ban hunting on their land. His third book, *Plight of the Otter*, was described by *Living Land* magazine as 'A mysterious, disturbing work that invites comparison with Gavin Maxwell's *Ring of Bright Water* and Henry Williamson's *Tarka the Otter*'. His new book, *The Vanishing Countryside*, will be published in June. Michael Ashton, 38, was born in York and educated at Central University, where he gained a degree in botany. His new book will be as controversial as his first three. His first book, *A Poisoned Heritage: Britain's Rivers and Waterways*, identified those industries and local authorities that were polluting our rivers and forced many of the offenders to change their practices. Michael Ashton's new book, *The Vanishing Countryside*, shows how thousands of acres of British countryside — woodland, wetland and moorland — have been destroyed in the last ten years. Michael Ashton taught botany in a secondary school for six years and then became a full-time writer. His new book identifies the government departments, local authorities and private developers who are responsible for the destruction. His new book is likely to be as controversial as his earlier work.

這一段文字的內容雖然是隨意排列，語言風格上也顯得重複囉

嗦，但它的主題是清楚的，講的是以環境問題為主題的作家米高‧阿斯頓 (Michael Ashton) 即將出版他的第四本書。

　　我們首先要做的是找出這段話的邏輯順序。只要大致讀一下，通過 His first book, His second book, His third book 等表達方式，我們就可以看出這段話應該以時間順序排列。由於前面這些短語表明了作家事業的不同階段，所以我們可以把整個段落按照時間順序來組織結構。可以用下面這個句子來開頭：

> Michael Ashton, 38, was born in York and educated at Central University, where he gained a degree in botany.

然後，就應該是他事業發展的下一個階段。寫的時候要注意避免不必要的重複：

> He taught botany in a secondary school for six years before becoming a full-time writer.

最後，我們可以用描寫他的事業發展最後一個階段的三個句子來結尾，寫的時候同樣要注意句子的流暢和句子結構的變化：

> Michael Ashton's new book, *The Vanishing Countryside,* not only shows how thousands of acres of British countryside — woodland, wetland and moorland — have been destroyed in the last ten years, but also identifies the government departments, local authorities and private developers who are responsible for the destruction. The *Vanishing Countryside* will be as controversial as his first three books.

　　這樣安排段落結構的好處在於其簡潔性，段落嚴格按照從過去到現在的記傳體順序來敘述。這樣雖然體現不出像上一個示範段落那樣由淺入深的層次，但它的優勢在於可以使描述非常有條理，並且最後得出相應的結論。這種段落結構安排方法的缺點在於可能造成段落的描述單調乏味，缺乏起伏感。

　　有時候，把最新發生的事情放在段落的開頭有利於傳記性材料的敘述，因為這樣可以讓讀者得到一種即時感，並且，通過這樣的結構段落，還可以使讀者馬上瞭解到所描寫人物的成就、現階段的聲望以及他目前的情況等，而不一定非要知道他很久之前的甚至是不相關的，諸如他的出生及早期生活的情況。

　　作為示範的這個段落正是運用了上述這種結構方式。由於這段的主題不只是關於米高·阿斯頓這個人，而且還涉及到其書的號召力和所引起的爭議，運用這種結構方式，我們就可以在段首和段尾各用一個主題句。請看按照這種方式所寫的這段話：

A new book by Michael Ashton, the writer who campaigns on environmental issues, will be published in June. *The Vanishing Countryside* will not only show how thousands of acres of British countryside — woodland, wetland and moorland — have been destroyed in the last ten years but will also identify the government departments, local authorities and private developers who are responsible for the destruction.

Readers of Mr Ashton's three previous books now expect such dramatic disclosures. In his first book, *A Poisoned Heritage: Britain's Rivers and Waterways*, the author identified those industries and local authorities that were polluting our rivers, and forced many of the offenders to change their practices. He caught the public imagination again in *In at the Kill*, when his powerful descriptions and starkly revealing photographs of blood sports persuaded many landowners to ban hunting on their land. *Plight of the Otter*, his third book, was described by *Living Land* magazine as 'A mysterious, disturbing work that invites comparison with Gavin Maxwell's *Ring of Bright Water* and Henry Williamson's *Tarka the Otter*'.

Mr Ashton, 38, was born in York and educated at Central University, where he gained a degree in botany. He taught botany in a secondary school for six years before becoming a full-time writer. *The Vanishing Countryside* is likely to be as controversial as his earlier work.

可以看出，有關即將出版的新書的資訊構成了一個緊湊的語篇單位，形成了這段話的第一部分；此前三本書的詳細介紹同樣構成一個緊湊的單位，形成第二部分；關於所寫人物個人情況的傳記性材料構成了第三部分。其中第三部分的最後一句話是整個段落一個有力的結尾句，它不僅指出新書即將引起爭論，而且還與這段話開頭的第一句相呼應。這樣，整個段落內容的結構安排以及由此產生的對所強調內容的側重點，都與前面那個關於報紙與讀者關係的示範段落不同。這樣的段落結構就與描寫人物的新聞稿或新聞故事大致相似：把人們最關心的話題放在前兩段中，並使短小的第三段保持活力，一氣呵成。

對於這種以及其他類似傳記性的描寫還有一個要求，就是在敘述中要儘量避免重複使用人物的名字 (如Michael Ashton) 或者對人物的某一種同樣的稱呼，如the author或him等，但也不能過於刻意地使用不同的人物指稱，以防陷入我們在前一章中提到的「過於優雅」的文體風格。在上面這段範例中，第一段為人物的指稱用的是Michael Ashton, the writer who campaigns on environmental issues；在較長的第二段裏用的是Mr Ashton, the author和he；第三段裏用的則是Mr Ashton和He。這裏用這些不同的方式來對所敘述的人物進行指稱和辨別已經足夠了。

資訊編排

文章段落的寫作，與其說是檢驗我們的寫作技巧，不如說是鍛煉我們給所收集的資訊分類的能力。大多數作者對於給資訊的大致分類並不覺得困難，並且還發現，如果列出資訊的條目，並給每條資訊加上一個適當的標題，分類就會顯得更清楚。

然而有些作者卻不太善於組織段落中的資訊和構成整個文章的各個段落。段落的內部結構與整個文章的段落結構的區別主要體現在規模大小上，它們實質上是屬於同一問題，因而都可以通過適當的結構組織方法來解決。我們通常採用的主要方法有兩種，一是按照時間順序來組織材料，一是按照主題順序來組織材料。

◆ 時間順序編排

如果我們所掌握的寫作材料能夠以月、年、世紀等來進行時間上的分類，那麼最簡單的方法就是把材料按照從過去到現在、由遠及近的時間順序來安排。可以用這種方法來編排段落的主題有很多，從歷史研究到傳記和自傳，從體育報導到戲劇評論等都可以按照時間順序來編排，因為這些題材都可看作是線性的時間遞進過程。有關旅行方面的題材也可以用這種方法來寫，因為任何一個行程都既有地理方位的順序又有時間上的順序。

如果覺得一味地按照這種從過去到現在的時間順序來安排段落過於死板，還可以對這種模式加以改變，就像在前面關於Michael Ashton的那個示範段落中一樣，先敘述當前發生的事，

後敘述以前的事情，也就是在描述完當前的情況之後，再按照時間先後順序加以敘述，這樣讀者就可以瞭解事情發展的來龍去脈，明白當前情況的由來。不管是寫一個段落還是寫更長的篇章，結構都要嚴謹且均衡。

如果稍加編排，段落或篇章的結構還可以有更多的變化形式。例如，我們可以把過去和現在進行比較，通過不斷地切換對比，不同期間發生的情況就能更加明白地呈現在讀者面前。在論文或者報告中，交替出現的對比結構最好每隔三段以上出現一次，因為如果時間順序的切換頻率過高就容易使讀者產生混亂。

這種寫作手法的各種變化形式，不僅適用於寫那些有明顯時間順序的主題內容，還可用於幾乎任何可追溯其過去發展歷史的主題，如通俗文化、城市治安、美國小說、兒童連環畫、一個足球俱樂部或一個鄉村板球俱樂部等。用這種寫法來組織段落結構，就可以把所描述事物的過去的情形與人們對它的評價與現在的情況相互交織，互相滲透，對比和比較也給我們所寫的文章增加了活力和張力。需要特別注意的是，不應把敘述的重點放在對事情過去情況的描述，以免使我們所寫的任何主題的文章都變成一種歷史研究。

散文、報告和論文所論述的同一主題中往往包括兩個或更多的話題，這些話題相互關聯但又彼此不同，每個話題都有其本身的時間歷程，所以對這樣的文章所提出的結構方面的要求更多。這方面的文章有很多，如一個關於二戰期間英國軍用飛機的研究課題，或者一項對於兩個或更多家商店的經營情況，或對於雇主的地區性調查，或者關於英國經濟在連續三界政府執政下的發展情況的報告等。

　　寫這樣的文章時，為了易於把握文章的結構，可以在寫作的規劃階段把文章的主題分為幾個部分，每個部分中包括幾個話題。例如，如果寫關於英國軍用飛機的研究課題，就可以分為三個部分：戰鬥機、轟炸機和偵察機，每一部分都可以按照時間順序分別敘述，「轟炸機」一部分還可以進一步分為四個話題：惠靈頓式轟炸機、斯特靈式轟炸機、哈利法克斯式轟炸機和蘭喀斯特式轟炸機，每個話題又可以用一兩個段落來敘述。

　　這樣，這個課題報告就可以分成幾個分別以時間順序組織成的部分。但是，我們有時會發現在不同部分的內容之間相互引用，在講到轟炸機一部分中，我們可能時常會提到二戰中幾種主要的英國戰鬥機，如噴火式戰鬥機和颶風式戰鬥機。同樣，在講到惠靈頓式轟炸機這一小部分時，可能還會參照或對比其他轟炸機。可以看出，實際上按照時間順序組織段落或篇章結構時，也要多少考慮一些主題內容方面的因素，這樣寫出的文章要比只以時間順序為主線的文章顯得更加靈活，更加全面。

◆ 主題編排

　　如果所寫的內容不能以時間或空間順序來編排，那麼就要按照主題來編排段落，也就是編排材料的方式要最能夠體現所寫的主題。這也是我們一般處理抽象或近乎抽象的主題時所採用的方法，如關於宗教、哲學、道德、教育、人的價值和人的性格等。由於人物性格是戲劇、小說以及詩歌中一個永恒的主題，我們這裏就可以用一篇論述關於格雷厄姆‧格林 (Graham Greene) 小說中幾個中心人物的文章為例。

　　在規劃文章的階段，我們還是先要把文章的整個主題劃分

為幾個組成部分；同時為了便於主題的把握，我們還可以把要寫的人物以及人物的性格列一個清單。我們甚至還可以按照小說的出版日期，分別起草文章的不同部分，如小說 *The Heart of the Matter*（《事件的中心》）中的人物亨利・斯科比（Henry Scobie），小說 *The Quiet American*（《靜靜的美國人》）中的奧爾登・派爾（Alden Pyle），*Our Man in Havana*（《我們在哈瓦那的人》）中的吉姆・沃姆德（Jim Wormold），以及 *The Honorary Consul*（《榮譽領事》）中的查雷・福特那姆（Charley Fortnum）和埃德瓦多・普樂（Eduardo Plarr）。但是在收集整理資料的過程中，我們會發現，如果把對小說中各個人物的敘述截然分開，就會使文章成為包括四五個相互獨立的部分，而顯得不連貫，缺乏整體性。為了使文章形成一個連貫的整體，我們必須把所收集的資料進行通盤考慮，對不同的人物進行相互參照和比較。一些傳記性的諸如生平介紹之類的資訊對於人物的區分和對比是很有用處的，但我們所寫的是一篇關於格林所塑造的人物的文章，因此更為重要的應該是展現出這些人物的所做和所想，以及他們怎樣對待家人，怎樣對待朋友，怎樣面對現實中的危險、孤獨、絕望和誘惑等。這些性格特徵也正構成了這篇文章的主題。

　　按照主題來安排文章的結構方面，主要有三種編排材料的方法。第一，可以採取一種均衡的結構，就像前面我們看到過的第一個示範段落那樣，使對有關大報和小報資訊的敘述處於同樣重要的地位。這一段結構的關鍵，取決於其開頭句和結尾句，就是說，如果保持這兩句話不變，所討論的內容（即大報和小報）不變，那麼即使改變段落中的敘述順序，也不會影響段落的意義及效果。

　　第二種方法是按照資訊的重要性，由低到高的順序編排材料，逐句逐段，有系統地過渡到最後的結論，就像前面的第二個示範段落那樣，經過一系列的陳述和鋪墊，最後得到的結論是「報紙的讀者也是一種商品」。

　　第三種方法實際上是第二種方法的一個變形，就是把材料按照重要性由高到低的順序來編排材料，正如前面講到的關於作家Michael Ashton的那個示範段落一樣。

　　按照主題來安排文章的結構方面，要求我們必須做出兩種選擇。一是要選擇上面所講的三種方法中哪一種最適合我們所寫的材料，是均衡地安排資訊呢，還是按照資訊的重要性由低到高的順序呢，抑或是與此相反的順序呢？第二個選擇中其實包括一系列的選擇，因為一旦我們選擇了三種結構方法中的一種，我們接下來還要繼續選擇段落中句子的順序，以及文章中段落的順序等。雖然只有作者自己才能做出這些選擇，但有一些指導原則還是會對我們有幫助。

◆ 劃分主題結構的指導原則

　　如果段落中的每項內容或者整篇文章中的每個段落都具有相同或相似的重要性，這種情況下，我們的選擇餘地就很小，一般採用均衡結構，使整個篇章的排列整齊有序，其最終結構的形成主要由開頭句和結尾句來決定。

　　如果所要敘述資訊的重要性或難度有所不同，就要按照重要性或難度遞增或遞減的順序來編排篇章結構。某條資訊的重要性往往可以用我們人類的價值觀念為標準來進行評價，例如，如果討論的是關於人的生死、安危、苦難，或者是人的愛恨、忍耐力、固執，以及教育和愚昧等，這些資訊顯然是比較

重要的；再有，有些資訊具有全人類所關注的重要性，如關於地球的狀況和我們周圍的環境的話題；有時，某些資訊的重要性在不同的範圍內或不同的規模上有不同的體現，如足球運動員的轉會費、犯罪率、長時間異常炎熱或寒冷的氣候等；有時候，資訊的重要性還可能體現在其獨特性或創新性上，如第一例心臟移植、國會補選中的意外結果或一種服裝的最新款式等。

判斷所寫的段落或文章中所使用材料難度的方法之一，就是先對預期的讀者進行一下評估。如果讀者數量越少且越具有專業性，則我們所寫的東西越容易被讀懂。例如，假如我們的讀者是一位課程教師或者是一位主考官，我們就可以認為他完全能夠理解我們所寫的具有一定知識水平的內容；如果我們的讀者是大量的非專業人士，那麼我們的敘述就要詳細、清晰，語言簡單。但有一點要注意，不管我們的讀者是一個人還是一百萬人，他們的智力水平都可能會與我們相當，或者超過作者本人，所以如果我們擺出一副盛氣凌人、自作聰明的樣子，就會使讀者產生敵意，最終失去讀者。

然後我們還要選擇按照重要性遞增還是遞減的順序來編排材料，哪一種較為合適。如果所寫的是一篇學術論文或是需要大量解釋和例子的文章，就應使用從次要到重要資訊遞增的順序，文章每個段落中的內容也應該循序漸進，這樣，所給出的證據或例子才能不斷使論點得到加強，也才能讓讀者信服我們的觀點。

如果所寫的文章想要儘快地吸引讀者的注意力，就應使用從重要資訊到次要資訊遞減的順序，這種順序尤其適用於當我們所掌握的資訊材料具有即時性或具有新聞價值的時候，正如

我們在前一部分中所看到的那樣，這種結構方法多用於新聞報導中，因為這樣的結構可以只用開頭的幾句話或幾段話就能引起讀者的興趣，從而把整個篇章讀完。這種資訊重要性遞減的順序也適用於傳達帶有不同程度緊迫性的資訊，如警告、指示或建議等。在這樣的篇章中，越是緊急的內容，越要放在靠前的位置。

結構變化

結構的多樣化可以給文章增添活力，增強讀者閱讀的興趣，因此我們要注意句子和段落結構的靈活多變。運用一定的寫作技巧不僅能使我們所寫的文章富於變化，避免單調乏味的重複，就是我們自己讀起來也會感到賞心悅目。如果一味地重複使用關鍵字、句子的開頭詞，甚至重複使用同樣的句子結構和句子長度，讀者就會感到厭煩，並且這種缺乏變化還會被讀者認為是作者能力不足的一種表現，這樣就會失去作者的威信和讀者的信任。正如本書前言中所說的那樣，如果讀者信不過作者所使用的語言，他們又怎能相信作者所傳達的資訊呢？

如果在嚴格的時間限制下或者在考試時進行寫作，就很難做到使文章的結構多樣化，但是如果在經過精心準備的條件下，就不應寫出像下面這樣缺乏變化的段落：

> The *Northern Chronicle* is a weekly newspaper and is published every Thursday. A member of the Northern News Group, it was established in 1899. It sells for 35 pence and has an average circulation just in excess of 35,000. Its circulation area is Normouth and the surrounding villages. It contains between 20 and 26 pages,

and includes the occasional supplement, such as the
'Home and Garden' section which came with the 16th
April issue.

這一段中包含了多種資訊，但由於第三、四、五句的開頭重複
使用了It, Its和It，並且這些句子的結構也相似，就使得原本要
表達的資訊表達不清。結構上的重複所造成的後果，就是讓
讀者覺得作者所表達的意思也是重複的，因為雖是不同的資訊
內容卻使用了相同的表達形式。第一個句子中的a weekly newspaper and is published every Thursday也有重複現象，其中的
every Thursday已經包含了weekly的意思。另外，第四句話重複
了前一句中的circulation，也是沒有必要。我們來看看這段話經
過修改之後的情況：

The *Northern Chronicle*, a member of the Northern
News Group, was established in 1899. Published every
Thursday at 35 pence, the *Chronicle* has a circulation
of just over 35,000 in Normouth and the surrounding
villages. Editions range from 20 to 26 pages and include occasional supplements such as the 'Home and
Garden' section in the 16th April issue.

只是通過簡單地變換一下段落中每句話的開頭詞，或者變
換一下文章中每一段的開頭，就可以使我們所寫文章的風格千
變萬化，如果再加上句子長度和結構的變化，就更能使文章充
滿活力，更能吸引讀者的興趣。

敘述方法

從本章講述段落和前一章講述句子的的介紹中，我們可以
看出，寫作中這種逐行、逐句、逐段的線性特徵，使得任何一

篇文章都有一個敘述結構；同時這兩章還表明，我們可以使用多種方法去編排文章的結構，以使文章更具感染力。我們比較容易忽略的是，文章除了敘述結構之外，還有敘述角度和敘述節奏的問題，把握好這些因素，我們就可以使文章取得更佳的效果。

◆ 敘述角度

敘述角度包括作者在其所寫作品中的角色以及參與程度等許多複雜問題，但我們這裏只考慮其中較簡單的規律，即作者的視角往往決定了讀者的視角，而且作者具有控制視角的主動權。

這一規律可以用電視這一可視媒體來更加形象地說明。電視節目錄製暴徒與警察之間的對抗時，攝錄機鏡頭一般是跟在警察身後，因此電視觀眾在收看新聞時的視角就與攝錄機和警察的視角相一致，並且觀眾的情感變化和對事件的客觀判斷也與此視角相一致。如果觀眾想從相反的角度看待同一事件，必須要有意識地去控制自己的思維才能辦到。與此相似，如果電視報導的是一場體育比賽，一般就站在觀眾的視角進行報導。但是如果把攝錄機安裝在一輛一級方程式的賽車上，或把一部微型攝錄機裝在滑雪靴上，或是板球外場門柱上，這時的視角其實就變得與體育活動某個參與者相一致了。

寫作時的道理也是一樣，我們可以從旁觀者的視角來寫，也可以從參與者的視角來寫，如果有必要，甚至還可以從一個視角跳轉到另一個視角。如果你所寫的文章有理有據，那麼從你自己作為作者的視角來寫讀者也是會接受的，也就是說讀者會從你所站的立場來看待所描述的事物。如果你所寫的文章風

格獨特，內容準確，即使讀者是冷靜挑剔的主考官，他也同樣會接受你的觀點。

非文學類作品的作者與小說家或戲劇家不同，一般不需要就描寫角度做較大的調整，但如果一旦需要做出調整的話，就要很明確地把這種視角的變化表示出來。例如，如果所寫的報告中敘述的事情涉及到勞資雙方、生產者與消費者或學校的教職員與學生等兩方或更多方的觀點，就要用明確的語言表明敘述角度或觀點的轉換。看下面的例子：

> Those were the views on pay and conditions expressed by the directors of Normouth Engineering Ltd. The employees expressed different views. 或者是：

> When the employees of Normouth Engineering Ltd were consulted, they expressed views that differed from those of the directors.

> A survey of 150 customers found that what they meant by the term 'Value for Money' was in sharp contrast to what the manufacturers meant.

> Interviews with over 100 students at Central University clearly established that students' expectations of higher education were not the same as the expectations of the academic staff.

敘述角度的變化方面，大的變化比微小的變化更容易把握，因為如果變化越小，所使用的敘述手段就越不容易讓讀者察覺，難度也就更大。但如果我們並不需要改變敘述角度，如在寫報告或摘要時，只需平穩地保持原有的描寫或敘述過程，這時就儘量不要讓讀者感覺到敘述手段的變化。

下面這段關於「驅逐愛爾蘭高地居民」這一時期的摘要中，句與句之間的轉接就顯得非常突兀：

It began in the middle of the eighteenth century. The clan system was breaking down in the Highlands and Islands at this time. This was due to the fact that the clans were defeated at the Battle of Culloden in 1746. After the battle some clan chiefs were executed, some were imprisoned, some went into exile like their leader Charles Edward Stuart. Also at this time some of the landowners wanted the land for sheep farming but the land was occupied by clansmen.

從這段話可以看出，作者對這一時期的歷史有所瞭解，但如果寫得連貫性再強一些的話，就會更具說服力。段落結構上的連貫也可以增強所敘述的歷史事件的連貫性，從而也就讓讀者更容易理解。這段話可以改寫為：

The long process known as the Highland Clearances began in the middle of the eighteenth century. After the defeat of the clans at the Battle of Culloden in 1746, the clan system was breaking down. Some clan chiefs had been executed, some were imprisoned, and others had gone into exile like their leader, Charles Edward Stuart. In the same period, land occupied by clansmen was wanted by some landowners for sheep farming.

改寫後的這段話以一個意思明確的主題句開頭，也避免了用 It 做句子開頭所帶來的意義含混不清。任何一個句子，尤其是一段話中的第一個句子，如果以 it 開頭的話，就容易使有些讀者感到意思不清或模稜兩可。另外，以 It began 或 It all began 開頭的句子用得過濫，已沒有了新意。類似的表達方法在修改之前的段落中還有 This was due to the fact that 和 Also at this time，而 This was due to the fact that 可以用一個簡單的詞 because 或 since 來代替。我們還可以從經過修改後的情況看出，由這些

表達方法所引導的資訊可以和其他資訊連接在一起，這樣就不會顯得零散。除了這些變化之外，修改後的段落使所表達的資訊更加緊湊，所使用的句子也在長度和結構上富於變化。這樣，就使得這段話的語言表達更加流暢和連貫，同時也使所表達的資訊同樣流暢和連貫，讀者也就更容易接受。

◆ 敘述節奏

敘述節奏是本章所要講述的最後一個寫作策略。任何一篇讓讀者產生節奏感的文章，都是取決於所寫事物的主題。不管讀者的閱讀速度是快是慢，一個本身就激動人心的主題會給讀者一種較快的節奏感，相反，如果所討論的話題本身輕鬆，必然會讓人感到節奏舒緩。因此，要想做到能夠人為地控制文章的節奏，我們必須採取其他的方法。

最簡單的方法是使用明確的語言表達方式，如果我們的文章想給讀者一個較快的節奏感，就可以直接用名詞speed及其同義詞，如：

> fleetness, haste, hurry, quickness, rapidity, swiftness, velocity.

用這些詞的形容詞和副詞也可以達到同樣的效果：

> fleet, hasty/hastily, hurried/hurriedly, quick/quickly, rapid/rapidly, rushed, swift/swiftly

此外還有一些相關的動詞：

> accelerate, dart, dash, fly, hurry, hurtle, race, rush, scurry, shoot.

這一寫作策略不僅可以控制文章的節奏，還能取得其他一些修辭效果，如表達憤怒、迷惑、自信、恐懼、貪婪和驚慌等感情

色彩。讀者可以通過這些用詞本身，體會到作者所要表達的思想感情。

使用這種方法也有不足之處，它容易使句子充滿指示性詞語，會讓讀者覺得作者在有意告訴他們應該怎樣思考。有些讀者不喜歡作者這種思想上的支配，這樣的讀者會更加注意你的寫作方法而不是你所表達的意思。

此外，通過創造性地使用某些句子結構及文章節奏，也可以達到控制敘述速度的目的，這種方法雖然不易讓人察覺，但與上述方法有異曲同工之妙，如：

> Barbara walked slowly along the shore. Shingle scrunched beneath her feet. She enjoyed the sound. The sea was calm. Mist drifted over the water. She heard the faint sounds of a boat. The boat was hidden by mist. She heard a slow creaking of oars. She heard a gentle rippling sound. She heard voices. The voices were muffled by the mist.

這段話中儘管使用了 slowly, calm, drifted, faint, slow, gentle 和 muffled 等詞，卻沒能表達出輕鬆、寧靜的意境，因為所使用的過於短小而且結構欠佳的句子，打斷了資訊的自然流動。如果把十一個短句合併為數量更少的較長的句子，我們就可以把原來斷斷續續的節奏變得更加平緩而連貫，使得原來顯得支離破碎的語篇變得更加流暢。下面是經過修改後的情況：

> Barbara walked slowly along the shore, enjoying the sound of the shingle that scrunched beneath her feet. Mist drifted over the calm sea. She heard the faint sounds of a boat that was hidden by mist: a slow creaking of oars, a gentle rippling sound and muffled voices.

原來的十一個句子減少到了三個，如果對句子結構再稍做修改，上面這段話的前兩句還可合併為一句：

> Mist drifted over the calm sea as Barbara walked slowly along the shore, enjoying the sound of the shingle that scrunched beneath her feet.

大多數讀者未能有意識地注意到文章的節奏感是由句子結構所產生的，因為他們認為節奏只與音樂或詩歌有關。然而，讀者可以本能地意識到文章的節奏對於控制文章中資訊的排列，以及對創造出恰當的語調和風格等寫作效果，都有一定的影響，而這些寫作效果對於文章意思的表達非常重要。如果作者能夠在毫不暴露寫作技巧的情況下，也就是讓讀者在毫無察覺的情況下達到上述寫作效果的話，文章就會給讀者留下更深刻的印象。即使有寫作方面專業知識的讀者同樣也會受到文章的感染，因為無論是在普通文章中，還是在詩歌、音樂或體育運動中，技巧的運用總能給讀者、聽眾以及相關活動的人帶來額外的愉悅。

第八章 | 文章布局及寫作

　　我們在大學裏就經濟、歷史或詩歌等多種多樣的主題所寫的文章屬於學術論文，而撰寫學術論文是一種學術活動，它要求我們必須遵循一定的寫作方法，這就使學術論文有著與眾不同的文章結構。

　　學術論文一般以對所討論話題及相關背景的介紹為開頭，如「今日英國的大眾消費廣告」就可以成為一個論述話題。在文章的醞釀期間，作者的觀點通常來自於對某一學術問題的好奇，並通過開放而敏感的思想表現出來。然而在論文的撰寫過程中，隨著不斷引入例證或個案分析作為論據，作者的觀點也會隨之產生變化。通過分析考查，我們就可能得出對這些論據的多種合理解釋，而這些解釋又可能進一步成為構成文章結論的觀點。

　　如果所發現的論據之間相互矛盾，我們就可以利用這些論據之間的不同之處，把個案研究轉變成對比研究。如果所提供的論據並不能說明問題，作者也要如實陳述，但這並不影響他在文章的最後以明確的觀點得出自己的結論。

　　相反，隨筆、雜文等一般文章只要按照作者個人的思路陳述，而不需要特定的論證過程，因此它所體現的主要是語言的使用技巧，不具有學術論文所要求的特定模式。當你在走進考場之後才知道所要論述的題目，並且要在一兩個小時之內必須

完成論文時，學術論文與一般文章之間的上述區別就表現得尤為明顯。撰寫一般文章的相對靈活自由，從某種程度上說，它無須為文章所論述的觀點提供證據或論據。此外，這種靈活性還表現在文章的內容──即作者的思想的表達方面，為表達思想所使用的語言及風格方面，以及為體現文章思想所使用的文章結構方面等。實際上，對於一般文章來說，語言、風格及結構本身就構成了文章的重要特徵，而在學術論文中這些特徵只是用來體現論證過程的載體或工具。

能夠表現一般文章的上述靈活性及語言的創造性的典型例子就是一些大報的專欄評論，這類文章用以表明報社或編輯的立場觀點、引導公眾輿論。報紙上的專欄評論屬於一般散文，而那些副刊作家在選擇文章主題及文章的寫作手法上都力求輕鬆愉快、語言活潑或辛辣諷刺，可以作為風格獨特的英國隨筆的範例。

我們上面對一般文章與學術論文之間的區別所做的描述之所以非常簡要，是因為初學寫作的人所需要的並不是泛泛而談，而是就如何開始著手寫作、如何展開論述一個話題、如何得出結論等方面具體而又切實可行的指導。

作者的心理障礙

報紙專欄作者雖是專業的寫作人士，也同樣會因思想尚未醞釀成熟或大腦處於麻木狀態致使思路混亂，從而不能馬上開始寫作。專欄作者知道他要寫的題目，知道他要採取的觀點，也知道文章要使用的風格和語調，但他就是寫不出文章的第一句話。這是一個普遍存在的問題，不過很多人並不明白其中的

原因。這種情況嚴重時，會持續幾天或幾星期，並且對小說家或詩人的影響要遠遠超過對新聞記者的影響，這一現象叫做「作者心理阻滯」。造成這種現象的主要原因有兩個。

原因之一是因為作者尚不明確自己在所要寫的文章中應該扮演什麼樣的角色。所有的作者在他們所寫的文章中都要起到一定的作用，但很少有作者會問自己這樣一個問題：我在所要寫的這篇文章應起什麼樣的作用呢？多數作者只是本能地而非出於自覺地意識到，他們必須使自己、或經過稍加改變的自己融入文章之中，這樣才能使所寫的文章真實可信。

有人會覺得這種說法有些牽強附會、故弄玄虛，而不屑一顧，但考慮一下下面這些情況，你就不會這樣認為：我們在撰寫履歷時總要把自己經歷中最好的一面通過陳述表現出來；我們有時在照相時會產生不自然或尷尬的感覺，當看到照片中的自己時又會產生與照相時稍微不同的感覺；或者在日常生活中，對比一下你和朋友們在一起時輕鬆狀態下的自己、和家人在一起時的自己或跟陌生人在一起時的自己，都會有所不同。

演員們都有著極強的角色意識，他們仍然在使用希臘詞persona來表達「角色」及其相關概念，就像劇作家們仍在使用拉丁語 *dramatis personae* 來表示劇中人物一樣。Persona 這個詞起初是面具的意思。演員帶上聖賢、魔鬼或是國王的「面具」，就會表演出這些人物的性格特徵來體現其身份。作者同樣也會帶上「面具」：一個憤世嫉俗的記者在撰寫頭版評論時，會變成客觀的道德家；一個中年的母親在創作犯罪題材的小說時會變成令人生畏的故事講述者；一個退休教師，看起來不過是個住在鄉間的普通人，卻能寫出頗具想像力的詩歌，得到批評界的讚

賞。作品中的角色使作者在日常生活中難以表現的部分身份特徵得以自由發揮或得到拓展。

你是否也是如此呢？你可能已經在所要寫的文章、小說或詩歌中為自己選好了一個角色，如果還沒有選定角色，或者尚不能確定自己在作品中的角色或所要起到的作用，你可以在草擬文章的初期先慢慢體會，直到為自己找到一張合適的「面具」，使你在寫作時既能夠揮灑自如，又可以伸縮有度。

產生心理障礙還有第二個原因。我們在寫一個句子之前先要在大腦裏進行構思。前文講到過，「大腦中語言」的形成過程是先由神經元細胞和神經鍵把電化學能轉變為語言，然後再轉變成標準英語。如果我們想寫一些新穎的東西（這裏是指和以前寫的東西不同，並不是指思想上具有獨特的創造性），就必須首先建立神經元與神經鍵之間的新的連接，這也正是大腦的功能之一。從這種意義上講，我們的大腦在我們的生命存在期間始終都在不斷地更新自己。但是大腦建立新的連接的時間是難以預料的，從幾秒鐘到幾年時間都有可能。

如果你在開始寫文章時感到建立新的連接比較困難，尤其在考試的情況下，你就只好使用大腦中已有的連接，也就是大腦已經存在的語言。這樣寫出的開頭第一個句子可能不如你所希望的那樣新穎獨特、引人注目，但它畢竟可以開啟你的思路。

但是，使用現成的、大腦中已有的語言時，要注意避免兩種情況，一是避免使用詞典上有關相關話題的定義，如：

The *Shorter Oxford English Dictionary* defines an advertisement as 'a public announcement'.

二是要避免使用相關話題的引語，如：

Samuel Johnson in his series of essays, *The Idler*, wrote, 'Promise, large promise, is the soul of an advertisement.'

之所以要儘量避免使用這些文章的開頭方法，是因為它們都是些陳詞濫調，即使具有像散文大家約翰遜那樣的洞察力，也難使這些寫作手法再產生出任何新意。另外，讀者們也會把這樣的寫作手法看作是作者才思枯竭或投機取巧的表現，也就是說，這表明作者已經沒有更好的想法，或者根本沒有花時間去認真思考。那麼怎樣才能寫好文章的開頭呢？奇妙之處在於，我們只要把上述兩種陳腐的用法稍作改變，就能成為可以接受的文章開頭。

文章的開頭

我們可以把前面提到過的字典定義式的平淡無奇的開頭變成下面的寫法：

The *Shorter Oxford English Dictionary* leaves many questions unanswered when it defines an advertisement as 'a public announcement'.

然後你就可以在文章中就廣告所帶來的問題進行討論，並提出一些解決方法。再看另外一種類似的開頭方法：

No dictionary definition, not even the *Shorter Oxford's* definition of an advertisement as 'a public announcement', can capture the complexity of modern mass-consumer advertising.

同樣，這個開頭也表明了文章要論述的內容，即探討現代廣告的複雜性。再看下面這個開頭：

No dictionary definition can capture the ingenuity and diversity of modern mass-consumer advertising. The *Shorter Oxford's* definition of an advertisement as 'a public announcement' gives no indication of the fact that advertising is the main form of popular culture in the Western world.

顯然，從這個開頭可以看出，文章的隨後部分會以一種積極的，甚至是熱情洋溢的語調進行論述，最後得出的結論很可能是：現代廣告不僅是一種大眾文化形式，而且是一種大眾藝術形式。

對於引言形式的開頭，同樣有幾種變換方式。例如前面提到的約翰遜那段引言，就可以變成下面這樣的形式：

When Samuel Johnson wrote, 'Promise, large promise, is the soul of an advertisement', he probably had in mind coffee houses, inns, theatres and publishers, the main advertisers in the eighteenth century. He could not have imagined the multicolour fantasies of power and pleasure promised by modern advertising.

以此為開頭，文章接下來要分析的當然就是現代廣告豐富多彩的創意和想像。再看下面這個開頭：

'Promise, large promise, is the soul of an advertisement', wrote Samuel Johnson in the middle of the eighteenth century. Today, the promise is even greater, but it has less chance of being fulfilled than the promise in a syndicated horoscope.

這樣開頭的文章，後文討論的很可能就是目前「時尚」廣告所做的虛假承諾。下面這個開頭方式也會引出內容類似的文章：

When Dr Johnson wrote, 'Promise, large promise, is the soul of an advertisement', in the middle of the

eighteenth century he was clearly being ironic. Advertisements have no soul.

　下面這個例子説明同樣的寫作技巧還可用於其他主題的文
章。《觀察家》(*The Observer*) 雜誌上的文章曾引用美國劇作家
阿瑟・米勒 (Arthur Miller) 的 A good newspaper, I suppose, is a
nation talking to itself 這句話作為開頭，就顯得平淡無奇。但我
們可以換一種引述方法，把文章的開首句改寫為：

> The American playwright Arthur Miller was probably
> thinking of affairs of state, of politics and human rights,
> economics and the arts when he said that a good news-
> paper is a nation talking to itself. But when a nation
> talks to itself the dialogue includes gossip, rumour, scan-
> dal and fantasy.

有了像上面這樣一篇文章的起始段，可以使我們在後文或者探
討有關小報和大報的問題，或者就這兩種報紙進行對比研究，
留出了足夠自由發揮的空間。

　一個可靠而有效的文章開頭方法，就是使用事實性的陳
述，這樣可以讓作者能夠從多種角度進行論述。如：

> Mass-consumer advertising has infiltrated many areas
> of modern life.

> The mass media newspapers, magazines, independent
> radio and television depend on advertising for their
> survival.

　最後要提到的一種文章開頭方法使用起來要冒一定風險，
但也是值得的，因為如果運用得當就可以寫出引人入勝、充滿
創意的開頭。這種方法就是用一個主題句，以一種與眾不同
的、甚至是能引起爭議的陳述表明你的觀點，定下文章的基

調。這種開頭方法可以很明顯地表明你作為作者在文章所扮演的角色。下面是一些例子：

> Newspaper readers as well as newspapers have become commodities in the battle for advertising and circulation.

這句話是講段落寫法的一章裏一個示範段落中的結尾句，但它也可以成為一個很好的文章開頭，後文可以討論廣泛的話題，如大報與小報，兩種報紙在廣告和社論等內容方面的比較，兩種報紙不同的新聞價值，以及它們的讀者群和發行量等。下面這個例子我們在前面已經提到過：

> Mass-consumer advertising is now the main form of popular culture in the Western world.

下面這個例子是關於一個不同話題的有趣的開頭：

> Slang transforms the human predicament into the human comedy.

我們使用上述這種給文章的開頭方法，其危險之一在於，我們可能自認為機智詼諧、富於創意的文字形式在讀者看來也許就顯得幼稚而滑稽。另外一個危險在於，由於這樣的開頭已經大致劃定了文章後文的寫法，因此它所劃定的範圍越窄，作者在後文論述主題時所受的限制就越大。當然這樣開頭也不無好處，好處之一就是，即使我們這樣寫出的開頭並不像我們想像的那樣機智活潑且充滿創意，但我們至少可以使所要論述的話題更加突出，並使讀者能夠更準確地抓住文章的主題。

這裏，新聞寫作中的一些技巧是值得我們借鑒的。以上提到的這種文章開頭的方法就類似於新聞報導中的「導語」或「角度」。從事新聞寫作的人，尤其是在報導新聞事件或者撰寫新聞特寫的時候，一般都儘量避免以抽象化、概括性的描述作為開

頭，也較少用統計數位作開頭，因為這樣的開頭缺乏個性，不容易吸引讀者。新聞報導者在接受寫作培訓的過程中，就懂得了在報導新聞事件時要注意抓住新聞事件中人性化的方面，並且從人性化的角度著手寫出新聞報導的導語。尋找新聞事件中人性化的方面，可能會造成侵犯他人隱私的不利影響，但它的好處在於可以使一篇可能顯得空洞無物的新聞報導增加許多人情味。

像下面這樣的導語，記者在寫作時就應儘量避免：

Homelessness in the Grantown area has risen by 27 per cent in the last year.

記者應該把這篇特寫或新聞特寫的開頭寫成如下這樣：

Grace Garland and her two small children — three-year-old Martin and four-year-old Ben — live in one small room of a Grantown hotel where they share a bathroom with two other families. The Garlands, and over 6,000 other people in Grantown, are homeless.

缺乏經驗的記者可能寫出這樣的開頭：

A growing number of disabled people in Grantown are gaining a new sense of purpose and a new self-confidence through the work of the Grantown Disabled Support Group.

而編輯則可能會更喜歡這樣的開頭：

Mike Giles raised over £3,000 for charity last year when he completed a half-marathon and two five-mile fun runs — in a wheelchair.

Mike (37), of 29 Almond Street, Grantown, has found a new sense of purpose and self-confidence since he joined the Grantown Disabled Support Group last year.

當然，特寫和隨筆是兩種不同的體裁形式，各有不同的寫作規範。儘管如此，隨筆作者也可以從寫得較好的新聞體裁文章中學到諸如即時性和人性化的特點。

文章的展開

要把一個話題展開，寫成一篇五百到一千字的文章，最好的方法是先收集足夠的論據，如事實、例證、引述或個案研究等，然後把這些材料組織起來，結構成篇。在有關段落寫法的一章中，已經介紹過怎樣把資訊編排成連貫而有序的段落，怎樣用字典上的定義或引語來做段落的開頭句或者結構段落，在「文章的開頭」部分，還介紹了如何寫作廣告以及如何在整個文章中抓住報紙讀者的注意力等。這裏，我們再介紹幾種其他拓展文章話題的方法。

一種極端的方法就是選擇一個你持有反對意見的話題，諸如單一歐洲貨幣或歐洲國家、體育運動的業餘性的終結、大學教育的費用以及建設更多的公路等等，因為反對意見可以使寫作顯得更有力度，當然這種反對意見要在一定的控制範圍之內（controlled），並且建立在大量證據的基礎之上才更加行之有效。你還會發現，在探討反面意見的過程中，不管是在調查研究階段還是在寫作階段，你必須就所探討的話題提出明確的觀點。

你還應該注意在適當的情況下運用對比研究的方法，因為當就兩個事物進行對比時，你會發現一加一大於二。這裏的意思是說，當把兩個話題放到一起進行對比的過程中會產生出第三個新的話題。對比通常是對兩個事物、兩種思想或兩種政策

進行的研究，但作者還可以就不同的敘述角度進行對比，這樣，雖然所論述的主題不變，但你可以從不同的視角加以闡述。這種寫作手法的危險性在於，文章中贊成和反對的兩種觀點可能會相互抵銷，並且不斷迅速變換的視角會使文章的形式和風格，像舞劇中的對白一樣滑稽可笑 (a form of pantomime prose)，好像一方說：「哦，是的，我沒問題！」，而另一方卻說：「哦，不，你不行！」

在文章中產生對比的方法之一就是可以用提問的方式，如：

What would be the effect on the news industries if all mass-consumer advertising were to cease?

Who can believe the promises in mass-consumer advertisements?

Does slang satisfy some social or personal need that cannot be met by standard English?

Does the division between broadsheet and tabloid news-papers mark a division in our society?

在一篇大約一千字左右的文章中，一般只能有少數幾個這樣的問題，問題太多就會使這種方法顯得做作而生硬，而且這些問題還不能是反問句，必須要有明確的回答，因為如果使用沒有答案的反問句就會在作者與讀者之間的對話中產生出一個空白，而讀者是很有可能不願意去填補這一空白的。

提問可以用來做文章的主要轉捩點。你的思路當中的每個新階段都要與前一階段緊密相聯，或者與之融為一體，使之看起來就像前一階段的自然過渡，這樣才能使文章形成一個連貫的整體。提問就可以用來引出文章中的一個新階段，不只是一個新的話題，而且是一個新的觀點。例如，在一篇有關俚語的

文章中，你可以討論生活中使用俚語的各個方面，並佐之以例證，隨之你就可以通過下面這樣的提問方式來改變討論的方向，轉換敘述角度：

> Does slang satisfy some social or personal need that cannot be met by standard English?

運用類似的方法，你也可以在討論大報和小報的內容差別時，提出這樣的問題：

> Does the division between broadsheet and tabloid newspapers mark a division in our society?

問題可以用做一個新段落的開頭句，或者主題句。如果把問題放在一段話的末尾，而在下一段中給出答案，其效果也是相同的。

當然，用來標誌思路中新階段的其他方法還有很多。從一個階段到另一個階段的時間轉換可以用下面這樣的表達方式：

> Mass-consumer advertising was transformed by the introduction of colour television and newspaper colour supplements in the 1960s.

> Newsprint was rationed during the Second World War, but by the mid-1950s newspapers began to publish more pages.

時間的轉換還可以用更加簡單的方法來實現：

> As we enter the twenty-first century we may find ...

> A common practice in the nineteenth century was ...

> A century later, we find that ...

> Between 1980 and 1990 there was little change ...

> Since 1990, there has been rapid change ...

同樣的方法還可以用來表示空間的轉換：

> In France, too, the problem of ...

> Conditions in the north of England, however ...

> When he returned to the United States he found ...

我們還可以用很多其他方法在幾乎任何類型的文章中進行敘述角度的轉換，看下面的例子：

> Turning to foreign policy, the President said, ...

> On the problem of violent crime, the Prime Minister warned that ...

> In his poems as in his novels, Thomas Hardy explores the themes of ...

> Another Scottish poet, Hugh MacDiarmid, was a contemporary of Edwin Muir's, but MacDiarmid's vision of Scotland is ...

> There are irreconcilable differences between the news values in the broadsheet press and those in the tabloids ...

> Compared to the *Daily Telegraph*, the *Daily Mirror* is ...

文章的結論

文章的結論應該是建立在其所有論點和論據基礎之上的合乎邏輯的結果。由於任何對論據的合理解釋都是能夠讓人接受的，所以你就可以把你對論據的解釋作為文章的結論。例如，《每日電訊報》(*Daily Telegraph*) 和《衛報》(*The Guardian*) 的兩個報社不同的社論撰搞人，可以在同樣論據的基礎上，得出截

然不同的結論。但是，如果你寫了一篇七百五十字的文章，所論述的觀點是現代大眾消費廣告是一種社會邪惡，你就不能在文章的最後五十字中說廣告是無害的；如果你在整篇文章中所論述的是大報或者普通報紙是反對專制獨裁的有效手段，你在文章的結尾就不能說報紙是資本主義社會維護一黨專政的工具。

　　另外兩種形式的結論也應該儘量避免。一種是口號、標語式的結尾，如：

　　　　Someone should do something about it.

或者是這類口號、標語的變形：

　　　　The local council should take positive action to end this abuse.

　　　　The government should intervene now before it is too late.

如果文章所寫的是關於地方或中央政府的職能的問題，像上面這樣的結論也未嘗不可，但如果用在話題輕鬆、面向普通讀者的文章中就不太適合了。

　　第二種結論方式可能會引起讀者的極大不滿，這種方式就是在文章的結尾處引出一個比整個前文更有遠見或更加耐人尋味的新的話題或新的思路。這樣不僅使文章令人驚奇地偏離了主題，而且會使所寫的整篇文章內容大為遜色。這種使文章的結論作為新的思路開始的現象，正是前文提到的作家心理阻滯的表現。我們要就某個話題展開思路需要花時間，我們在大腦裏建立新的連接需要花時間，這是我們產生獨特思想的源泉，並且把我們的思路按照新的連接進行構建同樣需要花時間。當我們的思路最終步入了軌道，我們會發現考試時間已經到了。

　　上面講到的關於文章結構中的開頭、發展以及結論等方面

的原則在下面三個範文當中都有體現。每篇文章中的開頭部分，都至少在某種程度上決定了文章的敘述角度。

下面第一篇範文的開頭先提出了支持大眾消費廣告的觀點，在隨後的段落中對這個主題展開論述。

Advertising: A Case for the Defence

No dictionary definition can capture the ingenuity and diversity of modern mass-consumer advertising. The *Shorter Oxford*'s definition of an advertisement as 'a public announcement' gives no indication of the fact that advertising is the main form of popular culture in the Western World.

Britain began to adopt American techniques of mass-consumer advertising in the 1950s, but it was not until the late 1960s, after the introduction of colour television and newspaper colour supplements, that British advertising became a major form of popular culture.

Today, with the exception of the BBC, most of the mass media — television, radio, newspapers and magazines — depend on advertising for their survival in their present forms. Independent radio and television are dependent on advertising for over 95 per cent of their income, the remainder coming from publications and sales of programmes; broadsheet newspapers and most magazines are 75 per cent dependent.

Advertising is not confined to the news media; it is our most widely shared cultural experience. Advertisements appear on bill-boards and shop fronts, in railway, underground and bus stations, on buses and taxis. They appear in sports grounds and, in the form of sponsorship, they sustain football, rugby, cricket, athletics, golf, snooker, darts and bowls. So completely have we accepted advertisements we even wear them on shirts and sweaters, shoes and boots, baseball caps, umbrellas and hand-luggage. But it is in the colour magazines and on television that modern advertising is most vivid, inventive and witty.

In a finely printed colour magazine the subject of the advertisement — the perfumed woman, the powerful car, the succulent food — assumes and almost luminous form. The art director and photographer use their knowledge of composition, colour, texture, lighting and camera angles to produce intensely realized, sometimes idealized, images. It is not the fault of the advertisers if their pictures are more alluring or more revealing than the editorial photographs in the same publication. Nor is it the fault of the advertising copywriters if their texts are wittier, happier or more literate than those of the journalists.

Television has the added elements of sound and movement that allow the advertiser to transform the still lives of magazine advertising into the entertaining dramas of television advertising. Indeed, television advertising is a recognized form of entertainment that has attracted eminent film directors while they have been 'resting' between films. Alan Parker (*Midnight Express*) directed the amusing Cinzano and Birds Eye advertisements; Ridley Scott (*Blade Runner and Alien*) directed the nostalgic Hovis advertisements; Ken Russell (the televised *Lady Chatterley's Lover* as well as feature films) directed the acrobatic, melodramatic Black Magic advertisements. Other cinema directors who have made television advertisements include Lindsay Anderson, Jack Gold, Joseph Losey, Karel Reisz and John Schlesinger.

These directors have created cinema in miniature: there are identifiable central characters, often with casts of supporting characters or even crowds of extras; there are story-lines that have a clear development and resolution; the locations and the background music heighten the emotion just as they do in the cinema, but without the violence. If television advertising is something of an insiders' game in which directors and advertising agencies try to impress each other, then the viewer benefits through the humour, the inventiveness, the sheer creativity of some of the work.

Television and colour magazines confirm that mass-consumer advertising is not only the main form of popular culture in the Western world; it is a highly popular form of minor art.

Moralists still argue that mass-consumer advertising is a corrupting influence, but without this income, newspapers and magazines would be smaller and more expensive, and most independent radio and television companies would cease to exist. Sport, too, would be affected: if sponsors withdrew their support there would be fewer clubs, fewer events, fewer sportsmen and women. The loss, not only of entertainment but of information, education and employment, would be a greater social evil than the alleged evil of mass-consumer advertising.

But is anyone really corrupted by advertising? Is it not the case that the vast majority of people now regard advertising in the same way as they regard horoscopes, or football pools, or television soap operas? We may read the horoscope and momentarily fantasize that we are going to be rich and famous again, or that yet another beautiful woman or handsome man is going to fall in love with us, but we know the horoscope is merely a silly and harmless entertainment, just as we know that most television soap operas are fantasies, and that we have as much chance of winning a fortune on the football pools as we have of hang-gliding across the Atlantic.

Mass-consumer advertising comes into the same category, except that advertisements are always good news and always have happy endings.

第二篇範文以反對廣告的觀點做開頭，然後分別從道德和政治兩個方面加以論述。看下面的文章：

Advertising: The Face Behind the Mask

When Samuel Johnson wrote, 'Promise, large promise, is the soul of an advertisement', he probably had in mind coffee houses, inns, theatres and publishers, the main advertisers in the eighteenth century. He could not have imagined the multicolour fantasies of power and pleasure promised by modern advertising.

What mass-consumer advertisements promise is not the reality of power and pleasure but a fantasy, and the aim of the fantasy is not to inform or enable the television viewers or the readers of colour magazines but to manipulate them by arousing their fear, their greed and their hope.

Advertisements for soaps, perfumes, cosmetics and toiletries play on the personal fears of women. Some advertisements imply that women are inferior as wives and mothers and that they are betraying their husbands and children if they, the women, do not get the weekly wash sparkling clean with the advertised brand of washing powder. Similarly, women who do not use the advertised brands of soap or toothpaste are implicitly accused of being unclean and therefore socially unacceptable. And women who do not use a certain perfume or shampoo or deodorant will be unacceptable as sexual partners. The advertisements promise an end to these fears if women buy, and go on buying, the advertised products.

The promise of a better life is also implicit in food and drink advertisements, which are designed to arouse the appetite and to promise instant gratification. Advertisers and the psychologists who advise them say that the central element in this area of advertising is *appetitiveness*, but this is simply another word for *greed*.

In what is sometimes euphemistically called *lifestyle advertising*, the promise of gratification is symbolic rather than physical, but the promise is no less real or powerful for offering to relieve emotional rather than physical hunger. Some car advertisements are clearly designed to arouse, and symbolically to fulfil, a masculine wish for power. Television advertisements show the driver exerting power over the environment, over the police, over business rivals and, almost inevitably in this genre of advertising, over women.

A common factor in most of these forms of advertising — perfumes, clothes, cars, holidays, food and drink — is that the fantasy promise of self-improvement masks the underlying appeal to self-indulgence. By arousing our fears, our greed and our fantasies of power, the advertiser is manipulating not only our spending habits but our way of life and our vision of life, because the advertiser encourages us to see all things as commodities which are available at a price. And the price is greater than the advertisers and their powerful clients would have us believe.

The advertising agencies' wealthiest clients are multinational corporations: oil companies, drug companies, motor manufacturers and others. Some of these organizations have annual incomes that are greater than the national incomes of the countries in which they operate. The organizations exert enormous influence. They may persuade a government to produce crops for export while the people of the country go hungry. They may force down the price of raw materials so that the supplier country is trapped in debt. They may use their influence to hold down the price of labour and thus the people's standard of living.

International capitalism, often described as the free market, is primarily concerned with the control of commodities, raw materials and labour costs, and with the manipulation of interest rates, currency exchange rates and investment capital — all with the aim of increasing productivity and profit. The free market is not interested in people except in their roles as producers or, more importantly, as consumers, of the market's goods and services.

To emphasize consumption when we live in a world of limited resources that are unevenly divided among the world's population and that in some cases, for example, oil and natural gas, should be carefully conserved rather than rapidly consumed — to emphasize this is irresponsibility on a global scale.

Mass-consumer advertising is the human face on these inhuman forces. Advertisements address us in a language of caring familiarity about our physical appearance, our attraction to members of the opposite sex, the state of our health. They speak knowingly, too, of our emotional states, our fears and hopes and dreams; they even suggest how these dreams might be realized.

But when we look behind the mask we see that the free market is not interested in our personal freedom. As consumers we are encouraged to experience only the fantasy, the illusion, of power and pleasure; the realities of power and pleasure rest partly with the advertising agencies but mainly with the organizations that are the agencies' clients.

第三篇範文探討的是關於俚語的問題。

A Pickled Wally — Slang and Society

Slang transforms the human predicament into the human comedy. It punctures pomposity and pretentiousness, reduces our ideals to bawdy jokes, and even turns tragedy into farce.

Slang is an alternative to standard English and expresses an alternative, unofficial, attitude to life, a way of thinking as well as a way of speaking. The differences between the two forms of language are most obvious when they deal with serious issues or intimate circumstances: money, wealth and poverty; food, drink and drunkenness; crime, police, prison and prison officers; the human body and bodily functions; emotional or extreme states of mind; and death.

Someone who is mentally ill, or more commonly someone you describe as mad because you strongly disagree with him, is *barmy, loony, loopy, nuts*; is a *bampot* or a *nutter*; is *off his nut, off his rocker* or *off his trolley*. He might also have been called *bonkers* until tabloid newspapers redesignated that word as slang for sexual intercourse. Someone who dies *snuffs it* or *has bought it*, or in an earlier age might have been said to have *kicked the bucket* or *popped his clogs*. Someone in prison is in the *nick*, the *clink* or the *slammer*. Features of the human anatomy — *bum* for buttocks, *bonce, noddle* or *nut* for head — are renamed. So too as are bodily functions, for example *crapping* for defecating and *piddling, riddling* or *widdling* for urinating.

One human condition alone, drunkenness, has generated dozens of slang words and phrases, a few of which are: *bevvied, blotto, canned, groggy, legless, lit-up, pickled, pissed, plastered, sloshed, smashed, stoned, tiddly, tight.*

The examples above confirm that slang punctures pomposity, but the examples also show that some slang expressions are so intent on denying not only the formalities but also the grim realities of life, so intent on shutting out the pain, that sometimes the result is itself black and brutal comedy. A standard English statement like *The fool was so drunk he was arrested* becomes the harsh humour of *The wally was so pissed he got nicked.* But the main effect of slang is to make the condition or the problem it describes sound less ominous, less threatening, almost friendly at times. *A hairy shunt in an old banger,* for example, sounds less serious than a *hair-raising crash in an old car.*

Slang also makes the occasion or the condition seem more vulgar in both senses of the word: of the common people, and unrefined or coarse. As a result, slang in its vulgar, unofficial way is as far removed from standard English as euphemism is in its over-refined or sanitized way. The standard English words *poor, moneyless* or *indigent,* become the slang *skint, broke, strapped* or *in stook,* and the euphemism *financially embarrassed.*

The two registers, slang and euphemism, are also ways of avoiding taboos, that is, forbidden words or forbidden topics. Although there are now few if any absolute taboos in Western society, there are still words that are thought to be too obscene, or too indelicate, for use in public or in polite company. A key word is the standard English *lavatory. Lavatory* itself — the word originally meant a washing place — was once a euphemism, but is now seen as being too blunt and has been replaced by the more widely used *toilet; loo* remains a colloquial term, hovering on the edge of polite usage but not acceptable in formal standard English. The many euphemisms for lavatory include *the men's room, the ladies' room, the Gents', the Ladies',* and the phrases *to wash your hands, to go upstairs, to freshen up.* Slang avoids all delicacy in words like *bog, crapper* and *lavvy,* a diminutive of *lavatory.* Euphemism avoids the taboo by skirting delicately around the edge of the subject; slang takes a more direct stance and uses words that defy or mock the taboo.

Does slang, then, meet some social need? It meets the need to discuss taboo subjects, as we saw in the paragraph above, but it meet another, more important need. Many slang terms — *nosh, gob, lolly, pong* — are widely understood, but distinct social groups or subcultures have their own slang vocabulary. The slang of the comprehensive school differs from that of the boarding school, and the slang of both differs from that of men in prison; the slang of jazz musicians differs from that of journalists.

Journalists' slang include the terms *bleed,* to print a photograph to the edge of a page; *blow-up,* to enlarge a photograph; *crop,* to reduce the size of a photograph; *kill,* to abandon an article; *pix,* pictures or photographs; *puff,* favourable publicity; *splash,* the main news story on the front page.

Slang registers like these are so distinctive that they function like codes, uniting the members of the subculture or speech community and excluding others. To that extent, slang still meets the need for secrecy, or at least for solidarity, implied in the French loan word *argot,* which is now a synonym for *slang.* The word originally meant the language of thieves and rogues, and although *argot* has outgrown that meaning it remains a useful reminder of the separate, sometimes subversive, nature of slang.

Because the various registers of slang develop in isolation from each other and from written standard English, they are highly volatile forms of language. The 1950s' terms, *spiv*, *ned* and *teddy boy*, now seem absurdly archaic, and so too do the 1960s' expressions, *fab*, *groovy*, *hip* and *cool*. Slang also varies from one age group to another, and even from one social class to another.

Clearly, slang meets several needs. It reduces the pompous to the comic and the intimidating to the familiar. It confirms the identity of a professional or social group, and at the same time it excludes those who do not know the language. It is an affirmation of life, a vulgar and defiant humour in the face of adversity. And in meeting these needs, slang reminds us yet again of the flexibility, the diversity and the vitality of the English language.

第九章 | 書信和報告寫作

書 信

　　為行使普通公民的權利，我們有時要寫一些正式的申訴信給稅務局、地方議會、議員、商店經理或是某家報紙的「讀者來信」欄目。我們所寫的申訴信越是切中要害，就越容易得到重視。

　　為了把這類書信寫好，我們必須遵守一些寫作技巧上的規則，例如，書信的開頭和結尾必須按照標準格式書寫，在信紙頂端，或是在信紙右上側，必須寫明你的通訊地址；在緊接地址的下方，或在信紙的左側，還要注明寫信日期，至於要不要把電話號碼也包括在內，就要由寫信人自己決定了。

　　在你所寫的地址和日期下方，在信紙上靠左邊的地方，要依次注明收信人的姓名、職位以及地址。如果你對收信人的姓名和職位不太清楚，就應該首先打電話給收信人所在的機構，可以向電話接線員說清楚你要寫信的目的，並尋問有關主管人士的姓名和職位。如果實在不能確定相關人士的姓名和職位，還可以使用你認為比較恰當的職位頭銜，如：總經理、公關部主任、計劃科長等。切記要寫清楚誰是收信人，否則，如果你的信寄給一個規模較大的組織或機構，就很可能從一個部門轉到另一個部門，也許幾個星期後才能轉交到有關負責人士的手中。

出於禮貌和稱呼上一致的考慮，寫給個人的信一定要用收信人的名字作為稱呼語，如Dear Ms Drummond或Dear Dr Marsh等。如果寫給某工作職位的收信人但又不清楚該人的性別的話，通常要用Dear Sir or Madam這樣的稱呼來開頭。有時候，還可以直接用職位來做稱呼，如Dear Editor, Dear Councillor或Dear Chairman。

有關書信結尾的規則十分簡單。如果你在書信開頭的稱呼中使用的是人名或職位名，如Dear Ms Drummond或Dear Editor，結尾就要用Yours sincerely（注意，這裏Yours中的字母Y要大寫，sincerely中的s要小寫）和你的名字。如果開頭的稱呼用的是Dear Sir, Dear Madam或Dear Sir or Madam等，就要用Yours faithfully和你的名字結尾。如果你是以某個機構代言人的身份寫信而不是以個人名義寫信的話，在信的末尾你除了寫清自己的名字之外，還要注明身份，如Ms Jane Thomson, Press Secretary, Grantown Camera Club或Dr Victor Arne, Chairman, Cradle Bay Civic Society。

書信的內容要依你所傳達資訊的性質而定，但有些指導原則對大多數情況都是適用的。首先，在信的第一段中要準確指出你寫這封信的目的，隨後的句子和段落再對這一目的詳加説明。如：

> I write to confirm the reservation I made by telephone today. The reservation is for a single room, with dinner, bed and breakfast, from the evening of 20 September to the morning of 25 September, 19--.

> As Secretary of Grantown Camera Club, I write to thank you and your Company for generously sponsoring our annual exhibition.

I write to complain about the excessive delay by Grantown Council Planning Department in dealing with my application for planning permission.

在尋問、建議或表示申訴的書信中，要想辦法儘量使收信人容易接受你的請求。例如，在上面的第三個例子，是一個向規劃部主任提出的申訴，寫信人可以這樣來寫：

My planning application is entirely straightforward and could be dealt with as a purely routine item of business. Even if your department wished to put my application to the Planning Committee, this could have been done at one of the Committee's monthly meetings.

在你所寫的信中，要使你所使用的詞彙和句子產生出最恰當的語調，以達到你所要達到的目的。為此，可以使用中性的、不帶任何感情色彩的語言。如果用語的語調咄咄逼人，或者帶有威脅或諷刺的語氣，往往不如使用積極、平和的語氣更能達到預期的效果。這一點在你所寫的信要交由第三者進行仲裁時尤為重要，我們從下面的規則中就能體會到這一點。

在書信結尾處，還要簡要重複一下你寫這封信的主要目的。例如在寫給規劃部主任的那封申訴信中，可以用下面這樣的寫法來重申寫信的目的：

I suggest that one of these two procedures, routine approval or submission to the Planning Committee, be followed now.

由於申訴信比其他正式書信更難寫也更重要，因此我們還要注意如下一些規則：

• 除非你自己是某一領域的專家，否則的話，不要跟專業人士談論專業問題；

- 如果考慮到自己沒有足夠的時間、精力和金錢
  去打官司，就不要以訴訟相威脅；

- 不能以非法手段相威脅；

- 信中要指明可能作為仲裁者的第三方。有一些
  固定的、不需花費什麼代價的申訴程式，如向
  國會專員或調查官提出申訴，向諸如出版或廣
  播委員會這樣的正式申訴機構提出申訴，或是
  向地方議員、國會議員、歐洲議會議員等提出
  申訴。

下面我們把以上列出的這些寫信的指導原則運用到一個假設的
情況當中。可以假想，某人認為地方議會的規劃部在處理她的
申請時有嚴重的拖延行為，於是她寫了如下這封申訴信給該部
的主任：

25 St Michael's Lane
Cradle Bay
Grantown GR1 1BC
Telephone: Grantown
(1234) 56789

23 May 19——

The Director of Planning
Planning Department
Grantown Council
High Street
Grantown

Dear Sir

I write to complain about the excessive delay by Grantown Council Planning Department in dealing with my application for planning permission.

On 11 February 19—— I sent a completed application form for outline planning permission for the construction of a one-storey extension to the rear of my house at 25 St Michael's Lane, Cradle Bay, Grantown. The application was acknowledged by your department in a standard letter dated 20 February 19——, but I have received no further response since that date.

I have made five telephone calls and two personal visits to your department in an attempt to discover how my application is being processed. On each occasion members of your department were unable, or unwilling, to tell me what decision had been reached or what progress had been made in processing my application. This lack of response is wholly unsatisfactory.

My planning application is entirely straightforward and could be dealt with as a purely routine item of business. Even if your department wished to put my application to the Planning Committee, this could have been done at one of the Committee's monthly meetings. I suggest that one of these two procedures, routine approval or submission to the Planning Committee, be followed now.

I shall copy this letter to my local Councillor, Mrs Alice Desai, and to my Member of Parliament, Mr Matthew Ray.

Yours faithfully

Ms Dika Riesl

　　經商的人也要寫申訴信，有時寫給地方政府，有時寫給中央政府的部門，有時又是寫給同行業的人。在第二個假設的例子中，木材供應公司 Grantown Timbers Ltd 的運輸部經理傑克‧哈福德先生(Mr Jack Hartford) 發現，為該公司提供汽車維修服務的汽車修理場 Malley Auto Servicing 的服務質量有所下降，而且情況非常嚴重，必須提出一個正式、書面的申訴。可是這次情況又有些特殊，因為哈福德先生與修理場的老闆喬治‧摩里(George Malley) 不管在社交場合還是在業務上彼此都非常熟悉。於是哈福德先生先打電話非正式地就此事與摩里先生進行商談，然後把電話交談中的主要內容在正式書信中再加以強調。由於這個例子是一個商戶寫給另一個商戶的信，開頭和結尾就和前面一個例子有所不同。這裏，發信人的地址中要包括電話號碼和傳真號碼，在結尾的簽名中既要寫明發信人的姓名，又要寫明他的職位。另外，這種書信應該採取一種正式的語氣，但在最後一段中，語氣既要肯定，又要保留調解的餘地。看下面的例子：

Grantown Timbers Ltd
Grantown Industrial Estate, Grantown GG1 2PQ
Telephone: 9876 543210　Fax: 9876 543 2100

10 November 19--

Mr George Malley
Proprietor
Malley Auto Servicing
London Road
Grantown GG2 5SP

Dear George

I write to confirm the main points of the telephone conversation we had today, 10 November.

There has been a serious decline in the quality of service provided to Grantown Timbers Ltd by Malley Auto Servicing in recent months.

On several occasions between August and 1 November this year your mechanics failed to correct serious faults in our vehicles. The faults included:

> electrical circuits on a Mercedes 20 tonne truck
> steering on a Volvo X97 tractor unit
> steering and brakes on a Ford Escort van
> roll bar on a Trex 50 all-terrain vehicle

and several other less serious faults on five Grantown Timbers vehicles.

In addition, your invoices for July and August this year include accounts for work that was not done by you. These errors, notably for new exhaust systems for two Mercedes trucks and complete sets of tyres for three of our Land Rovers, were drawn to the attention of your Accounts Department at the time. Despite this, your Accounts Department has re-submitted these invoices to Grantown Timbers Ltd.

On a less serious point, my drivers report that their vehicles are being returned in a dirty condition, with oil stains on seat covers and interior panels.

This quality of service is wholly unsatisfactory and cannot be allowed to continue. Unless there is an immediate improvement I shall be forced to close our account with you.

I understand that you have been experiencing serious problems with two employees and that you are in the process of appointing a new floor manager and a cashier. I hope these problems will soon be resolved so that our two firms can resume the excellent working relationship we had until this year.

With good wishes.

Yours sincerely

Jack Hartford
Transport Manager

報　告

　　所謂報告 (Reports) 是指對所作調查以及由該調查所得出結論的陳述。報告可以是某機構對其運作情況所做內部調查的結果，或者也可以是由外部、獨立的調研人員所進行調查的結果。報告的結構和風格通常是由某機構的內部慣例來決定，但有些特點對所有報告是共通的。

1. 報告應該具有事實性、客觀性，因此，它的遣詞造句要注意使用中性用語，並不摻雜任何個人感情色彩。報告還應該像下面幾點所要求的那樣，要有一個邏輯性較強的、有序的結構。

2. 一篇報告首先要指出進行某項調查研究的必要性。這一部分在報告中可以用背景 (Background) 或導言 (Introduction) 做標題。

3. 報告通常還應包括參照條款 (Terms of Reference)，也就是展開調查研究和撰寫報告的條件、標準以及所遵循的規則。

4. 報告要說明報告撰寫者所採取的步驟 (Procedure)。這些步驟包括說明調查的範圍和規模、調查所採用的方法（包括專家的驗證、對相關人員的採訪、隨機調查、調查問卷和實地考察）以及使用這些調查方法的原因。

5. 調查結果 (Findings) 是報告的重要組成部分，它是對調查發現的客觀、嚴謹的陳述。

6. 至此，報告的撰寫者就可以得出他們的調查結論 (Conclusion)，即對調查發現的合理解釋。

7. 如果通過調查研究的結果發現了問題所在，還要提出如

何解決問題的建議 (Recommendations)。結論和建議可以分別作為報告的兩個部分，也可以放在一起作為一個部分，冠之以結論和建議的標題。

撰寫報告的這些指導原則在下面兩個類比真實情況的例子中都有所體現。其中的第一個例子是關於法氏食品有限公司 (Fasta Foods Ltd) 的報告，這是一家為賓館和餐飲業提供食品的食品加工公司。由於公司的管理部門認為該公司存在嚴重的經營管理問題，於是請求一家獨立的經營管理諮詢公司的三位專業人士迅速作出一份有關公司管理方面的報告。這份報告次序分明，全賴運用點列及標題的方式。下面的這份報告應該附帶一份附函和一份包括統計、成本和分析等專案的附錄。

The Recruitment, Retention and Promotion of
Staff of Fasta Foods Ltd

A report by Gascoigne, Whistler, Vaughan
Management Consultants

CONFIDENTIAL

Introduction

In the past two years Fasta Foods Ltd has had difficulty in recruiting and retaining appropriate staff. The average annual turnover of staff in the two-year period is 24 per cent, ranging from 8 per cent in the Administration and Accounts Departments to 39 per cent in the Production and Delivery Departments. At a meeting of the Management Committee of Fasta Foods on 5 September 19--, it was stated that the problems of staff recruitment and retention were affecting the profitability of the Company. The meeting agreed that Gascoigne, Whistler, Vaughan, Management Consultants, be commissioned to investigate the problem as a matter of urgency and to report back to the Management Committee of Fasta Foods within one month.

What follows is the report by Gascoigne, Whistler, Vaughan.

1. Procedure

Gascoigne, Whistler, Vaughan interviewed all Heads of Departments of Fasta Foods individually. Questionaires were issued to all employees to be completed anonymously, and this produced 157 replies, a response rate of 78 per cent. A copy of the questionnaire and a summary of the main findings are enclosed with this report; summaries of the interviews are also enclosed.

2. Findings

2.1 Recruitment

It was found that Fasta Foods has no consistent policy on the recruitment of staff. Some vacancies, particularly in the Accounts Department, are advertised in the local press; candidates required to apply in writing, the best candidates are invited for personal interview and the final selection is made on the basis of the written application and the interview. Other employees, notably in the Production, Delivery and Plant Maintenance Departments, are recruited through local Job Centres or by word-of-mouth and personal contact with existing employees. Staffing in the Production Department sometimes resembles a system of casual labour rather than full-time employment.

The lack of a clear and consistent policy on the recruitment of staff means that there is no corporate view of the kind of experience, qualifications, age profile or personality required of new recruits. Consequently, there is no corporate control over the standards of new recruits.

2.2 Wages and Salaries

Several complaints were received about wages and salaries. On investigation, however, it was found that the wages of employees on hourly rates compare favourably with those in other local industries. Monthly salary levels are slightly above the national average for the food and drink industry.

2.3 Training

Fasta Foods has no policy on in-service training. New recruits may be offered advice by their Heads of Department or supervisors, but this is done in a random, unstructured way. Fasta Foods does not take advantage of the experience and expertise of existing employees.

2.4 Promotion

Although Fasta Foods has no written policy on promotion, the practice is to promote existing staff, normally on the recommendation of the Head of Department.

It was found that several employees promoted from existing staff within the last five years had insufficient experience or ability to meet the demands and responsibilities of their new, higher level posts. This has led to recurring irregularities in stock control which have seriously affected production flow, and to recurring interruptions to delivery programmes which have damaged customer relations.

The quality of promoted staff, along with topic 2.5, Conditions, proved the most controversial. Ninety-eight of the 157 respondents to the questionnaire expressed some degree of dissatisfaction with or mistrust of their immediate superiors.

2.5 Conditions

Fasta Food meets the minimum statutory requirements for health and safety at work, but Gascoigne, Whistler, Vaughan received eighty-four complaints from the hourly paid staff about conditions. Complaints referred to the lack of cleanliness in toilets, in the refectory and in the workplace generally. The segregated refectories, one for hourly paid workers and the other for salaried staff, was bitterly resented by many respondents. Complaints were also received about the lack of parking space and the lack of a nursery for the children of women employees.

3. Recommendations

3.1 Promotion

As a matter of urgency we recommend that Fasta Foods introduce a clear policy on promotion.

We recommend:

    (a) that all promotions be centrally controlled by the Personnel Office

    (b) that all candidates for promoted posts must complete an appropriate application form

    (c) that short-listed candidates, three where possible, be interviewed

    (d) that interviews be conducted by at least two senior members of

Fasta Foods, one of whom should normally be the Personnel Manager or the Assistant Personnel Manager

(e) that existing staff should be promoted only on merit.

Staff who are promoted on these criteria will be more effective as managers, leaders and exemplars.

3.2 Conditions

We strongly recommend that the working environment of hourly paid employees be improved.

We recommend:

(a) that the Management Committee consider ending the segregation of the adjoining refectories, which already share the same kitchen and menus

(b) that new furnishings and fittings be provided for the hourly paid refectory

(c) that the hourly paid refectory, the toilets and the workplace generally be maintained at a higher standard of cleanliness

(d) that the Management Committee consider the establishment of a nursery for the children of employees. Estimated cost of nursery provision are shown in the Appendix to this report

(e) that an annual ballot be held for company parking spaces, other than parking spaces for promoted staff.

We believe that these changes will remove the main sources of conflict between management and employees, and between salaried staff and hourly paid employees. Fasta Foods would then be in a better position to retain good staff and also to reduce the absentee rate.

3.3 Wages and Salaries

We recommend that Fasta Foods' monthly newsletter publish the wage and salary scales of other employers in the area and other major companies in the food and drink industry. This will demonstrate that Fasta Foods' rates are above average.

3.4 Training

If Recommendations 3.1 (a) to (e) were introduced, there would be no need for extensive training. As a short-term measure, however, we recommend that some promoted staff be required to attend in-service training; the training could be given by experienced members of the existing staff.

Training of two hours per week for a trial period of eight weeks could be introduced at one month's notice. An outline training programme is included in the Appendix.

We believe that the proposed changes would lead to more effective management, more harmonious management-employee relations, and a greater degree of job satisfaction for a majority of employees. These changes, in turn, should result in better recruitment and retention of staff and, as a consequence, improved efficiency, productivity and profitability for Fasta Foods.

Signed: Gardner Vaughan
for Gascoigne, Whistler, Vaughan
1 October 19--

第二個實例是一份公司內部報告，其結構比上一份實例報告更加嚴格，它在「發現問題」一部分中所提到的各個條目在隨後的「結論」和「建議」中都有所體現，而且由於「建議」中的 (b)、(c) 兩項緊密相關，它們就被放到了一起，作為一個部分。

Carlton Crates and Containers Ltd

Mr Wilf Sutton
Managing Director

Report on Carlton Crates and Containers Gazette

Background

During the period from June to 1 November this year, formal complaints about inaccuracies in the Company's house journal, *Carlton Crates and Containers Gazette*, were made by the Chairman of the Company and by the Secretary of the Women's Hockey Section. Informal complaints about the content and quality of the magazine were also received during the same period.

1. Terms of Reference

The Managing Director, in his memorandum of 15 November 19--, instructed the Personnel Department to investigate complaints about the Company's monthly house magazine, *Carlton Crates and Containers Gazette*, and to make recommendations.

2. Procedure

Between 20 and 27 November, interviews were conducted with all Heads of Departments and with members of the committee of the Staff Association. Between 30 November and 15 December brief interviews were conducted with non-promoted staff in all departments, a total of thirty persons.

3. Findings

(a) Printing

On four occasions in the last six months the house magazine has been delivered late by the printer. For example, the September edition, which should have been delivered by 28 August, did not arrive until 13 September, by which time several events listed in the magazine had already taken place.

The finished product is of poor technical quality: design and layout are old-fashioned, photographs and other illustrations are badly reproduced, and the quality of printing is inconsistent.

(b) Contents

Recent issues of the magazine have contained many typographical errors, notably misplaced captions for photographs. In the July edition the picture caption for the dog show, 'Boxer Bitch is Champion', appeared beneath the picture of the Women's Hockey Section; the photograph of the Company Chairman and his wife was captioned 'Congratulations on the biggest catch of the season — a 10 lb trout'; the names of some of the visiting French trade delegation were printed in the adjoining article, 'This Month's Recipe'.

(c) Staffing

The magazine is edited by the Advertising Manager and his staff, none of whom have previous experience of editing. There is no clear system for the collection of news items from Company clubs and societies or from individual employees, nor is there an agreed system of distribution of the magazine throughout the Company.

4. Conclusions

(a) Printing

Complaints about the quality of the printing, and the delivery service by the printer, are fully justified.

(b) Contents

Editorial control, for example, proof-reading and layout, is inconsistent and occasionally erratic. This has caused distress to the Chairman and his wife, and to members of the Women's Hockey Section.

(c) Staffing

The Advertising Department has neither the expertise nor the time required to produce a better quality monthly magazine.

5. Recommendations

(a) Printing

The printing of the magazine should be put out to competitive tender on the basis of print quality as well as cost. Quality and delivery should be specified in any contract with a printer, and should be closely monitored.

(b) Contents and (c) Staffing

A part-time editor should be appointed, either from within the Company or by advertising the post; alternatively, the Company could commission a freelance editorial consultant. The editor should exercise close control over contents and production, and should monitor the service provided by the printer.

Each department should nominate a departmental reporter who would undertake information-gathering and news-gathering on a continuous basis. The Staff Association should be encouraged to use the magazine to publicize all Staff Association events. A free 'small ads' service should be offered to all employees.

Monthly distribution of the magazine could become the responsibility of the Mail Room.

Additionally, it is recommended that the title of the Company's house magazine be changed from *Carlton Crates and Containers Gazette* to the simpler title, *Carlton Gazette* or *Carlton News*.

PJ Minster
Assistant Personnel Officer
22 December 19--

附錄一：
常用語法術語

adjectives 形容詞

adverbs 副詞

antecedent 先行詞

antonyms 反義詞

apposition 同位語

article 冠詞

    definite article 定冠詞

    indefinite article 不定冠詞

case 格

clauses 從句

    adjective *or* descriptive clauses 修飾性從句

    adjective sub-clause 定語從句

    adverbial clauses 狀語從句

    adverbial clauses of cause 原因狀語從句

    adverbial clauses of effect 結果狀語從句

    adverbial clauses of manner 方式從句

    adverbial clauses of method 方法從句

    adverbial clauses of place 地點狀語從句

adverbial clauses of purpose 目的狀語從句

adverbial clauses of reason 原因狀語從句

adverbial clauses of time 時間狀語從句

descriptive sub-clause 修飾性從句

embedded clauses 嵌入式從句

exclusive descriptive *or* adjective sub-clauses 非包含性定語從句

inclusive descriptive *or* adjective sub-clauses 包含性定語從句

main *or* principal clauses 主句

noun clauses 名詞性從句

conjunctions 連詞

content words 實義詞

contractions 縮略

determiners 限定詞

function words 功能詞

gender 性

359

gerund 動名詞

homonyms 同音異義詞
homophones 同音異形詞

inflections 曲折變化
intensifiers 強化
interjections 感歎詞

modal auxiliary verbs 情態助
　動詞
monosyllabic word 單音節詞彙
mood 語氣
　imperative mood 祈使語氣
　indicative mood 陳述語氣
　subjunctive mood 虛擬語氣

nouns 名詞
　abstract nouns 抽象名詞
　collective nouns 集合名詞
　common nouns 普通名詞
　concrete nouns 具體名詞
　countable nouns 可數名詞
　foreign nouns 外來語名詞
　non-countable nouns 不可
　　數名詞
　plural nouns 複數名詞
　proper nouns 專有名詞
　singular nouns 單數名詞
　verbal noun 動名詞
number 數
numerals 數量詞
　cardinal numerals 基數詞
　ordinal numerals 序數詞

object 賓語

parentheses 插入語
participles 分詞
　past participle 過去分詞
　present participle 現在分詞
person 人稱
phrases 短語
　adjective phrases 形容詞短語
　adverbial phrases 副詞短語
　linking phrases 連接短語
　noun phrases 名詞短語
　preposition phrases 介詞短語
plural 複數
polysemy 多義詞
polysyllabic words 多音節詞
predicate 謂語
prefixes 字首/前綴
prepositions 介詞
pronouns 代詞
　emphatic pronouns 強調代詞
　reflexive pronouns 反身代詞
　indefinite pronouns 不定代詞
　interrogative pronouns 疑問代詞
　personal pronouns 人稱代詞
　relative pronouns 關係代詞
punctuation 標點符號
　apostrophe 撇號
　brackets 括弧
　colon 冒號
　comma 逗號
　dash 破折號
　ellipsis 省略號
　exclamation mark 感歎號

full stop 句號

hyphen 連字號

inverted commas 引號

question mark 問號

semicolon 分號

sentences 句子

complex sentences 複雜句

compound sentences 複合句

compound-complex sentences
複合–複雜句

spelling 拼寫/拼法

split infinitives 分裂不定式

subject 主語

suffixes 後綴/尾碼

syntax 句法

tenses 時態

future continuous perfect tense
將來完成進行時

future continuous tense 將來進
行時

future perfect tense 將來完
成時

past continuous tense 過去進行
時

perfect continuous tense 現在完
成進行時

perfect tense 現在完成時

pluperfect continuous tense 過去
完成進行時

pluperfect tense 過去完成時

present continuous tense 現在進
行時

simple future tense 一般將來時

simple past tense 一般過去時

simple present tense 一般現在時

singular 單數

verbs 動詞

auxiliary verbs 助動詞

compound verb 複合動詞

finite verbs 限定動詞

intransitive verbs 不及物動詞

irregular verbs 不規則動詞

main verbs 主要動詞

phrasal verb 短語動詞

regular verbs 規則動詞

reporting verbs 引出提問的動詞

transitive verbs 及物動詞

verbs of command 指令動詞

voice 語態

active voice 主動語態

passive voice 被動語態

word classes 詞類

word division 斷字法

word formation 構詞

索 引

363

本社出版其他CASSELL英國語言參考書

《*Cassell* 英語常用詞組用法詞典》

Rosalind Fergusson編著・盧思源編譯

- 收錄了一萬多條英語新近常用詞組，包括成語、諺語、俚俗語、慣用語等。
- 針對中國人學習英語的特點和需要，編譯者在原詞典的基礎上增加了七千多條情景生動的例句，以說明每一詞組的用法，令讀者觸類旁通，學以致用。
- 帶有典故的詞組，均注明來源。
- 雙色印刷，編排清晰；詞組按關鍵詞的英文字母順序排列，查閱方便。
- 重點學習及需要牢記的詞組，均特別標出，以加深讀者記憶。

編著者Rosalind Fergusson是資深的編輯及撰稿人，曾撰寫及編輯多部字典及參考書。

編譯者盧思源教授，英國語言文學教授。盧教授除撰寫多部英語研究專著及主編多部英漢詞典外，還發表過數十篇英語研究論文。

213 × 142 mm　　646頁
ISBN 962-201-076-1 (精裝)
　　　962-996-078-8 (平裝)

《*Cassell* 常見英語錯誤》

Harry Blamires著・李經偉譯、姚乃強審校

很多讀者學習了多年的英語，仍然犯上不必要的錯誤，主要原因是我們每天接觸的英語報刊、雜誌或電台節目，都犯上同樣的錯誤，在耳濡目染之下，難免受到影響。本書從英語刊物及電台節目中，搜集了大量經常會犯錯誤的英語字彙及會話，按英語字母順序列出，供讀者快速查閱，避免錯誤。

譯者李經偉，現為中國人民解放軍外國語學院英語系英語教授。

審校者姚乃強，現任中國人民解放軍外國語學院英語系教授、博士生導師。曾參與和主編十多部英漢和漢英詞典，如《美國蘭登書屋韋氏英漢大學詞典》、《商務學生英漢詞典》等。

213 × 142 mm　　約350頁
ISBN 962-996-107-5